In this timely book, Jo~~e~~
in American history an
rent schism that has spl............ ~~....~~ unity and imperils the future of
American democracy. Since whites are declining demographically, they
have resorted to district gerrymandering and voter suppression. Feagin
envisions reforming these undemocratic institutions and developing "a
new and truly democratic constitutional convention at which all U.S.
population groups are fairly represented and at which the central goal is
creating a truly multiracial democracy."

—**Stephen Steinberg**, *author of* Counterrevolution:
The Crusade to Roll Back the Gains of the
Civil Rights Movement

White Minority Nation is truly a touchstone at this turning point in U.S.
history. With unparalleled eloquence, Feagin brilliantly offers a compel-
ling, in-depth look at the perils of white supremacy and eloquently shares
the potential for ordinary and elite Americans to attain an authentic multiracial democracy in the coming decades. The dazzling scope, depth,
and breadth of this commentary set the book apart, offering unparalleled
insight into current realities and a pathway to mobilizing concerted action
toward social justice and a more inclusive society.

—**Edna Chun**, *Chief Learning Officer,*
HigherEd Talent, Columbia University School of
Professional Studies

This book is packed with analyses and critiques of social science claims
about how white society might respond as they become a numerical minority racial group. Dr. Feagin examines multiple data points and common interpretations that do not stand up to current reality. The reality is
that the U.S. is becoming a majority-minority nation. Feagin's breakdown
of the white distress, horror, and resistance to losing the country is fasci-
nating. However, white supremacy will not die without a fight.

—**William A. Smith**, *Professor of Education,*
Culture & Society, University of Utah

The January 6 insurrection was horrifying, but Joe Feagin contextualizes
it as one of many ongoing expressions of white anxiety and grievance that
may reach a crescendo as we near 2050. With meticulous scholarship and
no-nonsense prose, Professor Feagin traces the vast and disturbing 250-year
history of how white fear of immigrants and persons of color was invented
by elites and stoked by unscrupulous news reporting, a process that continues to dupe whites and endanger blacks and browns today.

—**Kirk Johnson**, *Professor of Sociology and African*
American Studies, University of Mississippi

White Minority Nation

Written by a leading scholar of U.S. racial studies, this is the only book yet to comprehensively analyze the societal implications of the U.S. becoming a white minority nation as demographic changes bring people of color into the majority. Joe Feagin traces important societal changes since former president Donald Trump declared white nationalists at Charlottesville among the "very fine people on both sides," up through recent, highly publicized calls by the white far-right to challenge supposed "white replacement." Feagin details a range of U.S. social, political, and demographic issues commonly described in terms like the "browning of America," "the coming white minority," the "minority-majority nation," and "white genocide." He thoroughly unpacks these terms with data and comprehensively explores related critical issues, accenting and documenting the larger historical societal context, the big-picture view of four centuries of persisting foundational and systemic racism, and the many challenges to it by Americans of color.

The U.S.'s major demographic shift is already driving major divisions between Americans and their political parties. It will continue to do so in coming decades. What will the racial and other societal structure of the U.S. look like by the 2050s?

Joe R. Feagin is Distinguished Professor and Ella C. McFadden Professor in Sociology at Texas A&M University. He has published internationally recognized research on U.S. racism, sexism, and political economy issues. Over six decades he has written or co-written 78 scholarly books and over 200 scholarly articles.

White Minority Nation

Past, Present and Future

Joe R. Feagin

Routledge
Taylor & Francis Group

NEW YORK AND LONDON

Cover image: © Shutterstock

First published 2023
by Routledge
605 Third Avenue, New York, NY 10158

and by Routledge
4 Park Square, Milton Park, Abingdon, Oxon, OX14 4RN

Routledge is an imprint of the Taylor & Francis Group, an
informa business

© 2023 Taylor & Francis

The right of Joe R. Feagin to be identified as author of this
work has been asserted in accordance with sections 77 and
78 of the Copyright, Designs and Patents Act 1988.

ISBN: 978-1-032-41821-6 (hbk)
ISBN: 978-1-032-41817-9 (pbk)
ISBN: 978-1-003-35988-3 (ebk)

DOI: 10.4324/9781003359883

Typeset in Bembo
by codeMantra

Contents

Acknowledgments

I would like to thank my family for their love, patience, and support as I have spent long hours on this project over the past three years. I would also like to thank my many students and colleagues for their insightful comments on and support for this broader project over many years now. These latter folks include, to name just a few, Kirk Johnson, Sean Elias, Ried Mackay, Carly Jennings, George Yancy, Dudley Poston, Rogelio Sáenz, Joachim Singlemann, Jennifer Mueller, Maria Chávez, Stephen Klineberg, Dean Birkenkamp, Edna Chun, Kimberley Ducey, Eileen O'Brien, Melissa Ochoa, Kimberley Ducey, Mark Fossett, Mark Gottdiener, Randolph Hohle, James Baldwin, KangJae Lee, Anthony Weems, Philip Ewell, Terence Fitzgerald, Bill Domhoff, Eddie Telles, Jingqiu Ren, Carly Jennings, Sam Cohn, Holly Foster, Herb Perkins, Russell Feagin, Jessie Daniels, and Holly Foster. I would also like to thank my talented research assistant, Ried Mackay, for doing the excellent abstracts for this book's chapters.

Introduction

A White Minority Nation and Societal Upheaval

> I was terrified. I was scared of failing my people, my poetry. But I was also terrified on a physical level. Covid was still raging, and my age group couldn't get vaccinated yet. Just a few weeks before, domestic terrorists assaulted the U.S. Capitol, the very steps where I would recite…. [and] I was going to become highly visible—which is a very dangerous thing to be in America, especially if you're Black and outspoken and have no Secret Service.[1]
>
> (Amanda Gordon)

Amanda Gorman, the 22-year-old National Youth Poet Laureate, presented her poem "The Hill We Climb" at the January 2021 inauguration of President Joe Biden. Terrified but determined, she spoke poignant words from the Capitol steps that a few days before were stormed by violent terrorists shouting white nationalist slogans and seeking to stop a fair election Biden had won. He had won with votes from millions of young Americans like Amanda Gorman. This is the sad reality of contemporary America.

In Gorman's recollection commentary to the *New York Times*, she underscored why she, her family, and friends were terrified about what white Americans like these terrorists might try to do to her that day. She explains that her mother had her practice crouching so her mother could shield her body from bullets, while some friends sent her messages about getting a bulletproof vest. Another relative warned her to "be ready to die" if she did present at the Capitol. After an uneasy night before, she courageously decided she had to present in spite of fright and fear because of what the poem might achieve for freedom and justice and because she stood in a long line of Black women and men who had done the same: "We're descended from freedom fighters who broke their chains, and they changed the world. They call me."[2]

DOI: 10.4324/9781003359883-1

The Coming White Minority Nation: Hostile White Responses

Amanda Gorman's and her family's worries about white supremacist danger and violence were, and still are, quite realistic. In August 2017, a month after a Ku Klux Klan rally in Charlottesville, Virginia, hundreds of angry white conservatives flooded that city to protest for the societal goals of the country's resurgent white nationalism. One specific focus of this "Unite the Right" protest was the city's plan to remove a statue of slave-holding Confederate general Robert E. Lee. White supremacist protestors with flaming torches marched around the University of Virginia campus yelling slogans like "You will not replace us" and "Jews will not replace us."[3] This sensational white riotous event, which included the murder of a counter-protester by a white rioter, was one of the largest assemblies of neo-Nazi and other white nationalists in recent U.S. history. Already spreading across the world's conventional and social media, their white supremacist slogans aggressively repeated ideas about whites being replaced in the U.S. population by people of color. In recent decades, these old white racist ideas have dramatically resurfaced and been reworked by influential white nationalists in both the U.S. and Europe.

Significantly, the Charlottesville white nationalists protested near a university established only for white men by slaveholding founder and principal author of the Declaration of Independence, Thomas Jefferson, himself an outspoken white supremacist. These white marchers, many with Make America Great Again (MAGA) hats tying themselves to the new President Donald Trump, heralded white supremacist goals and precipitated racist conflict and violence. President Trump seemed to condone the extremist protests, weakly condemning them as part of a display of "hatred, bigotry and violence on many sides—on many sides." There were, he insisted, "very fine people, on both sides." He thereby included many openly white supremacist protesters. On a recurring basis—before, during, and after his presidency—Trump has endorsed and exploited the overt racist framing of white supremacist activists in Charlottesville and across the country, generally for his political gain.[4] With openly anti-immigrant and other racist rhetoric, he has effectively encouraged supporters to continue their aggressive white nationalistic actions to the present day.

Trump's persistent MAGA ("Make America Great Again") theme has barely concealed its underlying implication of "Make America White Again." Clearly, that is the way many followers took its meaning. Subsequent themes that Trump experimented with, "Make America Great Again, Again" and "Keep America Great," signaled to followers that message of enhancing and preserving a white-dominated country. In the MAGA theme, one hears strong echoes of past white commitments to systemic racial segregation turning into renewed calls for systemic racial segregation in the present. His theme is mostly *not* a sign of white frustration with the U.S. government's or U.S. corporations' globalization and international standing, as some have suggested, but rather a *nostalgic* theme about the white-desired racial character of U.S. society being fully white in dominant power and privilege.

To this point in time, the most dramatic and serious of violent MAGA political attacks was motivated substantially by white fear and anger over the country's growing demographic diversity and associated threats to white power and privilege. This was the insurrectionary attack on the Capitol in Washington, D.C. on January 6, 2021, the first in U.S. history. About 95 percent of the several thousand attackers were white, most of whom were male, and at least 10 percent were directly linked to far-right white supremacist and other extremist groups. Striking too was the average age of these insurrectionists. The media's video coverage constantly showed that the majority of them were middle-aged and older (see Chapter 2 for details).

Virtually all were Trump supporters, with many carrying Trump political signs and yelling MAGA slogans. Numerous insurrectionists carried symbols of white racial supremacy, including Confederate battle flags and crosses and other symbols of resurgent white Christian nationalism. Many had weapons of various kinds and used their signs as weapons, including in violent attacks on many police officers. Most appear to have been motivated by white supremacist theories such as the "great replacement theory," a theory reflecting white fear and anger about the significant population growth, and increasing political power, of Americans of color (see Chapter 2). National surveys have indicated those who attacked the Capitol had much support in the larger white population. A Monmouth University poll in spring 2021 found that 27 percent of white respondents felt that the anger behind the insurrection was fully or partially justified. This survey percentage likely translates into *millions* of adult white Americans.[5]

Writing in the influential *Foreign Affairs* policy journal, historian Charles King has underscored the reality that a large and increasing segment of the white population views racial integration and nonwhite Americans'

> broader social empowerment as an existential threat, and the country's institutions have proved weak when challenged by [white] officials determined to subvert them. If one were analyzing another country similarly placed in history, the warning lights for the fate of democracy would be flashing red.[6]

Demographic Change: White Conservative and Liberal Reactions

Among all the world's predominantly white nations, the U.S. is well on its way to being the *first* to experience becoming a white minority nation. In summer 2008, the U.S. Census Bureau announced its population projection that the U.S. would transition demographically to this white minority condition by the 2040s. By then, the Bureau estimated, a significant majority of an estimated 429 million Americans will be people of color.[7] Much media attention followed this dramatic news. These are more than just numbers on paper, for the political, economic, and other social impacts of this coming change have been hotly debated and protested. In recent years, demographic definitions and projections have often been politicized, in both popular and scholarly debates over the "coming white minority" and the "browning of America."

Indeed, demographic projections have long been used to attack, retard, and support societal change. A certain demographobia, fear of white[8] population decline, is endemic in many conservative white groups in European and North American societies. As social scientist Michael Rodríguez-Muñiz has emphasized, *actual* population trends are not necessarily "objective conduits for political progress, just as they are not objective harbingers of disaster." How official announcements of such trends are viewed "by any given social grouping is, to a great extent, the result of practical and political attempts to make sense of population dynamics."[9] That is, population politics often shapes how officially announced demographic data are interpreted.

Unsurprisingly, the emerging majority-minority reality has had a major impact on the U.S. Republican Party, especially in regard to white Republican concerns and fears about voters of color. Republican members of Congress had substantially supported the Voting Rights Act in its 2006 renewal. However, just seven years later, most Republican members of Congress moved to a diametrically different position. The Republican majority signaled support of a reactionary 2013 Supreme Court decision destroying a key voting rights provision in that Act that protected voters of color.[10] Additionally, in the period between 2006 and 2013, another key event took place, the election of the country's first Black president, the Democrat Barack Obama. That too likely affected the view of conservative white Republicans in Congress and elsewhere as they negatively envisioned a current and coming decline in white political-economic power and privilege.

In contrast, many white liberals in Congress and elsewhere have countered this contemporary white supremacist resurgence with more positive readings of the country's racial demographic changes. For example, in a 1998 commencement address at Portland State University, President Bill Clinton was hopeful about the racially diverse U.S. future, which he viewed as "changing at breathtaking speed."[11] Countering commonplace white nativism—white hostility to nonwhite immigration—Clinton celebrated the increasing U.S. racial diversity generated by a now decades-long history of democratized immigration. Recognizing that most of these immigrants have been people of color, he insisted:

More than any other nation on earth, America has constantly drawn strength and spirit from wave after wave of immigrants.... Today, largely because of immigration, there is no majority race in Hawaii or Houston or New York City. Within 5 years, there will be no majority race in our largest State, California. In a little more than 50 years there will be no majority race in the United States.

Even at that point in time, Clinton could see the unusual speed with which this demographic change was happening and, unlike white nativists, put a positive spin on it. These immigrants of color and the so-called browning of America were good for the country. The immigrants

are revitalizing our cities. They are building our new economy. They are strengthening our ties to the global economy, just as earlier waves of immigrants settled the new frontier and powered the Industrial Revolution. They are energizing our culture and broadening our vision of the world. They are renewing our most basic values and reminding us all of what it truly means to be an American.[12]

Two decades later in speeches during the 2016 presidential campaign, then Democratic Party candidate Hillary Clinton also spoke favorably of immigrants of color, and she was bluntly critical of the country's persisting white racism. In speeches and other commentaries she repeated several times her antiracist view that "Ending systemic racism requires contributions from all of us, especially those of us who haven't experienced it ourselves."[13] During her Democratic Party convention speech, she said: "So let's put ourselves in the shoes of young Black and Latino men and women who face the effects of systemic racism, and are made to feel like their lives are disposable."[14] It appears that the white liberal Clintons have been significantly influenced by their friends and acquaintances of color, especially those who are among the Democratic Party activists.

Unmistakably, these white politicians and other whites in the liberal wing of the U.S. ruling elite are paying more, and often relatively positive, attention to the experiences, views, and concerns of Americans of color. As I will show in a later chapter, recent surveys indicate that an important minority of whites are not fearful of nonwhite immigrants or of demographic changes toward a nonwhite majority nation (see Chapter 5). This large white subgroup appears to recognize these ongoing population changes will reshape historically white institutions and, to a degree mostly acceptable to them, gradually incorporate immigrants and other people of color within them.

Nonetheless, today a great many white Americans, often a majority, remain supportive of very conservative local, state, and federal political candidates and other societal leaders who reflect their fears of becoming a white minority nation and their desire to resist racial demographic change and related democratizing political change, especially in regard to how such changes affect traditional white power and privilege. I will return to the issue of this socio-political divide among whites in Chapter 5.

Conclusion: A Country on Fire?

In her candid 2021 book *The Reckoning*, Mary Trump, the niece of ex-president Donald Trump underscores the deep racial background lying behind the January 6, 2021, Capitol insurrection and other aspects of contemporary systemic racism. With unusual racial savvy for a white American, she connects many current racist events to long centuries of traumatic white racial oppression:

> What does the fallout from the calamitous year that was 2020 have to do with this country's origin story? I would argue, everything.... [Consider] our tragic beginnings; the ensuing transgenerational trauma inflicted on both the overwhelmed Native American and enslaved African populations; the white majority's tendency to exclude perceived out-groups from the protection of civil society; the evolution and reemergence of white supremacy; our society's insistence upon silencing those who have suffered because of our cruelty, indifference, and ineptitude; the economic and racial disparities that have only worsened since 2016; our devaluing of human life; the increase in anti-Black policies like voter suppression and gerrymandering; the resurgence of lynching as a means of terror and control.[15]

As a psychological expert on trauma, she speaks of these numerous societal traumas as resulting from centuries of white racial oppression, racial inequality, and a white racist framing that buttresses the white unwillingness to redress these highly destructive past and present conditions. In her view, these ongoing racial traumas have shaped the social fundamentals of this society, generation after generation, and generated a current situation of extreme national political emergency:

> Our country is on fire—literally, metaphorically—ravaged by flames, disease, and civic strife, all of which have been fanned by the willful indifference of a significant minority. The danger has abated but not passed. The flames are waiting to jump the line.[16]

Notes

1 Amanda Gorman, "Why I Almost Didn't Read My Poem at the Inauguration," *New York Times*, January 20, 2022, https://www.nytimes.com/2022/01/20/opinion/amanda-gorman-poem-inauguration.html (accessed February 10, 2022).

2 Ibid.; see also Isabel van Bruges, "Amanda Gorman Reveals Physical Terror, Mom's Shooting Fears Over Inauguration," *Newsweek*, January 21, 2022, https://www.newsweek.com/amanda-gorman-joe-biden-inauguration-poet-shooting-fears-1671517 (accessed February 10, 2022).

3 White nationalism is, according to historian Kathleen Belew, the "idea that white people are going to unify together as one national polity either in a white homeland or a white nation—or even in a white world—through the violent killing or exclusion of other people." See Sean Collins, "Trump Once Flirted with White Nationalism. Now it's a Centerpiece of His White House," vox.com, July 21, 2020, https://www.vox.com/21313021/trump-white-nationalism-supremacy-miller-bannon-immigration (accessed February 18, 2022).

4 Sheryl Gay Stolberg and Brian M. Rosenthal, "Man Charged after White Nationalist Rally in Charlottesville Ends in Deadly Violence," *New York Times*, August 12, 2017, https://www.nytimes.com/2017/08/12/us/charlottesville-protest-white-nationalist.html?action=click&auth=login-email&login=email&module=RelatedCoverage&pgtype=Article&region=Footer (accessed April 2, 2021).

5 "Monmouth University Poll," February–March 2021, www.monmouth.edu/polling (accessed March 22, 2021).

6 Charles King, "The Fulbright Paradox: Race and the Road to a New American Internationalism," *Foreign Affairs*, July/August 2021, https://www.foreignaffairs.com/articles/united-states/2021-06-18/fulbright-paradox (accessed June 20, 2021).

7 David Goldman, "America 2050: Minorities in Majority," CNNMoney.com, https://money.cnn.com/2008/08/13/news/economy/america_2050/ (accessed July 23, 2021).

8 Note: Unless otherwise noted, I use the term "whites" in this book to mean European-descended whites (those the U.S. Census terms non-Hispanic whites), the long-dominant U.S. racial group, and I use "nonwhites" and "people of color" for groups long defined and subordinated as racial groups by those dominant whites.

9 Michael Rodríguez-Muñiz, *Figures of the Future: Latino Civil Rights and the Politics of Demographic Change* (Princeton, NJ: Princeton University Press, 2021), pp. 203, 205, 213.

10 Glenn Rocess, "White Supremacists Have Already Lost the Race War," Medium.Com, https://medium.com/our-human-family/white-supremacists-have-already-lost-the-race-war-7c6c56747492 (accessed July 23, 2021).

11 Bill Clinton, "Commencement Address at Portland State University in Portland, Oregon," Weekly Compilation of Presidential Documents, www.gpo.gov, Volume 34, Number 25 (Monday, June 22, 1998), pp. 1120–1125.

12 Ibid.

13 Quoted in Danielle Moodie-Mills, "Was Clinton's Speech about Privilege or Personal Responsibility?" https://www.nbcnews.com/news/nbcblk/oped-was-clinton-s-race-speech-pandering-or-personal-responsibility-n520356 (accessed July 15, 2021).

14 Victoria M. Massie, "Hillary Clinton Said 'Systemic Racism' in Tonight's Speech. That's Major," vox.com, July 29, 2016, https://www.vox.com/2016/7/29/12320118/hillary-clinton-speech-systemic-racism (accessed July 15, 2021).

15 Mary L. Trump, *The Reckoning* (New York: St. Martin's Publishing Group, 2021), Kindle. Loc. 142–143.

16 Ibid.

Chapter 1

Population Realities
Popular and Scholarly Debates

Past history should always be taken fully into account when assessing the likely future history of a country. This is especially true for gauging the coming future of the U.S. as a white minority nation. Understanding its long history of invader colonialism, systemic racism, and expansionist imperialism is essential. Indeed, white far-right organizations have long attempted to suppress an honest foregrounding of and accurate teaching of that highly oppressive history, clearly as part of forestalling challenges to white political–economic dominance as long as possible into the future.

Diverse Historical Immigration and Imperialism

That U.S. historical background has involved some of the planet's largest migrations, so much so that the U.S. is often called a "nation of immigrants." In the first centuries, these migrations took place mostly within the globalizing imperialistic systems of a few European countries, and they included the involuntary migration of enslaved Africans for more than 240 years and the parallel voluntary immigration of white European workers and their families.

Certainly, the imagery of a nation of immigrants is inaccurate in some key respects, for there were *already* millions of Indigenous people on the North American continent long before those voluntary and involuntary immigrants arrived. In the 16th and 17th centuries, European immigrants invaded a geographical area that had many established Native American nations (the first "settlers" there), who had been resident for thousands of years. English and other European invaders thus began a long history of highly exploitive colonialism that featured repeated territorial dispossession of the Indigenous settlers there. The racialized exploitation of people of color has been a constant feature of what became the U.S. ever since. Early and later white invaders spoke of seeking liberty for themselves, yet created that liberty at great cost to often resisting Indigenous peoples.

DOI: 10.4324/9781003359883-2

Early on, the English (soon, "British") colonizers and their descendants in the North American colonies rationalized their often violent invasions and taking of Indigenous lands—and after 1619 their enslavement of Africans to work those lands—in terms of a dominant Eurocentric worldview, an assertive white racial framing of their new society. From these early decades to the present, ideas about the racial superiority of white Anglo-American culture and institutions have been central in the dominant white racial frame that rationalizes continuing racial oppression. In addition to many racist stereotypes and prejudices, this white frame includes racist myths and narratives about this society, numerous racist images, an array of white racialized emotions, and strong motivations for discriminatory actions targeting people of color. That omnipresent white racial frame has at its center a very positive orientation to whites as generally superior and virtuous and a negative orientation to racialized "others" generally viewed as inferior and unvirtuous.[1]

Typically, elite whites have decided what these dominant societal narratives and myths are. From this country's beginning, they and their ordinary white followers have viewed its economic development and geographical expansion in terms of grand myths such as the "right of discovery," "human progress," and "manifest destiny" accenting the virtues and superiority of white Western civilization. Americans of color have long taken exception to such white virtue and superiority framing. Recently, for example, the pioneering African American physicist Chanda Prescod-Weinstein has written that these elite whites' idea of who is

> human was entangled with an early form of Manifest Destiny for men: from the point of view of the Europeans who eventually founded the United States and Canada, someone is human if they are a propertied European man, and if someone or something is a European man or a state representing them, then they have a legal right to all the property they can get their hands on. Patriarchy isn't just prejudice against women but instead a total system that says (white) men can own anything, including the capacity to determine other people's rights or even—in the instance of white empiricism—the ability to determine when evidence is required in determining reality.[2]

Departing significantly from empirical reality, an early white European myth about the Indigenous lands they invaded was that they were largely uninhabited ("terra nullius"). This was an intentional virtue-signaling misrepresentation since most areas were certainly known then to be inhabited.[3] The scholar Raewyn Connell has emphasized the fact that white conceptions of the territories they invaded have typically neglected the already well-cultivated reality of those places and the huge negative impacts of their colonizing dispossession of the material foundations, and thus impoverishment, of non-Western societies there.[4]

"Civilizing" people of color—such as Native Americans and African Americans—has long been viewed by European Americans as a highly virtuous goal. In the Western philosophical tradition that accents John Locke, as historian Imani Perry puts it,

> The construct of "man" for Locke was a relation of property.... Locke's definition was a relation that depended on sovereign authority. As Europeans traveled the globe, the sovereign authority granted them rights to property relations that were also effectively rights of conquest.[5]

Unmistakably, the equating of human progress with expansion of European civilization and geographical scope mythologizes the highly destructive consequences for millions of people of color over centuries of this imperialism.

The northern European colonizers were initially a numerical minority on the east coast of North America, but by the late 1700s they had become a majority in what was by then termed the U.S. In the first (1790) census of the new U.S. about 80 percent of the population of 3.9 million was white, with the rest mostly being African Americans. Most Native Americans were not counted. The number of Native Americans then is estimated at about 600,000, down dramatically from their number in the colonized areas—estimated to be at least 3.8 million—at first contact with European colonizers. Strikingly, all U.S. censuses since this first one in 1790 have measured in some fashion the racial identities of those being surveyed. This early counting shows how central *white-imposed racial identities* have been from the beginning of U.S. history.

Soon after the new U.S. was founded, especially from the mid-19th century to the early 20th century, much additional white and nonwhite immigration came from areas within the growing U.S. sphere of trade and influence in Europe, Asia, and Latin America. U.S. capitalists, mostly white men, have long pressed for importation of nonwhite workers from other countries, long ago putting in place the U.S. population trajectory to becoming ever more nonwhite. This country's globally linked capitalistic development was well underway a century before the U.S. industrial revolution put it among leading Western nations in the late 19th century. That early capitalistic development created great wealth for its white capitalists. To take a major example, this country's Black enslavement system—often developed on stolen Indigenous lands—connected early white agricultural capitalists and their plantations operated by enslaved African workers to the British and other European slave trade. Soon too, early British industrialization created textile mills needing huge amounts of U.S. slave-grown cotton. A little later, the New England textile mills needed much of that cotton as well. U.S. merchants and shippers, again almost all white men, prospered as well. These interconnected capitalistic realities brought significant wealth for many white families in both northern and southern states.[6]

Over time, for more than two centuries, the prosperity and wealth of white Americans, and indeed of many white Britons, was built substantially on land and labor theft from these Americans of color. White America became prosperous *because* African America and Native America were racially oppressed and greatly impoverished. The racially privileged access of whites to critical socioeconomic resources, especially during the long slavery and Jim Crow eras (about 18 family generations, for 80 percent of our history), became a persisting foundation for white individual and family wealth to the present day. Whites' unjust enrichment over about 21 generations now is a core family wealth reality of U.S. society. Intergenerational transmission of this unjust enrichment is the mechanism that keeps a majority of white families' resources and wealth generally significant— and this country's racialized wealth inequality persisting if not permanent. This is true for white middle-class families, as well as for the wealthy white elite (see Chapter 4). Note too that, more recently in this long history, a white-run federal government gave discriminatory access to some important economic and social resources to newer whites, principally immigrants with northern or other European ancestry, from the mid-19th century well into the 20th century. These included mostly working class Irish, German, and Scandinavian immigrants in the mid-19th century and mostly working-class immigrants from southern and eastern European countries later on. These substantial resources included lands for farming, mining, and lumbering.

Adding to the African American and Native American populations, other people of color were incorporated into a U.S. society dominated by Americans of European ancestry from the mid-19th century well into the 20th century. They included many nonwhite immigrants from Mexico, China, Japan, and the Philippines. Thousands of Mexicans were involuntarily incorporated into the U.S. as a result of an imperialist Mexican American War in the 1840s. They did not actually migrate, as the newly imposed U.S. border crossed over them. A few decades later more came in from Mexico as migrant workers. By the 1850s, Chinese immigrants were brought in for railroad and other menial labor by white capitalists in Hawai'i and on the West Coast. Then, a few decades later, the 1920s U.S. anti-immigrant laws brought four decades of significantly reduced immigration to the U.S. Only after a 1930s Great Depression and a globalized World War II, in the late 1960s, did a much less racist U.S. immigration law allow more substantial migrations by immigrants of color to the U.S.

Currently, the U.S. has the largest number of immigrants among the world's countries, and immigrants of color make up a substantial majority of them. They have come to the U.S. for a variety of reasons, which include seeking better socioeconomic conditions, including job and educational opportunities, and reuniting with their American families. They include many working-class immigrants from Mexico and Central American countries, and numerous working class and affluent immigrants from China, other parts of Asia, and various Latin American countries. They and their descendants are helping to reshape the demography and certain U.S. economic and political realities, just as earlier generations of European immigrants did.

Significant numbers of these immigrants are linked in some way to past or present U.S. interventions in their countries. Recurring international interventions of the U.S. government and military, and of profit-seeking U.S. corporations, have increased migrations of many nationalities, with many people coming from countries like South Korea, Vietnam, Cambodia, Taiwan, the Philippines, and certain Middle Eastern countries. Critical global theorists argue that significant international migrations to the U.S. and other Western countries have been a consequence of political and economic crises left behind after these imperialistic countries' withdrawal from military or political-economic interventions in the less developed countries.[7]

In two decades or so, the U.S. population majority will be Americans of color. They will include very substantial numbers of descendants of voluntary and involuntary immigrants from areas that over four-plus centuries have been exploited, invaded, colonized, warred-in, or otherwise dominated by the U.S. or, as in cases like the African slave trade, by closely related European nations. That is, there are centuries-old global connections to constantly keep in mind when considering much U.S. immigration and its impacts, consequential historical and contemporary connections whose long-term demographic and democratic impacts, and ethical implications (e.g., reparations), were until relatively recently ignored.

Current Browning of America

Over the centuries since the founding of the U.S. in the 1780s, and to the present day, whites have been a substantial majority of the population, albeit now a gradually dwindling one. In 1980, the U.S. white percentage was 80 percent, but by the year 2000 that percentage had dropped to just under 70 percent. And in the 2020 Census, it was down to 57.8 percent. That recent Census found that U.S. racial diversity was increasing at a more rapid rate than expected. More than 40 percent of the population count was people of color, and for the first time in Census history, the white population had *decreased* over a decade (2010–2020). This population decline could be seen in many states, as well as in most cities over 100,000 and in most of the country's 3,100-plus counties.[8]

Moreover, the youngest completed generation of Americans—Gen-Z, a category usually set as those Americans born from about 1997 to 2012—is very diverse in its racial makeup. Indeed, the youngest segment of these Gen-Z whites and those in the still growing generation after them (tentatively named Generation Alpha), those babies born in years since 2007, constitute the first white cohort born as part of a racial *minority* group. To put it another way, children of color born since 2007 have always been a majority in this demographic category of Americans. Moreover, as of 2018, white children were a minority of children in 43 of the country's 100 largest cities, ranging from just 20 percent in Los Angeles to about 42 percent in Chicago.[9]

Clearly, the U.S. has moved dramatically from a mostly white and Black nation as of the 1960s to a much more diverse nation, a "microcosm of the world" as urbanist Stephen Klineberg has put it. Today, the U.S. is probably the most racially and ethnically diverse nation *in human history*.[10] The country's largest and most prosperous big cities (e.g., New York City, Los Angeles, San Francisco, Seattle, Chicago, Dallas, Houston, Washington, D.C., Atlanta, and Miami) vividly demonstrate to a perceptive visitor this fast-growing racial and ethnic diversity and the related healthy economic impacts that former President Bill Clinton has emphasized.

If future birth and immigration rates stay roughly similar to those of today, half the population will be people of color no later than the mid-2040s. By about 2050, according to Census Bureau estimates, a significant majority will be people of color. Note too that this major U.S. demographic change is occurring in a significant global context. Indeed, people of color in 195 countries, in most cases a population majority in each country, are now more than 80 percent of the world's total population.

White Population Future: Expanding or Contracting?

Much controversy has surrounded this Census Bureau estimate that around the year 2050, a significant majority of Americans will be people of color. Some demographers, journalists, and other social analysts have questioned this argument for a coming white population minority, raising the critical issue over who is, or will be, considered to be "white" as current and future decades pass. Among other arguments, these analysts argue that certain lighter-skinned Americans of color (e.g., certain Latina/os or Asian Americans), especially those who are mixed-race and middle or upper class, are rapidly being folded by dominant whites into the white racial category.[11] This alternative population scenario envisions these (former) Americans of color as being fully assimilated into an expanding-white

America and with substantial white racial privilege, as has happened with descendants of eastern and southern European immigrants since the early 20th century.

This assimilationist view assumes that the long-dominant European American group is, or soon will be, accepting and fully assimilating a great many of these particular nonwhites fairly and equitably into major, historically white societal institutions and will not continue to racially discriminate against them as in the past. It also assumes that the historical white-racist framing of these still phenotypically distinctive people of color is becoming dormant.

As articulated by several mainstream demographers and numerous contemporary media analysts, this idealistic view seems similar to the early 1900s idea of the U.S. being a "melting pot," such as in a famous 1908 drama of that name by the U.S. immigrant Israel Zangwill. However, these assimilationist social scientists indicate they are not arguing for a necessary full-scale "whitening" of people of color like earlier assimilation theorists did for the southern and eastern European immigrants, but instead view large numbers of Asian, Latina/o, and multiracial Americans of color as already blending into a *new* mainstream culture they contend is much more racially diverse, reciprocally and mutually adaptive, and increasingly egalitarian.[12]

Nonetheless, this theory of substantial and mutual assimilation into the long-dominant white category as applied to certain Asian, Latina/o, and multiracial groups is still largely white-framed. Interestingly, in the late 19th and early 20th centuries, the English term and concept of "assimilation" was *first* applied on a large scale to new immigrants by white scholars, politicians, popular analysts, and ordinary citizens operating out of traditional white racial frame. In that era, the Chinese, Japanese, and other Asian immigrants were considered to be "inferior races" that could *not*, both elite and ordinary whites insisted, successfully "assimilate" to the dominant white-Anglo-Saxon core culture and society.[13] For example, a major 1878 California Senate report argued vigorously that virtuous white male workers were at a major disadvantage in regard to Chinese immigrant workers there because white workers had real "families, a condition considered of vast importance to our civilization while the Chinese men have not" and because the Chinese

> can be hired in masses; they can be managed and controlled like unthinking slaves. But our laborer has an individual life, and this individuality has been required by the genius of our institutions, and upon these elements of character the State depends for defense and growth.[14]

Notice the virtuousness and centrality of both *whiteness* and of *white institutions* in this early version of the white racial frame. This view of these first large groups of Asian Americans was not limited to ordinary white workers in the West, as we see in the views of President Rutherford B. Hayes (1877–1881). He also held a view of the country having a "Chinese problem," saying publicly that he "would consider with favor any suitable [congressional] measures for discouraging the Chinese from coming to our shores."[15]

Today's assimilationist theories, although usually much more critical and nuanced, continue to assume that very substantial assimilation—often still unidirectional—to the long-dominant white Eurocentric cultural norms and folkways, and even more importantly to its major institutions, is the necessary and healthy path for non-European immigrants and their descendants. They view contemporary U.S. culture and society as now changing to a much less discriminatory, mutual-assimilation, multicultural mixture with white-institution-changing inputs from diverse immigrant groups, mostly immigrants of color, over the decades since the 1960s.

Now let us examine a range of issues regarding this assimilationist perspective in more detail to see if this view meshes with empirical realities revealed by research studies.

Who Is White? Imposing Racial Identities

The class-ascending socioeconomic achievements (e.g., in education, income, occupation) by some Americans of color, especially certain Latina/o and Asian Americans, are cited by the expanding-white analysts as a major sign that racial framing and discrimination have substantially declined and, thus, that the dominant white group is accepting large numbers of nonwhites into "white" America. But is the majority of European-descent whites really willing to expand the white category and its privileges by welcoming into that category large numbers of middle-class, lighter-skinned, and/or multiracial Americans of color? In assessing such an argument, we must consider seriously how these Americans are still racially viewed and treated by the dominant white group.

Being or not being seen as "white" is a *social construction*, one most impactfully constructed and maintained for centuries by powerful white men at the top of society and perpetuated by a myriad of their implementing acolytes and followers. In early North American colonies like Jamestown and Plymouth, "race" constructions were gradually institutionalized in the legal and other institutions by the English elite there. Initially, incoming colonists viewed themselves as English and identified with their English religious organizations. Soon, however, constant contacts with Native Americans and newly enslaved Africans led the colonial elite and other colonists to create white-framed, color-coded "race" categories based on phenotype that persist to the present day.[16]

Perceived racial phenotype still matters greatly for European-descent whites. Most Black, Asian, Latina/o, and other phenotypically distinctive Americans still have a physical "look" to whites that precludes them from being actually seen and treated by most whites as truly white.[17] In turn, this presents major barriers to their full assimilation into historically white institutions like that of millions of immigrants and their descendants originating from southern and eastern European countries during the 1890s–1920s era. If a person is perceived as phenotypically not white—as having nonwhite characteristics as defined by the white majority—they will likely never be able to assume a fully white identity with regular white privileges in everyday life. Regardless of their own view, that nonwhite identity will constantly be *imposed* on them by whites, especially those with power over them.

There is no social science research that I know of that shows that a *majority* of white Americans view any contemporary nonwhite group as actually being or becoming white in U.S. society. In one 1999 pilot study, we gave questionnaires to 151 self-defined white college undergraduates. Their task was to categorize a long list of major U.S. racial–ethnic groups into "white," "not white," or "don't know" categories. As expected, most students placed Irish Americans, English Americans, German Americans, and Italian Americans firmly into the white category. However, they reacted very differently to all the groups generally considered to be people of color. An *overwhelming* majority categorized all Asian American groups (e.g., Japanese Americans, Chinese Americans) as "not white." All the Latina/o groups (e.g., Mexican Americans, Puerto Ricans) were also categorized by a large majority of these students as *not* white. Very substantial majorities of these college-age whites did not view and categorize any of these Asian American and Latina/o groups as truly "white." This admittedly nonrandom sample's finding, which probably would be substantially replicated if done today, greatly contradicts arguments that a majority of whites are now, or soon will be, incorporating some nonwhite groups into a truly white racial status in their everyday white racial framing and, likely, their recurring interracial actions.[18] Other researchers examining issues of whether major segments of nonwhite groups such as Latina/o and Asian Americans are now viewed or treated as white by European Americans have come to a similar conclusion.[19]

In addition, the demonstrated white unwillingness to significantly expand the white racial category can be seen in studies of Americans of mixed-race parentage with significant white ancestry, a topic we can now examine in some detail.

Intermarriage and Multiracial Americans

The increasing numbers of racial intermarriages and of mixed-race Americans have received much media and scholarly attention in recent years.

Today about one in seven new U.S. marriages is biracial, most with one white partner and the other nonwhite—the latter most often Latina/o or Asian American.[20] Unsurprisingly, thus, in the 2010 U.S. census, 2.9 percent of respondents identified as multiracial, but a decade later in the 2020 census, with its significantly different racial choice questions, that percentage was nearly 9.8 percent. In regard to that statistical change, the 2021 Census Bureau report on multiracial Americans notes that it was "largely due to the improvements to the design of the two separate questions for race and ethnicity, data processing, and coding, which enabled a more thorough and accurate depiction of how people prefer to self-identify," and it was not a result of large-scale growth in that multiracial population.[21] Nonetheless, this group of Americans is significantly larger now than in it was in the latter part of the 20th century.

Scholars and popular commentators arguing that significant groups of Latina/o and Asian Americans are gaining major white status and privilege often foreground this population of multiracial Americans among them—that is, those who identify as belonging to more than one racial group including white (e.g., in the 2020 Census 2.7 million identity as Asian-white). In their view ever more people in this multiracial group currently are, or will soon become, a part of a new white population majority that will force major change in the country's traditional racial hierarchy. Indeed, celebrations of these multiracials and their increasing numbers have become commonplace in the mainstream media. For instance, *The Atlantic* magazine journalist Hua Hsu writes that in the near future that increasing numbers of these multiracial Americans will likely self-identify as "white," probably enough to significantly delay the development of a white minority nation.[22] Another article in the popular magazine *Psychology Today* titled "Mixed Race, Pretty Face?" accents the growth and allegedly greater beauty and health of lighter-skinned, white-Asian multiracials and their positioning as part of a "new white" America.[23]

Here we might note which racial intermarriages tend to be foregrounded by media and other societal analysts. Take the example of white-Latina/o intermarriages. Those intermarriages most often emphasized do not involve darker-skinned Latina/os of areas like south Texas and California, but rather certain lighter-skinned Latina/os from various U.S. areas. The latter come closer to traditional white phenotypical and normative preferences. However, if an expanding-white analysis mainly accents intermarriages involving white-presenting Latina/o Americans and other similar Americans of color, then it ends up generalizing from a small segment of all such intermarriages as the measure of nonwhite access to privileged whiteness.[24]

Many expanding-white analysts seem to assume that white partnering in interracial marriages results in most such couples, or at least their biracial children, being incorporated into expanded white America. However, the relevant data suggest the opposite may be more likely. For example, the leading demographers Dudley Poston and Rogelio Sáenz conclude in their review of demographic data that mixed-race marriages do not take people "out of the nonwhite group.... If anything, the increased numbers of mixed race-ethnic marriages will increase, not decrease the numbers of nonwhites in the U.S. population."[25]

That is, the children of such intermarriages are more likely than not to add to the number of Americans seen by most whites as phenotypically or otherwise nonwhite, and thus they will not be routinely treated by those whites as actually and fully white. That racial phenotype is typically determined by how their nonwhite parentage is perceived by whites in everyday situations. One social science research study assessed how white children actively categorized multiracial people who had specific white and Black ancestry that was unknown to those children. The children categorized these multiracial individuals as Black more often than white, thereby imposing a Black racial identity on them. When similarly tested, white adults did the same thing.[26] In addition, in a major interview study the parents of mixed-race (Asian-white) children reported that most whites misperceived or ignored their mixed-race ancestry and instead typically treated them in terms of their observable Asian phenotype and ancestry.[27] These and other contemporary data on the lived realities of multiracial children and adults indicate that most are *not* becoming well-integrated into an expanded-white status group. Nor is their increased numerical presence in U.S. society forcing a truly egalitarian treatment of them or a deconstructing of conventional white views of racial privilege.

We might also keep in mind that white Americans have a centuries-old history of viewing "racial mixture" as a degraded condition involving forbidden cross-racial behavior, a view dating back to the long slavery and Jim Crow eras. In addition, early on, the white racist framing of mixed-race Americans included what came to be known as the "one-drop rule," wherein even one ancestor who was known to be Black made a person Black. Operating over the centuries, this widespread framing reveals the refusal of most white Americans to view mixed-race people as "white." Even the liberal U.S. founder, Benjamin Franklin, argued long ago from the dominant white racial frame that white "amalgamation with the other color produces a degradation to which no lover of his country" can ever consent.[28] Subtle, covert, and blatant variations of that old white racist framing remain commonplace today.

Choosing Racial Identities and Discrimination

Quite relevant to arguments about an expanding-white racial category are the empirical issues of how certain often-cited Americans of color, including those who are multiracial, really view themselves and their recurring experiences. The current U.S. vice-president, Kamala Harris, exemplifies this typical mixed-race identification. She proudly identifies her mixed-race ancestry as involving a mother who is a Asian American and a father who is Black American, a relatively rare combination among American families. Even though far-right racist websites have insisted she has claimed to be white, this is false. She has never tried to present herself as white or different from who she actually is.[29]

Interestingly, one study of 46 mixed-race California adults found that those with Asian–white or Latina/o–white parents were able to self-identify successfully as either multiracial or white, likely depending on the social situation they were in. The study's authors speculate that some of these California multiracials could become part of an expanded white category.[30] However, other studies indicate that most mixed-race adults and children do not try to assert being white. Demographers Dudley Poston and Rogelio Sáenz have concluded from their research on changing racial composition of the youngest Americans that most multiracial children identify with their nonwhite backgrounds.[31]

In addition, a recent Pew Research Center analysis of adult Americans who reported in a national survey that their identity involves two or more racial groups found that a significant majority had always viewed themselves as mixed-race, with just 29 percent indicating they had *ever* thought of themselves as only one "race."[32] The Pew researchers also examined the discriminatory experiences of a larger group of survey respondents with near and distant mixed-race ancestry, not only those reporting two or more races in categorizing themselves but also those reporting one race for themselves but also reporting two or more races for a parent or grandparent. Their research report summarizes the better treatment that white-looking multiracials in this larger sample generally faced:

> Multiracial adults who said most people would describe them as White if they passed them on the street were also the least likely to say they had received poor service in restaurants, hotels and other businesses; had been treated unfairly by an employer in hiring, pay or promotion; or had been unfairly stopped by police because of their racial background.[33]

Unmistakably, white perception of a multiracial person's phenotypical look makes a crucial difference in the level of white discrimination in their everyday lives. In contrast, a majority of these Pew multiracial respondents said that *they* were "more open to other cultures and more understanding of people of different backgrounds."[34]

White Racist Framing and Discrimination: Blocking Integration

Operating from the still dominant white racial frame and its subframes, a majority of whites continue to discriminate against Americans of color in overt, covert, and/or subtle ways. Yet analysts accenting the expanded-white majority idea tend to downplay or ignore the research showing the still large-scale discrimination faced by Latina/o, Asian, mixed-race Americans, and other Americans of color. Many such analysts also exaggerate the significant improvement in white attitudes about racial integration suggested in national attitudinal surveys. For example, they argue that white attitudes in opinion surveys about racially segregated institutions have gotten much less supportive of such institutions since the 1950s.[35] While accurate for these brief survey questions, this improvement argument misses larger points about the superficiality of these expressed attitudes, their nesting in a broader white racial framing that is not interrogated, and the discrimination many of these respondents likely still engage in. Consider, too, that much of this major attitudinal shift in white attitudes on surveys about racial integration of major institutions mostly occurred before the 21st century. In addition, many whites' expression of positive racial integration attitudes on superficial opinion surveys probably reflects a desire for social approval and to appear unprejudiced publicly to a pollster.[36]

Most significantly, these apparently liberalized white attitudes seen in surveys regularly give way not only to white expressions of racist views in numerous everyday settings but also to much overt, subtle, and covert racial discrimination there. We know this to be true because of thousands of accounts of white racist framing and white discrimination by Americans of color in many in-depth interview studies, in-depth surveys, detailed ethnographies, and discrimination field testing. These contemporary research studies have documented an array of substantial white discrimination in employment, business, housing, health care, and politics, as well as on the street (e.g., hate crimes). Moreover, much of this white racist framing and discrimination targets racial groups, or large segments within them, that are supposed to be becoming white, such as Latina/o Americans, Asian Americans, and mixed-race people of color.[37]

For instance, citing empirical data on discrimination, scholars G. Christina Mora and Michael Rodríguez-Muñoz have explicitly criticized some demographers' arguments that many Latina/os are moving into a truly white status and privileges category. The argument "that on the whole they are becoming white underestimates the ongoing racial stigmatization and exclusion faced by many in this community."[38] Particularly striking is persisting racial discrimination that takes the form of aggressive anti-immigrant rhetoric and discriminatory actions: "Should we assume that mass deportations, which too often lead to the separation of Latino families, or inflammatory electoral campaigns will have no effect on how Latinos identify and understand their place in U.S. society for years to come?"[39] In their view, some social scientists' projections of Latina/os now, or soon, becoming part of an expanding-white majority are misguided because of the continuing U.S. politics of white supremacist and anti-immigrant agitation. Associated with this is the commonplace reality of other types of white racist framing of Latina/os in California and across the country. For instance, a recent interview study in the Los Angeles area found that the overwhelming majority of a random sample of 40 mostly well-educated whites racially framed the substantial and growing Latina/o population there very negatively. Significantly, these whites did not distinguish among the Latina/o Californians in terms of national origin, citizenship status, or generation, but emphasized that they *all* had a deficient culture threatening to "American values" and that prevented them from ever properly assimilating to white-Anglo mainstream culture. Clearly, these California Latina/os were *not* viewed as white or even as truly American. In addition, these whites were acting on this strong racist framing of Latina/os, as most indicated they had sought to live *racially segregated* lives away from them.[40]

Consider too that in interview studies most Latina/o Americans do not consider themselves as free of serious white discrimination or as being white-privileged in everyday experiences. They do not report themselves, or significant numbers of friends and relatives, gradually or rapidly moving into the category of white-privileged. Several research studies have found that substantial majorities of them report that whites do not view them as white, and they note much experience with everyday racial discrimination. Even if they sometimes mark "white" racial group on Census forms for their identity, this is usually a coping strategy in dealing with the limited options for that Census question and/or with conformity pressures of a white-dominated society, *not* a reconceptualization of their actual racial identity.[41] Note too that the U.S. Census and other official government programs, as well as many social science analysts using their data, portray Latina/o (Hispanic) Americans as being just an "ethnic" group whose members who can be "of any race," including white. This is inaccurate, as is suggested by data in the aforementioned Pew study. In that recent survey, researchers found that most Hispanic respondents viewed "being Hispanic as part of their *racial* background." That is, most are quite aware that white Americans consider them and their families as a "Hispanic race," and *not* as part of the "white race."[42]

Note too that several interview studies of Asian Americans have found that most do *not* view themselves as being or becoming truly white and white-privileged, although like all Americans of color they frequently conform to some assimilationist expectations of a still white-dominated society.[43] Unmistakably, thus, current research data show that the ongoing incorporation of Asian American and Latina/o immigrant groups, and their second and later generation descendants, into U.S. society has included much white discrimination and has *not* brought them to a societal status anywhere close to racial equality with white Americans. Full access

to, and equal status within, the historically white cultural and socioeconomic mainstream emphasized by the expanding-white social science and
journalistic analysts will require that the substantial majority of whites
no longer regularly frame these Asian American and Latina/o American
groups in negative terms—and not just in whites' racist stereotyping, but
also in whites' racist historical and contemporary narratives—and no longer
regularly discriminate against them interpersonally or institutionally.

The Case of Residential Segregation

As I discussed briefly in the Introduction, for centuries, most white Americans have been heavily committed to the country's comprehensive and
multi-institutional racial discrimination. Not even in the 1865–1877
Reconstruction era or the 1960s–1970s civil rights era did a white majority *ever* support comprehensive racial desegregation of major historically
white institutions—e.g., workplaces, schools, legislatures, and residential
areas. In fact, for centuries comprehensive desegregation of historically
white institutions has been a frightening *existential threat* in most white
minds, generation after generation from slavery days to the present. Even
efforts at something less than comprehensive desegregation just in one
historically segregated institution (e.g., in public schools since 1960s civil
rights era) have frequently been met by intense white pushback, including
backward movement to resegregation when whites deem that necessary.

To get a better picture of the scale of this persisting racial segregation,
let us consider in detail the major example of residential segregation and
its impacts and on life patterns. Over several centuries up to the present
day, most U.S. counties, towns, and cities have had substantial racial segregation in their residential and living patterns, in effect a racist structure
built into the country's rural and urban spaces. More than a half century
after the pathbreaking 1968 Fair Housing Act, this highly racialized geography persists, with severely damaging impacts on communities of color.
One recent study of 209 larger metropolitan areas found that 81 percent
were more segregated in 2019 than they had been in 1990.[44] As this report
summarizes, residential segregation is still

> one of the principal causes of group-based inequality, by separating
> people [of color] from life-enhancing resources, such as good schools,
> healthy environments, and access to jobs. This was the raison d'être
> for public accommodations segregation in the Jim Crow South: to
> maintain a racial caste system. But residential segregation does this
> with nearly the same wicked efficiency today.[45]

In all U.S. regions, the metropolitan areas still have a substantial degree
of residential segregation across them, and especially at the neighborhood

and community levels within them. A recent analysis of census data for the 100 largest metropolitan areas by demographer William Frey found that between the year 2000 and the 2015–2019 period the white share of their population had dropped from 64 percent to 54 percent. Still, the white population share of a local community where an average white individual lives was significantly higher, moving from 79 percent to a still very high 71 percent over that period. As he notes in his report, the highly segregated neighborhood experience of the "average white U.S. resident is far different than the national demographic profile would suggest." Elsewhere in his report he emphasizes "that despite the fact that people of color account for the vast majority of recent U.S. population growth, white residents almost everywhere—including those in the nation's most diverse metropolitan areas—continue to reside in mostly white neighborhoods."[46]

Frey also assesses the neighborhood segregation patterns for Black, Latino, and Asian Americans in these metropolitan areas. He finds modest declines in that racial segregation for Black and Latino Americans, but not for Asian Americans. In all three cases, however, their racial segregation indexes remain quite high.[47] A National Fair Housing Alliance report summarized the reality this way: "half of all Black persons and 40 percent of all Latinos live in neighborhoods without a White presence." Their report also shows significant racial segregation of Asian Americans from whites, though less than for Latina/o and Black residents.[48] Yet another recent analysis of still substantial Latina/o housing segregation notes that not only are the country's largest cities still highly segregated, "but the mid-Atlantic, the Midwest, and the West Coast—places where Latinos live—disproportionately make up the most segregated regions."[49]

Note too that research on suburban areas shows that Black Americans continue to be almost as segregated from whites *within* the suburban belts around cities as they were some decades back, while Latina/o and Asian Americas in suburbia are also still significantly segregated from whites.[50] In addition, where there is some significant racial integration of communities within central city or suburban areas, whites frequently take action there to lessen the possibility of equal-status interracial contacts for themselves or their families. For instance, one Los Angeles area study found that white suburban parents mostly "emulate their core-city counterparts, leveraging school enrollment to buffer their children from disadvantaged minorities living nearby."[51]

Moreover, in recent decades, numerous white families have taken yet more extreme segregating action because of their fear of increasing populations of color and residential desegregation in big cities or their suburbs. They are moving from those areas to whiter exurban and rural areas. Journalist Rich Benjamín has researched whites who have fled growing racial diversity in cities on the U.S. coasts. He tracked many of the fearful whites to heavily white exurban areas and mostly white or all-white towns, what he terms "whitopias." He shows that increasing numbers of these whites are

> homesteading in a constellation of small towns and so-called "exurbs" that are extremely white. They are creating communal pods that cannily preserve a white-bread world, a throwback to an imagined past with "authentic" 1950s values but with the nifty suburban amenities available today.... [These are] whiter than the nation, its respective region, and its state.[52]

Patterns and Impacts of Housing Discrimination

What accounts for persisting racial residential segregation? Clearly, an array of white discriminatory actions is the answer. Much research evidence shows that whites still aggressively engage in restricting the residential decisions of Americans of color in order to preserve centuries-old patterns of racial segregation. Repeatedly, housing studies using white testers and testers of color have found significant racial discrimination in rental and purchased housing. One federal study used large-scale field testing with a white tester and a tester of color in 28 metropolitan areas, and like others before it, found that Latina/o, Asian, and Black American homeseekers were much less likely than similarly qualified white homeseekers to be shown relevant housing options. Discrimination typically begins at the homeseeker's first phone call, as "renters whose race is readily identifiable based on name and speech are significantly more likely to be denied an appointment than minorities perceived to be white." When testers made in-person housing visits "renters who are identifiably Black, Hispanic, or Asian are shown fewer units than minorities who are perceived to be white."[53] Additionally, recent social science research has provided much information on how contemporary landlords implement this extensive discrimination. One interview and observational study of 157 rental housing landlords in four cities found that they "distinguish between tenants based on the degree to which their behavior conforms to insidious cultural narratives at the intersection of race, gender, and class."[54] Landlords with large complexes often use computerized racial screening algorithms, while those with smaller complexes mostly rely on their subjective racial assessments and home visits. This housing discrimination is especially burdensome for modest-income Black and Latina/o renters who face even greater white-racist framing by landlords, now facilitated by digital technologies, yet have fewer socioeconomic resources to counter it.

Clearly, the residential segregation of Americans of color has long been central to the operation of this country's very systemic racism. It links to many negative conditions and outcomes for families of color. One recent report on segregated communities in metropolitan areas found that this racial segregation has been shown by much data to have

> harmful impacts in terms of health, educational attainment, employment, income and wealth. This evidence supports our view that racial residential segregation is the mechanism that sorts people into advantaged or disadvantaged environments based upon race, and therefore is the taproot of systemic racial inequality.[55]

A concrete example they provide is the reality of poverty rates being much higher in segregated communities of color than in segregated white communities.

Additionally, this report's researchers further note that U.S. regions with "higher levels of residential segregation have higher levels of political polarization," a situation linked to white right-wing efforts to limit the political clout of segregated communities of color by district gerrymandering and voter suppression. In addition to these harmful socioeconomic, health, and political impacts of residential segregation, there are even broader societal impacts, especially the impossibility of creating in a highly segregated society "a national community with a sense of shared purpose and common destiny."[56] To buttress this conclusion, the report's authors quote the 1968 report of National Advisory Commission on Civil Disorders, the pathbreaking government report that first made the term and concept of *systemic racism* commonplace. That report concluded that replacing the country's Jim Crow racial segregation with full racial integration is "the only course which explicitly seeks to achieve a single nation."[57]

Intentional White Isolation

Central to the way in which whites, especially the elite, have organized this society's spatial and geographical arrangements is their concern, even obsession, with reducing unnecessary white contacts with African Americans and most other Americans of color. One aspect of persisting racial segregation is evident in data showing that most whites live largely separate lives outside a few impersonal settings like larger workplaces and public malls. Today, the substantial majority of whites still resist large-scale, socially intimate, and significant racial integration of personal and family relationships in their residential neighborhoods and communities. A Public Religion Research Institute survey found three quarters of whites had *not even one* person of color in their immediate friendship network. Many of the others had very few friends of color.[58] This socio-racial topography of most U.S. towns, cities, and rural areas has not resulted from chance. It has been most centrally and substantially shaped by recurring segregative and other discriminatory decisions by white real estate agents, white bankers, white home insurers, white politicians, and white families, indeed now for many generations.

Ironically, much data shows these whites opting for racial segregation are acting against some of their own individual and family interests. To take a major example, Centers for Disease Control (CDC) death-rate data show that whites are actually "safer in racially diverse areas—not only from violent deaths in general but specifically from guns, drugs, and suicides."[59] Diversity-fleeing whites seem to frame racial demographic change so negatively that they cannot visualize a U.S. that is not only more racially diverse but also more democratic and healthier, including for whites.

Indeed, whites intentionally living in isolation from and ignorance of people of color means that they do not have the knowledge and experience necessary to cope well with an ever more diverse U.S. future, much less to commit to two-way assimilation of Americans of color in U.S. society. As the prominent social science expert on racial segregation Gary Orfield has suggested, whites growing up in heavily white areas typically have "no skills in relating to or communicating with minorities."[60] In the near future, as the U.S. becomes more diverse, this white weakness will be a major individual and group disadvantage. Additionally, this will become more of an international handicap for a U.S. involved in international trade, politics, and diplomacy in a world where the major political and economic leadership is increasingly nonwhite and where non-European countries are ever more powerful economically and politically.

Melting-Pot Blending of Cultures: Contemporary Fictions

Now let us consider some other problematical aspects of contemporary assimilationist arguments about U.S. society. One contention in the scholarly arguments is that major elements of the home cultures of immigrants of color and their descendants have blended into, and thereby created, a dominant "melting pot" culture that is rapidly replacing the long dominant white-centered culture. And it is not just social scientists and other academic analysts who have accented this melting pot perspective. Mainstream journalists have picked up on it. For instance, the aforementioned *The Atlantic* journalist Hua Hsu envisions a true melting-pot culture. His major examples are musicians of color in the popular music sphere and the integration of people of color in certain sports and some mainstream movies. In his view major aspects of traditional white cultural dominance have already ended:

> Instead of the long-standing model of assimilation toward a common center, the culture is being remade in the image of white America's

multiethnic, multicolored heirs.... Just as Tiger Woods forever changed the country-club culture of golf, and Will Smith confounded stereotypes about the ideal Hollywood leading man, hip-hop's rise is helping redefine the American mainstream.... Pop culture today rallies around an ethic of multicultural inclusion that seems to value every identity—except whiteness.[61]

When referencing American "culture," those arguing strongly for a melting pot present and future frequently have popular entertainment in mind. For instance, they cite the increasing importance of people of color in popular music, in television and movies, and in other mainstream media. They also frequently cite the growth in restaurants offering popular versions of Latin American, Asian, or Middle Eastern foods.

However, apart from certain types of popular entertainment, such as music and a few major professional sports, most U.S. "culture"—more broadly construed to include all major societal institutions—is still heavily shaped by centuries-old white values, norms, folkways, and laws. And most of these institutions continue to be dominated by white, mostly male decision-makers at the top. Even much of our more diverse popular culture's organizational structure (e.g., the rap music industry) is dominated in top decisionmaking positions by white executives. Their white political-economic goals and power usually remain dominant and determinative, if sometimes less obvious than in the past. Clearly, the idealistic notion of a national melting pot with much *reciprocal* assimilation of whites and diverse other racial groups, and thus an end to white dominance, has not been accurate for this country's past, and it is not accurate now. Nor is it likely to be in the near future.

A critical consideration typically missing in the contemporary melting pot argument is the continuing *empirical* reality of white dominance in these major institutional areas. Consider contemporary U.S. food culture. When I lecture on how much U.S. popular culture is still aggressively white-controlled, some critics in the audience will counter with comments about how a diverse international array of foods is now dominant in that popular culture. They cite Chinese, Japanese, Middle Eastern, Asian-Indian, or Mexican food, and try to make the point that whites of European ancestry and their tastes no longer dominate much of U.S. food culture. There is certainly some truth to this reality of more diverse international foods, but such arguments usually miss some less obvious but critical and continuing societal realities.

A central empirical reality here is just how white-bastardized and white-controlled much of that popular cultural reality actually is. A central misunderstanding in the diverse-food argument has been underscored by former Commissioner of the U.S. Food and Drug Administration, David Kessler, in his important book, *An End to Overeating*. He illustrates this misunderstanding with contemporary food examples. In the U.S., he notes,

> bottled teriyaki sauce ... combines soy sauce and rice wine to mimic Japanese flavorings, putting an American spin on a classic Japanese cooking technique. The amount of added sugar makes it far sweeter than anything found in Japan. We've also invented new approaches to sushi classics—for example, mayonnaise-topped tempura shrimp now comes wrapped in rice as a sushi roll.... The dish we call "General Tso's chicken' is loaded with sugar, much to the consternation of the Taiwanese chef who created it.... Traditional Chinese cuisine also makes use of a lot more vegetables than are included in our versions.[62]

With many such examples, Kessler demonstrates how white-run U.S. corporations have aggressively added sugar, fat, and salt to—and otherwise significantly altered—many food items from across the world. So, in the U.S. case "Chinese food" is often not *real* Chinese food, and "Mexican food" is often not genuine Mexican food, and so on. Consider typical U.S. versions of Mexican food. Most European Americans had no idea of what tacos were before the 1960s. Founded by a *white* entrepreneur in 1962, Taco Bell's fast-food restaurants reframed, sanitized, and made palatable Mexican tacos and other Mexican food for a non-Mexican public. In this cross-cultural exchange between whites and Mexicans or Mexican Americans, the latter had little power to negotiate the conditions of this reframing and reworking of their traditional foods within a white-dominated food culture. Unsurprisingly, cultural exchanges across asymmetrical social power lines usually have this biased result. The lesser party has to give up a significant part of its *authentic* national culture in this process. This does not create a truly reciprocal and egalitarian melting pot culture.[63]

Indeed, working for the top corporate executives in the U.S. food industry, who are of course aggressively seeking added capitalistic profits, thousands of U.S. workers are constantly redesigning the world's foods to fit what Kessler calls white "American desires"—and, we might add, white American food and farming norms. Just *who* are these Americans with disproportionate power to redesign the world's foods, and to successfully manipulate via advertising, the media, and other avenues many U.S. (and ever more overseas) consumers to eat them? And, increasingly, to become seriously obese and otherwise diseased from eating too much of them? They are the mostly white, male, and upper-class decision-makers at the top of major U.S. food corporations. As of this writing, for instance, the seven top CEOs in the U.S. food industry are *all white*, and six are men.

More One-Way Assimilationism: Music Culture

We should note too that this white-controlled use of non-European cultural inputs into the dominant U.S. culture applies to earlier immigrants of color, including violently coerced immigrants from Africa, and their contemporary descendants. Over some decades now, there has been much discussion of how African American music and musicians have been assimilated into U.S. mainstream culture, to the point of changing that culture in a dramatic melting-pot way. Indeed, many white musicians and composers have drawn on African American music and musicians to develop this country's popular music sphere. White musicians and music producers have innovated in, or enhanced, their white popular music by taking ideas from Black musical innovations, ideas, themes, and types. However, this cultural appropriation has often been outright musical theft, and whites have regularly bastardized, whitewashed, or unacknowledged what they have done.[64] The idea that these and other nonwhite cultural inputs have resulted in major white cultural *replacement* are thus greatly exaggerated for the contemporary U.S.

In other areas of the contemporary U.S. musical scene, continuing white racial dominance is even more obvious. Consider Philip Ewell, an innovative African American music scholar who has openly challenged the white-framed and white-normed character of classical music education, as exemplified by the dominant Schenkerian theoretical analysis tradition. He has shown how the reality of white racism in music education has moved from overt racial exclusion to current white-racist assimilationist pressures. White-pressured, one-way assimilation is discriminatory, usually painful and harmful to its targets, and by no means an example of an equitable and egalitarian societal reality.[65] In an important research article, Ewell has noted that for decades

> music theory has tried to diversify with respect to race, yet the field today remains remarkably white, not only in terms of the people who practice music theory but also in the race of the composers and theorists whose work music theory privileges.... I posit that there exists a "white racial frame" in music theory that is structural and institutionalized, and that only through a deframing and reframing of this white racial frame will we begin to see positive racial changes in music theory.[66]

Responses to Ewell's well-researched arguments by some white music scholars have insisted that Black people can only become important in the Western musical canon if they fully assimilate to its white normative framing and structure. This insistence signals white entitlement to decide how, when, and for whom that one-way assimilation should take place—and, thus, how U.S. society actually "integrates" people of color.[67] Ewell has also heard from white music critics using hostile language:

> For exposing some of the more insidious elements of whiteness and maleness in American music theory, I have been called inept and incompetent, I've been called a racist, an idiot, a charlatan, a moron, a communist, a nitwit, an anti-Semite, a bigot and, yes, I have been called a [N-word].... And sometimes, astonishingly, such commentary appears in a purportedly peer-reviewed academic music journal.[68]

Indeed, racially exclusionary and/or hyper-assimilationist realities remain commonplace in U.S. higher education, well beyond music education.

White Assimilationism: Major Costs of Conformity

Consider too that scholarly and mainstream journalistic accents on a melting-pot U.S. culture frequently focus on popular culture and ignore the broader meaning of culture I briefly noted previously. That broader meaning of culture includes society's numerous major institutions—in the U.S. case, at least the capitalistic economy, legal system, political system, and educational system. In these major areas, for the most part, conventional white values, norms, folkways, and laws are still conspicuously dominant. Even as whites become a statistical minority of key U.S. states, and eventually of the total population, white dominance will likely continue.

For instance, over several centuries now, Americans of color, with diverse ancestries, have been forced to conform to the laws and norms of a legal system substantially based on English common law. They have also been forced to accept the "standard" American form of the English language. Of course, the dominant U.S. language has long been English, with the privileged dialects being those of middle-class whites and a linguistic framework imbedded with whites' implicit and explicit societal understandings. Other U.S. residents, including new immigrants and their descendants, must assimilate to that specific language and its imbedded understandings. Thus, a 2020 Pew Research Center poll found that majorities of Republican and Democratic Party members alike felt that speaking English was essential to being *truly American*. It may be that many of these respondents were implying a critique of those Americans who mostly speak Spanish, the second most spoken language in the U.S.[69] Note too that English has *not* been forced into sharing the national language spotlight with the Spanish language of many millions of Americans, today or in the past.

One-way assimilationist pressures create many painful problems for people of color. For instance, many white-controlled institutions screen people of color in or out based on whether they fit the white organizational norms and folkways. From ethnographic research on people of color entering certain historically white spaces, social scientists Glenn Bracey and David McIntosh have argued that, in addition to actual physical segregation, institutional segregation is maintained by means of white *race tests* that only allow a few conforming people of color to fully enter "white institutional space." In addition, people of color "who no longer consent to White normativity are quickly discovered and excised." They add that whites also "use cognitive tricks like subtyping, which define [certain] colleagues of color as special exceptions to their otherwise undesirable racial groups."[70] Much white discrimination has this important vetting dimension. A study by Ted Thornhill of admissions screening at historically white colleges and universities found that white admissions counselors tend to prefer Black students "predicated on their racial palatability." When they received inquiry emails from fictitious potential Black students, these admissions counselors were "more responsive to Black students who present as deracialized and racially apolitical than... those who evince a commitment to antiracism and racial justice."[71] These race testing findings are not limited to higher education, for much evidence suggests that contemporary discrimination in many types of historically white institutions includes screening for the "right kind" of people of color while excluding the "wrong kind." Those people of color screened out are frequently those who demonstrate some type of antiracist counterframing directed at institutionalized white racism.

Significantly, one interview study of affluent whites in a major Alabama city found that they generally accented a colorblind view of racial matters, so much so that they asserted they had positive views of certain Black neighbors. There was, however, a limitation in their racially framed views, as they *only* gave positive evaluations to Black Alabamans they felt were actively conforming to their white middle class norms.[72] Additionally, in their research, scholars Jonathan Rosa and Nelson Flores accent this one-way process of assimilation of people of color in contemporary U.S. society. In their view, contemporary white-dominated institutions frequently recruit exceptional people of color "to seek entry to white supremacist institutions and acceptance by white listening subjects." Furthermore,

> efforts to facilitate racialized populations' mastery of supposed [white] "codes of power"... are not empowering in the ways that are regularly discussed in sociolinguistics and related fields, but rather a mechanism for producing *governable subjects* that support the raciolinguistic status quo.[73]

Even diversity efforts in white-controlled organizations are often framed in terms of people of color being *useful* to a particular organization and *conforming* in a process of mostly one-way assimilation to its white-created norms and expectations. This is true in most mainline scholarly fields, including the physical sciences. A rare African American among U.S. physicists, Chanda Prescod-Weinstein, has recently written about racialized experiences and damage in her scientific field:

> like my enslaved ancestors, Black people in the twenty-first century—and other so-called minorities—in science are constructed as a commodity for nation building.... [N]one of this is about what society can do for people of color so much as what service people of color can provide to the national establishment. In this sense, it's not surprising that no one thought to talk to me about melanin, the wonderful biomolecule that historically was used as an excuse to mistreat my ancestors. But having that thought would require believing that physics was for Black people too, rather than that Black people, to the extent that we are welcomed in physics, exist to secure nationalist power.[74]

This society's intense white conformity pressures often have severe health impacts on Americans of color. In a well-researched documentary, the Japanese American researcher Janice Tanaka interviewed third-generation Japanese Americans about their long lives. The general public sees these well-educated, economically well-off Americans as very successful, yet the interviews revealed that many were dealing serious psychological distress, physical illness, alcoholism, or drug addiction. One major reason for their misery and difficulties was that their second-generation immigrant parents, who were U.S. citizens, had been unjustly interned as youth in U.S. concentration camps established by racist white officials during World War II. Coming out of that war, as young parents, many put great pressure on their third-generation children to carefully conform to white expectations and norms, likely seeking to prevent future discrimination by whites.[75] White-racist framing of Asian Americans has long had very negative consequences, including today in the form of the model minority myth that incorrectly assumes they adapt easily to white norms and face no problems of discrimination and other oppression in a still white-racist society. Unsurprisingly, researchers have found similar negative health effects from constant white conformity pressures among Latina/os. Most often experience white discrimination, but "some do it in a state of denial, that is, they deny the reality of anti-Latino bias, discrimination and prejudices around them. And they push their children into an Anglo-like existence."[76] This too can result in negative physical and mental health effects. In these Asian American and Latina/o research data, we observe yet more major weaknesses in the scholarly and journalistic arguments that there is an expanding-white America that includes large segments of these American racial groups on egalitarian terms, now or in the near future.

Future Assimilationism: More Appeasement

Numerous analysts of U.S. population change are forthright in asserting that Americans of color *must* allow whites and their Eurocentric culture and institutions to continue as dominant in the more diverse future.
They do not believe that U.S. society is now reciprocally assimilating, nor
should it do so. One non-U.S. analyst, Eric Kaufmann, a London politics
professor, argues that even if by 2050 there is much more intermarriage,
more mixed-race Americans, and a white population minority, there will
not be, and should not be, a new melting-pot America that is an egalitarian, multiracial democracy. There should be, at most, only what he terms
as a "whiteshift," which means a process in which historically white population majorities persist by absorbing "an admixture of different peoples
through intermarriage, but remain oriented around existing [Eurocentric]
myths of descent, symbols and traditions." Traditional white Eurocen-
trism in culture and society should be the present and future goal because rapid U.S. demographic change toward a white minority is already
creating within the dominant white population "an existential insecurity
channeled by the lightning rod of immigration," that is, great nativistic
anxiety over loss of white identity that feeds hostility to non-European
immigration and fuels the rise of a radical "populist" right in the U.S.[77]

As with the other assimilationist theorists, Kaufman's white appeasement perspective suggests that white Americans will *never* accept a real
mixed-race culture that abandons the Eurocentric sociocultural center. At
best, whites must be pressed to engage in "cultural work to adapt white
majority myths of origin and symbol systems to the new mixed population.... The declining unmixed white population would then need to
accept the rising mixed group and fuse with it." In this assessment, Kaufman demonstrates that he too has bought into a traditional white framing
of whites as just another "ethnic" group and argues that "identifying as
white, or with a white tradition of nationhood, is no more racist than
identifying as Black."[78] He insists that when whites fear immigrants of
color and aggressively defend their racial group interest, this racist defense
should be seen, as for groups of color, as just a "legitimate form of interest
group politics."[79]

Like many other non-U.S. analysts, Kaufmann does not seem to know
the long systemically and foundationally racist history of the U.S. He ignores the fact that whites are still the materially and structurally dominant
group that has gained great power and privilege over 21 generations of
extreme racial oppression and large-scale unjust enrichment at the expense of Americans of color. Unsurprisingly, thus, he favors a long-term
expanding-white process in which white majorities evolve "seamlessly
and gradually into mixed-race majorities that take on white myths and
symbols ... [and] include those of part-white background as white."[80]

Americans with *no* European ancestry should just accept and identify with this reworked national identity that is still centered on white sociocultural norms, traditions, and myths. If this does not happen, and an anti-racist critique and displacement of the white-racist past is foregrounded, he predicts much more aggressive white populist resistance and violent terrorism. If analysts and politicians anticipate this white resistance, they should begin a national whiteshift conversation about these realities, one he views as enabling "conservative whites to find a sense of ethnic continuity in the rising mixed-race population."[81]

In a somewhat similar late 1990s argument, the prominent sociologist, media commentator, and advisor to Democratic Party presidents, Amitai Etzioni, has offered a view of the racially diverse U.S. future as one that will likely be a responsible "monochrome society," by which he means one with a consensus on continuing Eurocentric "American values." He contends that most Americans already embrace the "same basic aspirations, core values, and mores" and likely will continue to do so in future decades, whether or not they have socio-racial backgrounds greatly different from the current white majority. Considering the U.S. situation from the 1990s to 2050s, Etzioni has naively claimed there is a "commitment by all parties to the democratic way of life, to the Constitution and its Bill of Rights, and to mutual tolerance," and that there is a common Eurocentric culture undergirding the country's racial-ethnic diversity. This culture is alleged to be accepted by all Americans, and it includes the "conviction that one's station in life is determined by hard work, saving, and taking responsibility for one's self and one's family." He has contended that, despite major racial differences, most Americans agree on the view of a society involving "shared responsibilities of providing a good society for our children and ourselves—one free of racial and ethnic strife."[82]

In his late 1990s perspective, Etzioni was clearly wrong in his futuristic optimism about all U.S. parties sharing a commitment to U.S. democracy, civility, and a country free of a racial strife, the last clearly refuted in the election of former President Donald Trump and its antidemocratic aftermath. It is contradicted by the widespread and continuing white support—even by some Republicans in Congress and state legislatures—for the terroristic insurrection at the U.S. Capitol in January 2021 and by continuing violence-oriented activism by white supremacist groups. Notably, Etzioni also left out a discussion of how his view of the U.S. future would look in regard to the still prevalent racial, class, and gender oppressions woven throughout major U.S. institutions.

Similarly naive optimism is found in various parts of the mainstream and social media. The political successes by people of color are often exaggerated or misperceived. The mostly white analysts in these media rarely analyze the reality of most politicians of color, who are usually rare in those highest political offices, that have had to markedly *conform* to long-existing white socio-political folkways to secure and maintain their high political positions. Consider these examples. Former Louisiana governor Bobby Jindal once wrote "it is time for the end of race in America." He has constantly operated out of a white racial framing that celebrates the culture and symbols of white America, including describing the Confederate flag as "a symbol of my heritage [that] has nothing to do with racism and hate."[83] Even presidential candidate Barack Obama operated out of white-sensitive strategies copied from the previously successful moderate campaigns of Black political candidates like Massachusetts senator Edward Brooke, Los Angeles mayor Tom Bradley, and Virginia governor Douglas Wilder. Like these successful Black politicians, he "generally shied away from racial controversy as he moved onto the national political scene. He did not run as a 'civil rights' candidate, and he generally distanced himself from what were perceived as 'black issues' on the campaign trail."[84]

Conclusion: Upholding White Supremacy

Without a doubt, there are major problems with the various scholarly and popular viewpoints accenting white racial interests and concerns by making the demographic future appear as one where there will *not* be a white population minority. Indeed, these arguments not only deny empirical reality but also help to sustain the centuries-old idea that the U.S. is and should always be a white-dominant country. They are clearly an example of white appeasement. As sociologists Cristina Morales and Rogelio Sáenz argue, the expanding-white

> efforts to minimize the thunder associated with the country becoming majority-minority for the sake of drawing less animosity against people of color may be seen as noble, [but] in reality it also is an effort to make whites comfortable with new demographic reality.[85]

Similarly, in his book on civil rights politics, Latino sociologist Michael Rodríguez-Muñiz points out that these white appeasement arguments leave out a serious consideration of their longer-term normative implications. That is, appeasement narratives "run the risk of legitimating sentiments of white loss and victimhood and reinscribing the sense of entitlement to dictate the terms of the future."[86]

Unmistakably, this view that the white racial group will, or must, expand unidirectionally by adding people of color acceptable to whites is white-framed. This view does not seriously consider the views of Americans of color, who might well ask: Why should white category expansion be a central U.S. concern and be foregrounded? *Why should traditional white cultural norms be the standard for groups of color to become acceptable residents and citizens in what claims to be a real democratic country?* As one Latina scholar recently underscored in a discussion with me about this expanding-white majority concept, "Why are we striving towards whiteness? Why is white-ness the default mix demonstrating inclusion?"[87]

In my view, the most important problem with social scientists' and other analysts' attempts to downplay the reality of a coming white minority na-tion by assuming multiracial Americans will or must become part of a white majority is that this view sustains centuries-old white supremacist framing of the U.S. as *necessarily* a white-dominant nation in terms of both popu-lation and dominant political-economic power. As demographers Dudley Poston and Rogelio Sáenz have noted, the rhetoric of social analysts

> that questions the authenticity of the U.S. becoming a majority-minority nation and that sees this shift as an illusion serves to up-hold the notions of white supremacy. White supremacy is a system that supports and maintains dominance of whites over people of color. Accordingly, it is impossible for the United States to cease being a country where whites dominate in all respects including demograph-ically. In the process, the discourse of those who deny the actuality of our country becoming majority-minority in the near future serves to allay white distress and horror over the possibility of losing their coun-try to nonwhites. ... a not-so subtle message reassuring whites that they are still in charge even numerically. Certainly, the standardization of all things white as the normal results in many whites not seeing that they have a race or a culture, for those things belong to nonwhites.[88]

Notes

1 See Joe Feagin, *The White Racial Frame*, 3rd ed. (New York: Routledge, 2020).
2 Chanda Prescod-Weinstein, *The Disordered Cosmos* (New York: Bold Type Books, 2021), p. 140.
3 William M. Denevan, "The Pristine Myth: The Landscape of the Americas in 1492," Unpublished Paper, Department of Geography, University of Wis-consin, Madison, Wisconsin.
4 Raewyn Connell, *Southern Theory: The Global Dynamics of Knowledge in Social Science* (Cambridge: Polity Press, 2007), p. 206.
5 Quoted in Prescod-Weinstein, *The Disordered Cosmos*, p. 140.
6 In this and next paragraph I develop further ideas in Joe R. Feagin and Kim-berley Ducey, *Racist America: Roots, Current Realities, and Future Reparations*, 4th ed. (New York: Routledge, 2019).
7 Raya Cohen, "Migration," *Global Social Theory*, https://globalsocialtheory.org/topics/migration/ (accessed June 29, 2022).
8 William Frey, *Diversity Explosion* (Washington, DC: Brookings Institution, 2015), Kindle Loc. 198, 305.
9 Dudley L. Poston and Rogelio Sáenz, "Young White Children are the Minority: The Demography of Whiteness Decline in the United States,"

Paper presented to Population Association of America meeting, St. Louis, Missouri, April 2021.

10 I am indebted here to discussions with sociologist Stephen Klineberg.

11 Richard Alba, *The Great Demographic Illusion* (Princeton, NJ: Princeton University Press, 2020); Dowell Myers and Morris Levy, "The Demise of the White Majority is a Myth," WashingtonPost.com, May 18, 2018, https://www.washingtonpost.com/opinions/the-demise-of-the-white-majority-is-a-myth/2018/05/18/60fc897c-5233-11e8-abd8–265bd07a9859_story.html (accessed May 25, 2021).

12 See Alba, *The Great Demographic Illusion.*

13 See Joe R. Feagin and Clairece B. Feagin, *Racial and Ethnic Relations*, 8th ed. (Upper Saddle River, NJ: Prentice-Hall, 2008), Chapters 1–2, 10.

14 "Appendix," *The Journal of the California Legislature*, 1878 Assembly, p. 47. I am indebted here to suggestions of sociologist Kirk Johnson.

15 Ronald Takaki, *A Different Mirror* (New York: Little Brown, 1993), p. 189.

16 See Joe Feagin, *The White Racial Frame*, 3rd ed. (New York: Routledge, 2020), Chapter 1.

17 See, for example, Rosalind Chou and Joe Feagin, *The Myth of the Model Minority: Asian Americans Facing Racism*, 2nd ed. (Boulder, CO: Paradigm Books, 2015; and Joe Feagin and José Cobas, *Latinos Facing Racism: Discrimination, Resistance, and Endurance* (Boulder, CO: Paradigm Books, 2014).

18 Joe R. Feagin and Danielle Dirks, "Who Is White? College Students' Assessments of Key U.S. Racial and Ethnic Groups," Unpublished Manuscript, Texas A&M University, 2004. On similar findings for Canada, see Maurice Berger, *White Lies: Race and the Myths of Whiteness* (New York: Farrar, Straus, and Giroux, 1999), pp. 41–42.

19 Again, on Asian Americans see Chou and Feagin, *The Myth of the Model Minority*; and on Latino/as, see Feagin and Cobas, *Latinos Facing Racism.* On mixed-race Americans, see the chilling data in Sharon Chang, *Raising Mixed Race* (New York: Routledge, 2015).

20 Frey, *Diversity Explosion*, Kindle Loc. 344.

21 Nicholas Jones, Rachel Marks, Roberto Ramirez, and Merarys Ríos-Vargas, "2020 Census Illuminates Racial and Ethnic Composition of the Country," Census.Gov., August 12, 2021, https://www.census.gov/library/stories/2021/08/improved-race-ethnicity-measures-reveal-united-states-population-much-more-multiracial.html (accessed August 27, 2021). See also U.S. Census Bureau, "The Two or More Races Population: 2010," September 2012, www.census.gov/prod/cen2010/briefs/c2010br-13.pdf (accessed May 17, 2013).

22 Hua Hsu, "The End of White America? *The Atlantic*, January/February 2009, https://www.theatlantic.com/magazine/archive/2009/01/the-end-of-white-america/307208/ (accessed May 13, 2013).

23 William Lee Adams, "Mixed Race, Pretty Face?" *Psychology Today*, January 1, 2006, www.psychologytoday.com/articles/200512/mixed-race-pretty-face (accessed May 13, 2013). I also draw here on Sharon Chang, "Mixed Race, Pretty Face," *RacismReview*, April 4, 2013, www.racismreview.com/blog/2013/04/04/mixed-race-pretty-face/ (accessed May 13, 2013).

24 I am indebted here to discussions with sociologist Randolph Hohle.

25 Poston and Sáenz, "Young White Children are the Minority."

26 Steven O. Roberts and Susan A. Gelman, "Do Children See in Black and White? Children's and Adults' Categorizations of Multiracial Individuals," *Child Development* 86 (November/December 2015): 1830–1847.

27 Sharon Chang, *Raising Mixed Race* (New York: Routledge, 2015).

28 Quoted in Ronald Takaki, *Iron Cages* (Oxford: Oxford University Press, 1979), p. 50. See also Claude-Anne Lopez and Eugenia W. Herbert, *The Private Franklin: The Man and His Family* (New York: Norton, 1975), pp. 194–195.

29 "Fact Check: Kamala Harris did not Switch from Identifying as Indian-American to Black," Reuters, https://www.reuters.com/article/uk-fact-check-harris-did-not-switch-raci/fact-check-kamala-harris-did-not-switch-from-identifying-as-indian-american-to-black-idUSKBN25H1RC (accessed June 30, 2022).

30 Jennifer Lee and Frank D. Bean, "Reinventing the Color Line: Immigration and America's New Racial/Ethnic Divide," *Social Forces* 86 (December 2007): 577–579.

31 Poston and Sáenz, "Young White Children Are the Minority." See also Chang, *Raising Mixed Race.*

32 Juliana Menasce Horowitz and Abby Budiman, "Key Findings about Multiracial Identity in the U.S. as Harris Becomes Vice Presidential Nominee," Pew Research Center, August 18, 2020, https://www.Pewresearch.org/fact-tank/2020/08/18/key-findings-about-multiracial-identity-in-the-u-s-as-harris-becomes-vice-presidential-nominee/ (accessed May 22, 2022).

33 Ibid.

34 Ibid.

35 See Alba, *The Great Demographic Illusion.* Several other social scientists have made this argument in discussions with me since 2020.

36 See Ivar Krumpal, "Determinants of Social Desirability Bias in Sensitive Surveys," *Quality & Quantity* 47 (June 2011), DOI:10.1007/s11135-011-9640-9

37 See detailed summaries of data on contemporary discrimination in Feagin and Ducey, *Racist America,* especially Chapters 5–6.

38 G. Cristina Mora and Michael Rodríguez-Muñoz, "Latinos, Race, and the American Future: A Response to Richard Alba's 'The Likely Persistence of a White Majority,'" *New Labor Forum,* April 2017, DOI: 10.1177/1095796017700124, pp. 1–6.

39 Ibid.

40 Celia Olivia Lacayo, "Perpetual Inferiority: Whites' Racial Ideology toward Latina/os," *Sociology of Race and Ethnicity* 3 (2017): 566–579; Gabriel San Roman, "Study: OC Whites Want Nothing to Do with Mexicans—But Asians Are Okay!" *OC Weekly,* August 22, 2016, https://www.ocweekly.com/study-oc-whites-want-nothing-to-do-with-mexicans-but-asians-are-okay-7440023/ (accessed February 11, 2018).

41 Paul Taylor, Mark Hugo Lopez, Jessica Hamar Martinez, and Gabriel Velasco, *When Labels Don't Fit: Hispanics and Their Views of Identity* (Washington, DC: Pew Hispanic Center, 2012); and Julie A. Dowling, *Mexican Americans and the Question of Race* (Austin: University of Texas Press, 2014). See also Mora and Rodríguez-Muñoz, "Latina/os, Race, and the American Future: A Response to Richard Alba's 'The Likely Persistence of a White Majority'"; and Feagin and Cobas, *Latinos Facing Racism.*

42 Horowitz and Budiman, "Key Findings about Multiracial Identity in the U.S. as Harris becomes Vice Presidential Nominee."

43 See Chou and Feagin, *The Myth of the Model Minority.*

44 Stephen Menendian, Samir Gambhir, and Arthur Gailes, "The Roots of Structural Racism Project: Twenty-First Century Racial Residential Segregation in the United States," Othering & Belonging Institute, University of California, Berkeley, June 30, 2021, https://belonging.berkeley.edu/roots-structural-racism(accessed May 24, 2022).

45 Ibid.
46 William H. Frey, "Neighborhood Segregation Persists for Black, Latino or Hispanic, and Asian Americans," Brookings Institution, April 6, 2021, https://www.brookings.edu/research/neighborhood-segregation-persists-for-black-latino-or-hispanic-and-asian-americans/ (accessed May 24, 2022).
47 Ibid.
48 National Fair Housing Alliance, *The Case for Fair Housing: 2017 Fair Housing Trends Report* (Washington, DC: National Fair Housing Alliance, 2017), p. 6. See also John R. Logan and Brian Stults, *The Persistence of Segregation in the Metropolis: New Findings from the 2010 Census, Census Brief Prepared for Project US2010* (Providence, RI: Brown University, 2011), pp. 2–3.
49 Russell Contreras, "U.S. Latinos Earn Less, Die Earlier in Segregated Areas," Axios.Com, June 24, 2021, https://www.axios.com/2021/06/24/latinos-earn-less-die-earlier-racial-segregation (accessed June 30, 2021).
50 Alana Semuels, "White Flight Never Ended," *The Atlantic*, July 30, 2015, https://www.theatlantic.com/business/archive/2015/07/white-flight-alive-and-well/399980/ (accessed November 13, 2017). See also Daniel T. Lichter, Domenico Parisi, and Michael C. Taquino, "Toward a New Macro-Segregation? Decomposing Segregation within and between Metropolitan Cities and Suburbs," *American Sociological Review* 80 (2015): 843–873.
51 Jared N. Schachner, "Racial Stratification and School Segregation in the Suburbs: Evidence from Los Angeles County," *Social Forces*, November 23, 2021, online, DOI.org/10.1093/sf/soab128 (accessed June 30, 2022).
52 Rich Benjamin, "Refugees of Diversity," *The American Prospect*, September 19, 2009, http://prospect.org/article/refugees-diversity-0 (accessed May 29, 2015).
53 Margery Austin Turner *et al.*, *Housing Discrimination against Racial and Ethnic Minorities 2012* (Washington, DC: U.S. Department of Housing and Urban Development, 2013), pp. 1–5.
54 Eva Rosen, Philip M. E. Garboden, and Jennifer E. Cossyleon, "Racial Discrimination in Housing: How Landlords Use Algorithms and Home Visits to Screen Tenants," *American Sociological Review* 86 (2021): 787–822.
55 Menendian, Gambhir, and Gailes, "The Roots of Structural Racism Project: Twenty-First Century Racial Residential Segregation in the United States."
56 Ibid.
57 Quoted in Ibid.
58 Robert Jones, "Self-Segregation: Why It's So Hard for Whites to Understand Ferguson," *The Atlantic*, August 21, 2014, https://www.theatlantic.com/national/archive/2014/08/self-segregation-why-its-hard-for-whites-to-understand-ferguson/378928/ (accessed November 6, 2017).
59 Mike Males, "There's a Myth That White People are Safer among Other Whites," *Yes! Magazine*, August 21, 2017, http://www.yesmagazine.org/peace-justice/the-myth-of-white-safety-in-white-numbers-20170821 (accessed January 1, 2018).
60 Quoted in George J. Church, "The Boom Towns," *Time*, June 15, 1987, p. 17. This Houston section draws on discussions with sociologist Gregory D. Squires.
61 Hua Hsu, "The End of White America?" *The Atlantic*, January/February 2009, https://www.theatlantic.com/magazine/archive/2009/01/the-end-of-white-america/307208/ (accessed February 2, 2021).
62 David Kessler, *An End to Overeating* (New York: Penguin, 2010), pp. 111–112. See also pp. 184–189.
63 I am indebted here to email exchanges with sociologist Randy Hohle.

64 Joe Feagin, *How Blacks Built America* (New York: Routledge, 2016), pp. 58–67.

65 Philip A. Ewell, "Music Theory's White Racial Frame," Annual Conference of the Society for Music Theory, Columbus, Ohio, 2020; and Philip A. Ewell, "How We Got Here, Where to Next? Examining Assimilationism in American Music Studies," webinar presentation, College of Fine Arts, University of Texas, Austin, November 9, 2020.

66 Ewell, "Music Theory and the White Racial Frame."

67 Ewell, "How We Got Here, Where to Next?"

68 Ibid.

69 Aidan Connaughton, "In Both Parties, Fewer Now say Being Christian or Being Born in U.S. is Important to Being 'Truly American,'" Pew Research Center, May 25, 2021, https://www.Pewresearch.org/fact-tank/2021/05/25/in-both-parties-fewer-now-say-being-christian-or-being-born-in-u-s-is-important-to-being-truly-american/ (accessed June 29, 2021).

70 Glenn E. Bracey III and David F. McIntosh, "The Chronicle of the Resurrection Regalia: Or Why Every Black Hire Is the First," *American Behavioral Scientist* 64 (December 2020): 1961–1974.

71 Ted Thornhill, "We Want Black Students, Just Not You: How White Admissions Counselors Screen Black Prospective Students," *Sociology of Race and Ethnicity* 5 (October 2019): 456–470.

72 Sandra K. Gill, *Whites Recall the Civil Rights Movement in Birmingham* (Cham, Switzerland: Palgrave Macmillan, 2017), pp. 79–84.

73 Jonathan Rosa and Nelson Flores, "Unsettling Race and Language: Toward a Raciolinguistic Perspective," *Language in Society* 46 (2017): 621–647. Italics added.

74 Chanda Prescod-Weinstein, *The Disordered Cosmos: A Journey into Dark Matter, Spacetime, and Dreams Deferred* (New York: Bold Type Books, 2021), p. 90.

75 *When You're Smiling: The Deadly Legacy of Internment*, produced and directed by Janice D. Tanaka, Visual Communications, 1999.

76 Nestor Rodriguez, personal communication. See José A. Cobas, Jorge Duany, and Joe R. Feagin, eds., *How the United States Racializes Latinos* (Boulder, CO: Paradigm Publishers, 2009).

77 Eric Kaufmann, *Whiteshift: Populism, Immigration, and the Future of White Majorities* (New York: Abrams Press, 2019), p. 6.

78 Ibid, pp. 670, 674.

79 Ibid., p. 676.

80 Ibid., p. 695.

81 Ibid., p. 71.

82 Amitai Etzioni, "The Monochrome Society," *The Public Interest*, No. 137, (Fall 1999): 42–55.

83 Shalini Shankar, "Better Off Brown: Why Bobby Won't be President but Piyush Could," Medium.Com, July 29, 2015, https://medium.com/@shalini_shankar/better-off-brown-why-bobby-won-t-be-president-but-piyush-could-948d62556744 (accessed June 26, 2022). I am indebted here to the suggestions of sociologist Kirk Johnson.

84 Thomas J. Sugrue, "A More Perfect Union? Barack Obama and the Politics of Unity," Gilder Lehrman Organization, https://ap.gilderlehrman.org/history-by-era/facing-new-millennium/essays/more-perfect-union-barack-obama-and-politics-unity?period=9 (accessed June 26, 2022).

85 Rogelio Sáenz and M. Cristina Morales, "Demography of Race and Ethnicity," in *Handbook of Population*, ed. Dudley L. Poston, Jr., 2nd ed. (Cham, Switzerland: Springer Nature, 2019), p. 170.

86 Michael Rodríguez– Muñiz, *Figures of the Future: Latino Civil Rights and the Politics of Demographic Change* (Princeton, NJ: Princeton University Press, 2021), p. 216.

87 I am indebted here to discussions with sociologist Melissa Ochoa.

88 Poston and Sáenz, "Young White Children are the Minority: The Demography of Whiteness Decline in the United States." I am indebted here to discussions with sociologist Dudley Poston.

Chapter 2

White Fear of Racial Change

Historical Context, Current Realities

In 2013, the food corporation General Mills ran a pathbreaking Cheerios cereal commercial on television, and then put it on YouTube online. Featuring a family with a white mother and a Black father interacting with their cute biracial child, the *YouTube* video has now been viewed millions of times and gotten both positive and negative reactions. Initially, numerous negative commentators dominated with language of white fear of racial change—for example, assertions that the commercial showed "racial genocide" and was "anti-white." In response to the initial negative reactions, many of them vicious, General Mills had to disable the comments section on the YouTube video.[1]

Recall that just a few years later, in August 2017, hundreds of angry white neo-Nazis and other white nationalists protested at the "Unite the Right" rally in Charlottesville, Virginia. They were shouting slogans from the nativistic "great replacement theory" like "You will not replace us." In surveys, millions of whites indicated they agreed with such extremist racist slogans. Indeed, just prior to their angry protests, the former Ku Klux Klan grand wizard, David Duke, had commented:

> This represents a turning point for the people of this country. We are determined to take our country back, we're going to fulfill the promises of Donald Trump, and that's what we believed in, that's why we voted for Donald Trump, because he said he's going to take our country back and that's what we gotta do.

In a later Twitter comment to Trump, he said that "I would recommend you take a good look in the mirror & remember it was White Americans who put you in the presidency, not radical leftists."[2]

White Racial Fear: Past and Present

Today as in the past, a great many white Americans have demonstrated this substantial fear or anxiety over being reduced in white power and

DOI: 10.4324/9781003359883-3

privilege by historically subordinated racial groups. As we see in these demonstrations, many aggressively foreground extremist ideas and terms like "white replacement" and "white genocide." Central to this array of racist concepts is the view that white dominance and supremacy require not only white-controlled institutions and culture but also numerical dominance as a majority-white U.S. population. Most whites are now aware of substantial population increases in Americans of color in recent decades, growth likely continuing far into the U.S. future. This browning of America is, as I suggested previously, a truly *existential* threat for a great many whites.

In his first major presidential address in 1933, the new president Franklin D. Roosevelt gave perhaps the most famous speech in U.S. history about public fears. In the midst of the 1930s Great Depression, he spoke as if he were speaking to future U.S. crises as well:

> This is preeminently the time to speak the truth, the whole truth, frankly and boldly. Nor need we shrink from honestly facing conditions in our country today. This great Nation will endure as it has endured, will revive and will prosper. So, first of all, let me assert my firm belief that the only thing we have to fear is fear itself—nameless, unreasoning, unjustified terror which paralyzes needed efforts to convert retreat into advance.[3]

Roosevelt was referencing the great fear of the future in a country then suffering through the very devastating socioeconomic impacts of the Great Depression. Nonetheless, his perceptive statement can be adapted to understand the negative societal consequences of the significant increase today in whites' unreasoning fears of major racial change.

In both the elite and the general population, whites have frequently worried about increased numbers of Americans of color, including immigrants of color, becoming too numerous and rising up against white-enforced oppression to create a freer and more equal societal status for themselves. Over these centuries, unfortunately, our U.S. educational system has not kept Americans well informed about our systemically racist history, including recurring resistance by Americans of color to white racism and their major role in expanding the freedom, democracy, and social justice loudly proclaimed in the country's centuries-old rhetoric. That important antiracist history has rarely been taught in any detail to young Americans, especially those below the college level, and indeed has generally been hidden from most Americans of all ages.

Moreover, a great many whites, and some others, are in vigorous denial of the country's long white-racist history, to the point of encouraging or allowing right-wing lawmakers to prevent it from being honestly taught in elementary and secondary schools. Many elite and ordinary whites have also tried to prohibit it from being taught in college courses and work-place diversity training. Currently, authoritarian censorship of such truth-ful teaching on the part of many right-wing political officials is advancing rapidly in this country. For an individual, psychologists define "denialism" as an unhealthy defense mechanism "in which confrontation with a per-sonal problem or with reality is avoided by denying the existence of the problem or reality."[4] Similarly, contemporary white *social denialism* in-volves a large group of Americans avoiding a serious societal problem and harsh social reality—in this case our extensive white-racist history—by denying its very existence.

Foregrounding the well-documented realities of this country's systemi-cally racist history is one goal of this book. This historical emphasis should help all readers better understand that current racial demographic changes are substantially an outcome of that complex racialized past. It should also assist in understanding that the many recent, and likely future, antiracist protests by Americans of color and their white allies against this country's systemic racism are a continuation of similar protests and other resistance in our long and racially oppressive past, including many protests against the white failure *ever* to implement this country's much heralded founding rhetoric of "liberty and justice for all."

Numerous demographic and other social analysts discussed in Chapter 1 recognize there is a pervasive and problematical racist framing of U.S. society in the contemporary white population, but they reject the data on the inevitable reality of a coming white-minority nation, at least in part, so as not to inflame the pervasive white sense of losing dominance and of ex-istential peril. By doing so, however, they help to keep the old white racist framing of white supremacy as dominant in this society. Unfortunately, today in the writings, speeches, and other expressive actions of elite and ordinary whites one still witnesses a great emphasis on and foregrounding of the hardcore center of this white racist frame that irrationally asserts white virtuousness in major societal matters—including superior white history, civilization, intelligence, physique, values, and morality.

Early White Fears: Immigrants, African Americans, Native Americans

Concern about or fear of certain new immigrants, especially those not considered at time of entry to be "white" or "white enough," goes far back to the first centuries of this country. The white elite and its polit-ical acolytes have a centuries-long history of anti-immigrant sentiment and actions. Prior to the 1787 creation of a U.S. Constitution, during the Revolutionary war, major leaders like General George Washington openly expressed negative views of inferior "foreigners," by which they usually meant new immigrants from Germany and Ireland. Soon, one of the first acts passed by the new U.S. Congress was the 1790 Naturalization Act explicitly limiting citizenship for new immigrants to those who were "free white persons." In the late 1700s, the British American founders in the new Federalist Party became concerned about recent non-British immigrants' political radicalism (e.g., that of French immigrants), especially their support for the emerging Democratic-Republican Party. The Federalist legislators passed a 1798 Alien Act giving power to English American President John Adams to deport those immigrants considered a political threat. The dominant English and other British Americans were often nativistic in regard to immigrants who did not know the English language. Even the liberal white founder Benjamin Franklin was hostile to inferior ("swarthy") German immigrants who, he feared, would soon "be so numerous as to Germanize us instead of us Anglifying them."[5] Yet more German and Irish immigrants entering during the 1840s and 1850s, often viewed by native-born whites as not white or as off-white, were targeted for much white nativistic agitation. Secret societies, such as the "Know-Nothing" movement, fought non-British immigration. White Know-Nothings were elected to state legislatures, Congress, and state executive offices, and they often precipitated or ignored violent attacks against these "undesirable" immigrants.[6]

Most in the founding white elite were generally antidemocratic in their thinking about less well-off whites such as these more recent immigrants and their descendants. These elite men generally agreed there was an "excess of democracy" in the country, and they especially meant among non-elite whites. They were disturbed that some of the colonies, and later as U.S. states, were too democratic in their political institutions, including political participation of the inferior new immigrants. For example, the Pennsylvania Constitution and its political structure did not have a

> Senate to overturn stuff that happened in the House. There was a president of Pennsylvania, but he couldn't veto laws. There were courts in Pennsylvania, but they also couldn't overturn laws. All you had to do if you wanted to get a law passed in Pennsylvania under their Constitution of 1776 was get it by the lower house, the only house, of the state legislature.[7]

In addition, the white male representatives there were elected annually and thus were directly obligated to the voters. Seeing this political structure as an excess of democracy, the elite white men at the 1787 Constitutional convention made the U.S. government much less democratic—with a House of Representatives with too-large districts, a Senate not directly elected by ordinary voters, and a president not directly elected by ordinary voters. Historian Woody Holton has summarized this counter-majoritarian reality: "You've got massive insulation between the people making decisions and the voters. And that is by design."[8]

Of course, one of the largest early and continuing immigrations to North America in this era was that forced on enslaved Africans. In several North American colonies, enslaved African and Native Americans were a substantial proportion of the population, sometimes a majority. In 1750, Maryland was 31 percent African American, Virginia was 44 percent African American, and South Carolina was 61 percent African American. Most were enslaved.[9] White worries over maintaining their dominant racial status and demographic majority in the colonies, and later in the U.S. states, were early on existential and commonplace, especially after uprisings and other types of resistance by enslaved Americans. At the U.S. Constitutional Convention, the leading Virginia slaveholder George Mason spoke of his great *fear* of slave revolts. In his view, the continuing slave trade would bring in more African Americans and make the new country ever less defensible and "more vulnerable," and he was referring to white vulnerability.[10] As a result, the elite white men there put Article 4, Section 4, in the new Constitution, which stipulates that the federal government must help state governments put down domestic violence, which included the slave uprisings many of these men feared.[11] In spite of their fears, however, the majority also supported or acquiesced in the continuing and profitable importation of enslaved Africans for two more decades. The majority of white men in this important Constitution-making elite, like the majority of those who signed the earlier (1776) Declaration of Independence, were or had been slaveholders or were directly involved in the slavery system as merchants, bankers, lawyers, and the like.

Moreover, as one can see from the white elite's highly racist statement about the menace of "merciless Indian Savages" in the Declaration of Independence, they also greatly feared the resistance of Indigenous Americans to white colonizing invasions. This was true for ordinary whites too. The scholar Cristina Beltrán puts it well: "With white citizens fearful that Indian attacks would 'annihilate' their 'infant communities,' frontier freedom represented an ongoing opportunity for white citizens to engage in practices of invasion, war, removal, and settlement."[12]

When whites' racial oppression and rationalizing racial framing are challenged by substantial resistance from those oppressed, whether in this revolutionary era, the 1860s Civil War era, the 1960s civil rights era, or the contemporary era, they often aggressively—verbally, violently, or both—assert their racial superiority. Every era since the first decade of white North American colonialism has seen many fearful whites organizing substantial military and policing forces to protect themselves against antiracist uprisings and other protests by oppressed nonwhite Americans, even those that are peaceful and democratic in their goals.

"The Menace of the Under-Man": Early 20th-Century Fears

White distress and anxiety over racial change accelerated again in the early 20th century. Leading white Americans—intellectuals, legislators, industrialists, and presidents—were developing and spreading strong versions of a white "race suicide" theory under that explicit label. Their arguments were forerunners of today's white supremacist arguments operating under the now commonplace labels of "white genocide" and "great replacement theory" (also known as "white replacement theory"). Developed dramatically in the decades after 1900 by academic eugenicists and other white supremacists, their concept termed "race suicide" emphasized what they saw as a great threat to white Anglo-Protestant American dominance of U.S. society.[13] The alleged threat stemmed from the failure of white Anglo-Protestant families to have enough children to counter the growing numbers of children of recent immigrants, then the mostly poor Jewish and Catholic immigrants from southern and eastern European countries deemed to be lesser European "races."

Still read by ardent white supremacists today, one influential white author was Madison Grant, an important zoologist and Republican intellectual who in 1916 published what became a much-cited racist book, *The Passing of the Great Race*. It went through multiple editions. Grant was a well-educated eugenicist who advocated numerous views associated with the scientific racism spreading in that period. He argued that the many new immigrant groups from southern and eastern Europe, such as the Catholic Italian and Polish immigrants, were *inferior racial groups* that would interbreed with and thereby destroy the dominant and racially superior white "Nordic race."[14] He further insisted these superior white Nordics faced "race suicide" from this and other types of racial intermixing:

> Neither the black, nor the brown, nor the yellow, nor the red will conquer the white in battle. But if the valuable elements in the Nordic race mix with inferior strains or die out through race suicide, then the citadel of civilization will fall for mere lack of defenders.[15]

About the same time, the Harvard-educated lawyer and historian Lothrop Stoddard published another highly influential book, *The Rising Tide of Color: Against White World-Supremacy*. Stoddard was also a white supremacist and argued there for the "overwhelming preponderance of the white race in the ordering of the world's affairs... the indisputable master of the planet."[16] Stoddard's book is a visual wonder that documents his great fear of a world populated by people of color, a book with maps showing just where the threatening inferior racial groups lived. The visual presentations are accompanied by strong words of fear and anxiety about how "colored" migration from these places to the Western world "is a universal peril, menacing every part of the white world."[17] Just two years later, the now famous Stoddard published *The Revolt Against Civilization: The Menace of the Under-Man*, which made quite clear that he feared the end of white Anglo-Saxon Protestant dominance in Western countries, especially the U.S. At one point, he asserts:

> For a long time past American biologists and sociologists have been coming more and more to the following conclusions: (1) That the old "Native American" stock, favorably selected as it was from the races of northern Europe, is the most superior element in the American popu-lation; ... that the more recent immigrants from southern and eastern Europe average decidedly inferior to the north European elements; ... that the negroes are inferior to all other elements.[18]

In this second book the only times he uses the word "white" are for that first category of native-born, superior white Anglo-Saxon Protestant "stock." There he also makes clear that the southern and eastern European immigrants are still in an inferior "off-white" limbo category between pure whites and very negatively stereotyped Black Americans. Note too that Stoddard was a fierce advocate of racist eugenics and the superiority of the racial-genetic inheritance of the superior white people—that is, an advocate of the rapidly spreading and influential scientific racism of this era. Unmistakably, Stoddard was fixated on "racial mixing."

Moreover, as historian Matthew Guterl notes, Stoddard's book about "the menace of the under-man" was internationally influential. It argued so well "for the segregation and sterilization of 'the unfit' (and especially immigrants into white nations) that it was quick translated into German, and played a key intellectual role in shaping the Nazi Holocaust."[19] In that era of racialized fascism, the genocidal Holocaust targeted what the Ger-man Nazis considered to be *under-men* (in German, *Untermensch*), not only European Jews but also the Roma and Slavic peoples in Europe.

Interestingly, in spring 1929, a multiracial Chicago cultural organiza-tion set up a debate on the topic of "Shall the Negro Be Encouraged to Seek Cultural Equality?" between Lothrop Stoddard and the leading Afri-can American scholar and NAACP activist, W. E. B. Du Bois. Stoddard had even cited Du Bois in *The Rising Tide of Color* book with regard to Du Bois's point that people of color across the globe were beginning to revolt against white domination. Before a crowd of several thousand, a majority African American, Du Bois went first and asked why anyone should not be able to seek societal equality, insisting that Black Americans have made remarkable socioeconomic progress since the end of slavery. He adds that such Black progress has never been the Nordic program. Their program is the subjection and rulership of the world for the benefit of the Nordics. They have overrun the earth and brought not simply modern civilization and technique, but with it exploitation, slavery and degradation to the majority of men.... They have been responsible for more intermixture of races than any other people, ancient and modern, and they have inflicted this miscegenation on helpless unwilling slaves by force, fraud and insult; and this is the folk that today has the impudence to turn on the darker races, when they demand a share of civilization, and cry: "You shall not marry our daughters!" The blunt, crude reply is: "Who in Hell asked to marry your daughters?"[20]

Here the insightful Du Bois references the centrality of the centuries-old white obsession over "racial mixing," in this case countering with the reminder that *whites* have intentionally forced much racial mixing under slavery conditions. Ironically, for generations now, the very idea of racial desegregation at the level of interracial relationships brings forth much white fear and anger about "racial mixing" stemming from Black not white actions. This racist perspective emerged during the slavery era when ordinary white southerners were constantly warned by elite whites in newspapers and from other elite sources that "without slavery, they would be forced to live, work, and inevitably procreate with their free black neighbors."[21] For instance, the white-run *Louisville Daily Courier*, in a border state with many enslaved Black people, warned ordinary whites that, if ever freed, many Black men would try to mate with "their" women and "amalgamate together the two races in violation of God's will."[22] To take another example, in the 1820s, the famous white artist Edward Clay published racist cartoon-like prints with images of white–Black couples and multiracial children, thereby visually illustrating white hostility to "race mixing" that allegedly would result from slavery's abolition. A few decades later in the Civil War era, white anti-abolition journalists in the North even created a new negative word "miscegenation" for such cross-racial relationships.[23]

Interestingly, though considered by many whites of the time a powerful American intellectual, Lothrop Stoddard made rather feeble replies to the sharp Du Bois commentary on racial matters and even claimed there was "Negro delusion" in seeking racial equality since the Civil War. Stoddard then laid out a bi-racialism solution he insisted could involve yet more "separate but equal" arrangements for Black Americans. In a savvy reply, Du Bois cited the extreme Jim Crow segregation already in place and firmly pointed out that Stoddard himself had *never* experienced a radically inferior Jim Crow rail car. Soon, the majority Black audience laughed the hapless Stoddard off the stage.[24]

Nonetheless, both Stoddard and Madison Grant had a major and continuing impact on powerful white media commentators and on leading white politicians in the White House and Congress. The famous Republican President Theodore Roosevelt, who proudly considered himself a scientific racist, praised Madison Grant's book *The Passing of the Great Race*, for its "grasp of the facts our people need to realize."[25] Roosevelt agreed with other racist eugenicists that there was a major contemporary problem of white "race suicide" because Anglo-Protestant whites were not having enough children. A few years later, Republican President Warren G. Harding said that he too rejected any social equality between white and Black Americans and cited Stoddard's book *The Rising Tide of Color* for supposed evidence that there was a global "race problem." His predecessor as president, the world famous Democrat Woodrow Wilson, had similar anti-egalitarian views that were supportive of Jim Crow segregation, and at the White House he actually celebrated one of the first U.S. motion pictures, *Birth of a Nation*, which is based on a hyper-racist novel celebrating the rise of the Ku Klux Klan.[26] Indeed, Wilson viewed the global role of the white-dominant U.S. during the World War I era as extraordinarily important and therefore that, initially, staying out of that war was essential because "white civilization and its domination over the world rested largely on our ability to keep this country intact."[27]

Numerous members of the U.S. Congress were likewise influenced by Grant, Stoddard, and other leading white-racist intellectuals. Among these was powerful Republican Senator Henry Cabot Lodge, a nativistic English American, who feared that current and potential southern and eastern European immigrants posed a serious "threat" to the U.S. social fabric. In his view, admitting more of these racially inferior European immigrants, most of whom were also not Protestants, would destroy the "superior Nordic race." Lodge, like other white supremacists then and now, linked his superior Nordic race notions to Protestant Christianity.[28] Repeatedly, we observe in almost all these racist commentaries by leading white politicians the early versions of the current "great replacement theory" now commonly asserted by U.S. white nationalists. Unsurprisingly, Lodge led other nativistic white members of Congress, the overwhelming majority, in passing highly racist anti-immigrant legislation. This included the major 1924 Immigration Act that excluded or limited most U.S. immigrants other than whites from northern European countries for decades, indeed until the mid-1960s.

Note too that Madison Grant and Lothrop Stoddard were not alone in fostering highly racist narratives and myths about U.S. history and society. Most other white intellectuals of their era held similar views. For example, prominent white historians writing before and during this era celebrated whites and white racial domination in their assessments of slavery and other U.S. history, including the history of U.S. immigration. Most took white domination and centrality as normal and did not problematize the country's systemic racism. For instance, the prominent pro-slavery Yale University historian, Ulrich B. Phillips, wrote very influential books like *American Negro Slavery* (1918) and *Life and Labor in the Old South* (1929) in which he portrayed Black Americans in overtly racist terms. There he argued that Black enslavement was essential to maintaining white social control over them. In his very influential view, the ruthlessly oppressive plantation system was a paternalistic necessity, and resistance by these enslaved Americans was alleged to be a reversion to alleged "savagery."[29]

Like Grant and Stoddard, Phillips and most white historians and other academic analysts of this era—including the major Phillips school of slavery historiography—operated out of a strong white supremacist version of the old white racial frame, one aggressively prizing white civilization and accenting Black racial inferiority. Like Stoddard and Grant, they helped to make the country's systemic racism seem a quite normal and natural state of affairs. Their recurring fears of African Americans and other Americans of color rising up against racial segregation and other oppression are evident in many of their scholarly and popular writings.

Even so, in this long era, numerous African American leaders and scholars, including the great W. E. B. du Bois, radically dissented from these white scholars' views of those enslaved and of the oppressive slavery system. Indeed, Du Bois's major historical book, *Black Reconstruction*, helped to shift later histories of U.S. slavery in a much more critical direction, including more historical discussions of the many positive impacts of African Americans and other people of color in building a more free U.S.[30] Du Bois and other scholars of color showed that hundreds of uprisings against slavery and other types of racial oppression were necessary and that such resistance efforts helped greatly in moving U.S. society in a more democratic direction.

White Racial Fears: The Contemporary Era

For generations now, majorities of white Americans have expressed much fear, anxiety, or rage about losing significant white dominance over Americans of color. This is more than an emotional and ideological issue for them, for it is ontological and existential—that is, about their very being and existence as *white* people. Since the 1950s–1960s civil rights expansion era, many examples of this can be seen in the extreme white reactions to civil rights movements and other efforts for multiracial democracy.

To take a major example, after running as an integrationist candidate in 1958 and losing to a segregationist, Alabama's famous George Wallace shifted dramatically to a segregationist position and won the governorship handily in 1962. He won the votes of huge numbers of ordinary whites who bought into his anti-Black views and other white supremacist views.

In January 1963, this new Alabama governor delivered a melodramatic inaugural speech at the Alabama State Capitol, on the spot where the slaveholder Jefferson Davis had been sworn in as president of the Confederate States of America a century earlier. His intensely white supremacist speech was directed specifically at the Black rights movement's desegregation efforts in his state. He asserted emphatically that "In the name of the greatest people that have ever trod this earth, I draw the line in the dust and toss the gauntlet before the feet of tyranny, and I say segregation now, segregation tomorrow, segregation forever!"[31] Of course, he had *white* people in mind as the "greatest people," and the tyranny he emphasized was the long overdue efforts of the federal government to accelerate racial desegregation of public schools and other historically white institutions throughout the Jim Crow South. Revealingly, Wallace and his white supremacist speechwriter firmly asserted what a great many whites did still believe in the South and the North—that the civil rights movement had gone too far and that much racial segregation was normal and desirable.[32]

Still, in spite of strong southern segregationist resistance, and under pressure from the U.S. civil rights movement and concerned about international publicity about and critiques of Jim Crow segregation (especially in decolonizing countries), the U.S. Congress managed to pass three important 1960s civil rights laws accelerating racial desegregation in several important societal areas, including employment, voting, and housing. However, over the decades since, white distress and fear over traditionally white-dominated institutions becoming too desegregated has led to much backtracking on the early civil rights progress. Civil rights laws and court desegregation decisions have often been weakly implemented by underfunded federal and state agencies that are overwhelmed by the extensive scale of discrimination or run by whites with weak or no commitments to civil rights goals. As a result, year after year, millions of white discriminatory acts still target Americans of color with little or no significant redress available.[33]

By the early 1970s, there was significant political pushback against the civil rights movement's partial desegregation successes. Since that era white Republican Party leaders have moved to what politicians and media analysts call a "southern strategy," one designed to play into white voters' racist fears and to attract them away from the Democratic Party once dominant in southern states. Since the Richard Nixon presidency (1969–1974), this reactionary Republican strategy has accented white voters' *racial* interests in the South (and soon spread to whites' racial interests elsewhere). This strategy has frequently used codewords and concepts like "states' rights," "racial quotas," "street crime," and "critical race theory" that are still commonplace in whites' racist framing of Black Americans, other Americans of color, and racial desegregation efforts.

In addition, since the 1970s, white pushback against desegregation and other racial change has taken the form of significant growth or expansion of white nationalist and other white supremacist organizations. These fearmongering organizations and their leaders have forcefully reasserted the decades-old contentions of racist leaders like Madison Grant and Lothrop Stoddard that whites are facing "race suicide" and threat of replacement as the dominant racial group. Increasingly, this alleged threat is termed "race genocide," such as by white nationalist leaders in groups like the National Socialist White People's Party. This neo-Nazi group's 1970s newsletter, like others on the racist far-right, published articles emphatically questioning the calls by environmentalists and other reformers for reducing U.S. and Western population growth. An example is their widely circulated article titled the "Over-Population Myth is Cover for White Genocide."[34] This fearmongering argument insisted that whites must reject contraception and *breed* many more children lest they become outnumbered by people of color in the country's future population.

Another example of these white nationalist groups and leaders was the influential neo-Nazi David Lane. He was a member of a white terrorist group, The Order, that killed several people, including a Jewish American talk show host, and engaged in robberies bringing in millions for white nationalist causes. Writing from prison, Lane successfully popularized the current "white genocide" concept in the 1980s and 1990s. He became famous for his terroristic "White Genocide Manifesto," in which he portrays the official U.S. government's efforts at racial desegregation of society as specifically implementing racial genocide.[35]

Since the 1990s, thousands of alarmed white nationalists have aggressively proclaimed versions of the white genocide argument. This white nationalist theorizing has been spread by an array of new racist organizations and by internet websites like "Stormfront" that get millions of viewers. Far-right research funding organizations like the Pioneer Fund have supported many white-racist researchers, including those seeking to prove the racial inferiority of Americans of color. Organizations like the New Century Foundation have had online conferences on the browning of America and of other countries, with openly expressed concerns about alleged white genocide and white racial survival.[36] Today, such extremist arguments appear throughout contemporary social media and other online blog posts by a large assortment of white individuals and groups, including the posts of recent white mass shooters. In a recent Google search that I did, the term "white genocide" appeared 2.9 million times on a great array of internet websites. Running this term in Google's Ngram program revealed it has also *sharply* increased in use in Google's huge catalogue of English articles and books since the 1980s.

Prominent White Conservatives' Fears: The 1990s and After

In addition to these white nationalist organizations and their extremist leaders, over the last several decades we have seen more mainstream conservative politicians, media commentators, and authors articulating a variety of similarly fearful themes about the browning of America in their writings, speeches, and organizing actions.

Consider, for example, the former White House Communications Director under right-wing President Ronald Reagan in the 1980s and later Republican presidential candidate, Patrick Buchanan. He has authored numerous white Christian nativistic and nationalistic books, media articles, and speeches. In one such commentary, he expressed his hope that U.S. "Judeo-Christian values" will be preserved and that "our Western heritage is going to be handed down to future generations and not dumped on some landfill called multiculturalism."[37] In fearful terms similar to those of numerous other white Christian conservatives, Buchanan accents the theme of protecting what he views as superior and highly virtuous white civilization, one needing to be vigorously protected for future white generations. In another media setting, Buchanan made a pointed racist comment that

> if we had to take a million immigrants in, say, Zulus next year or Englishmen, and put them in Virginia, what group would be easier to assimilate and would cause less problems for the people of Virginia? There is nothing wrong with us sitting down and arguing that issue that we are a European country, English-speaking country.[38]

By "people of Virginia" Buchanan clearly means whites, and *not* the substantial population in that state who are Americans of color—and who might be quite comfortable with such non-European immigrants. By Zulus he means Black Africans, yet Black Africans have been in Virginia much longer than Buchanan's own Irish ancestors. Here he accents his intensely white-racist framing, including nativistic fear of immigrants seen as unassimilable into a dominant Eurocentric culture. Explicit too is his viciously expressed view that U.S. culture cannot be healthy and multicultural.

Later on, in a 2008 article called "A Brief for Whitey," Buchanan again emphasized the centrality of white virtuousness in his racist framing. He insisted that African Americans should be *grateful* for having been enslaved, Christianized, and allegedly civilized by white Europeans. In addition, he argued that there should be a national conversation on race that would give supposedly silenced white Americans "a voice."[39] Already at that time, conservative white Republicans like Buchanan were fearful about the possible election of a Black man as president, which might somehow cut off the voices of white Americans. This was an odd and disingenuous argument because elite whites, then as now, were in nearly complete control of major mainstream media and in control of numerous newer social media outlets. Moreover, in his 2011 book *Suicide of a Superpower*, published by a leading New York publisher, the bombastic Buchanan echoes not only the white-suicide language of earlier white supremacists like Grant and Stoddard but also that of activists in contemporary neo-Nazi and other white extremist groups. He reiterates nativistic and nationalistic themes, alleging that the U.S. is disintegrating because of the "stunning decline" in white Christianity, white "American values," and white population dominance. He again fumes at the significant increase in immigrants and other Americans of color in the U.S. population and at the growing accent in many progressive organizations on increasing racial diversity and multiracial democracy.[40]

Today, Buchanan is not alone among the white elite in his strong white nativistic and nationalistic views. For example, consider Peter Brimelow, a former editor at the leading business magazine *Forbes* and onetime aide to the prominent conservative Republican Senator Orrin Hatch. Now the editor of a racist-right website, Brimelow has made similar arguments against immigrants of color and their descendants in his *Alien Nation*, an infamous book also published by a major U.S. publishing company. In his writings, he has regularly expressed great fear about an alleged decline of Western civilization from too many immigrants and other people of color. From his bluntly white-framed viewpoint, the "American nation has always had a specific ethnic core. And that core has been white." Back in the 1950s before racist U.S. immigration laws were eliminated and before there were large-scale civil rights movements, most Americans "looked like me. That is, they were of European stock. And in those days, they had another name for this thing dismissed so contemptuously as 'the racial hegemony of white Americans.' They called it 'America.'"[41] An immigrant from Europe himself, Brimelow established in 1999 the white supremacist VDARE website, which has continued to the present to attack contemporary nonwhite immigration and express other aggressively white-framed nativistic and nationalistic perspectives. Indeed, his *Alien Nation* screed has been republished recently in an ebook version, with a new foreword aggressively repeating his decades-old racist views. The book seems to be popular on the white racist-right, judging from its numerous positive reviews on the Amazon books website.

Countless other white U.S. and European intellectuals, media commentators, and politicians have recently expressed similar takes on these racial issues. For example, reviewing a demographic book on the browning of America, Christopher Caldwell, influential editor of the far-right *Claremont Review of Books*, has suggested that many Americans are not currently fearful enough:

In days when people spoke more freely about such matters, dramatic change in the dominant population of the world's dominant power would have been occasion for speculation and worry. About whether, for instance, as more of its citizens come from non-European back-grounds, the United States will change its idea of its cultural heritage.[42]

Oddly, in his fearful statements, he seems unaware of a long history of white Americans, from Madison Grant to the present, speaking *quite freely* about U.S. whites supposedly losing cultural and population dominance. In addition, the white British (and recently, American) historian Niall Ferguson alleges the last century has seen a general "descent of the West" and decline of Western civilization (i.e., of white European dominance) and in his view an unfortunate reorientation of the world toward Asian countries. Similarly, the white British government official, Mark Logan, has alleged that the once troubling "white supremacy is [now] history" and, rather amazingly and without evidence, that the "rise of China and other non-white societies" has effectively "disenfranchised white people."[43]

Beyond these prominent white intellectuals and officials, many other elite whites view the white U.S. population and culture as seriously threatened or even in major decline. For instance, in the late 1990s, my sociology colleagues and I crafted and supervised what appears to be the only large set of in-depth interviews on racial matters ever done with top members of the U.S. white elite, in this case more than 100 white men in high-level professional and corporate business occupations. Many expressed significant concern about the growing population of Americans of color, emphasizing commonplace white negative themes noted previously. Still, yet others viewed a more multiracial America neutrally, as more or less inevitable change, and a few even made positive comments on that racially diversifying trend.[44]

Donald Trump's White Nationalistic Demagoguery

In recent years, the former U.S. president Donald Trump has been the most visible and influential white nationalist in the country. Some decades back as a New York entrepreneur and powerful member of the East Coast elite, he kept much of his white-racist framing relatively low key, likely in order to ingratiate himself with an array of Democratic and moderate Republican Party officials and other powerful figures in his state. At the time he was primarily a wealth-seeking entrepreneur. Yet in more recent years, and with direct involvement in U.S. politics, he has more openly operated out of a strong racist-right framing. As African American journalist Ta-Nehisi Coates has noted, "It is often said that Trump has no real ideology, which is not true—his ideology is white supremacy, in all its truculent and sanctimonious power."[45] Or as Columbia University professor Bernard Harcourt has put it, Trump has seized on one of the prevailing white supremacist perspectives and tied "it to his unique blend of racism and xenophobia—his white nationalism—and in the process, has pushed the country apart."[46]

Since the mid-2000s, Trump has regularly traded in racist conspiracy theories such as when he attacked Democratic presidential candidate, and later president, Barack Obama in racist "birther" terms as not being American-born. Thereafter, in numerous speeches and other public comments before, during, and after his 2017–2021 presidency, he frequently accented other issues indicating white fears of the browning of America. Thus, he targeted immigrants of color with hostile racist commentary, often implying the old white replacement theories. In his first campaign for president, he framed Latin American and Muslim immigrants in racist terms, much like those of the earlier Lothrop Stoddard, as part of "invasions" of the U.S., and pressed hard for their partial or total exclusion. In conspiratorial speeches sometimes using mock Spanish, he then and later has alleged that the U.S. is "a dumping ground" for Mexico's "bad hombres": "When Mexico sends its people, they're not sending their best.... They're bringing drugs. They're bringing crime. They're rapists."[47]

Trump persisted in these racially framed views during and after his time as president. For example, during the 2018 midterm elections, Trump again insisted that only Republicans could save the country from immigrants of color, this time impoverished Central American refugees walking long distances to the U.S. An effective racist demagogue, he still repeatedly used anti-immigrant and white replacement language to play off of white racist fears of population change, saying "It's like an invasion.... They have violently overrun the Mexican border.... These are tough people, in many cases.... And a lot of men that maybe we don't want in our country."[48] Like most white nativists, Trump has routinely ignored social science evidence revealing the overwhelming majority of Mexican and other Latin American immigrants to be true refugees—that is, individuals and families fleeing political or drug-trade violence in their home countries and seeking jobs to support very impoverished families.

As president and subsequently, Trump's persisting attempts at building a bigger and longer border wall with Mexico signal an obsessive commitment to "great replacement theory" notions of protecting a fearful white America from alleged outside "invasions" of people of color. Detained Latin American immigrants, including children, were put into animal-like cages. In contrast, he never suggested a need to block external white immigrants, even celebrating Norwegian immigrants at one point as president. Moreover, frequently accenting the white replacement idea, Trump has retweeted far-right Twitter accounts asserting "white genocide" notions in regard to nonwhite demographic changes in the U.S.

and in South Africa.[49] Political scientist Kevin Arceneaux has argued that these Trump political

> appeals are about harnessing the power of the state to maintain white dominance…. They promise to go back to a time when whites were unquestionably at the top of the social hierarchy. These appeals are about keying into anger and fear, as opposed to hope, and they are about moving backward and not forward.[50]

Of significance too is that until Trump so vigorously articulated and expanded the anti-immigrant framing there was, as political scientist Ryan Enos has noted,

> mostly a consensus among Republican and Democratic politicians allowing for a continued welcoming of immigrants into the United States and keeping reactionary anti-immigrant politics off the table. There was also largely a consensus among most Democratic and Republican voters supporting this.[51]

Unmistakably, Trump has been able to garner much popular support for a renewed anti-immigrant framing of U.S. society much like that of the flaming white nationalists Madison Grant and Lothrop Stoddard a century ago. So far, as sociologist Douglas Massey has underscored, Democratic Party leaders have not pushed back hard enough against this renewed Republican xenophobia with strong reminders that the U.S. is a fabled "nation of immigrants," whose long immigration history encompasses the ancestors of most contemporary white Americans.[52]

Other Republican Leaders: Fearing Immigrants and Demographic Change

Unsurprisingly, white nativistic and nationalistic themes have been vigorously articulated by numerous other right-wing politicians, most extensively by those in the Republican Party, and especially since the rise of presidential politician Donald Trump. One influential figure is former U.S. House member Republican Steve King, who has asserted that the U.S. and Europe are facing threatening nonwhite migrations that will "replace" the dominant white populations. He has also articulated anti-Semitic tropes. For example, somehow blaming important Jewish figures like the philanthropic billionaire George Soros, King has emphasized a central argument in white replacement theorizing, that of too few white babies: "If we continue to abort our babies and import a replacement for them in the form of young violent men [of color], we are supplanting our culture, our civilization." In his aggressively white-framed view, undocumented immigration is a "slow-rolling, slow-motion terrorist attack on the United States" and even a "slow-motion Holocaust."[53] King has travelled frequently to Europe and become an important U.S. link to white nationalists and supremacists in European countries, including Germany and Great Britain. Additionally, King has been joined by numerous other white Republican politicians in parroting anti-immigrant, dangerous global elite, white cultural genocide, and other white nationalistic themes, including Florida State Senator Dennis Baxley, deputy leader of the Maine Republican Party Nick Isgro, Maine Governor Paul LePage, Maine Republican Party Executive Director Jason Savage, New York Republican member of Congress Scott Perry, and Texas Lt. Governor Dan Patrick.[54]

For example, in spring 2021, Representative Scott Perry parroted white replacement themes common to these and other Republican leaders: "For many Americans, what seems to be happening or what they believe right now is happening is, what appears to them is we're replacing national-born Americans, native-born Americans to permanently transform the landscape of this very nation."[55] As with most of these white nationalists, he meant *white* native-born Americans, for a huge proportion of native-born Americans have been nonwhite now for centuries.

Furthermore, for some years, far-right political groups like American Cause have regularly called on Republican legislators at the state and federal levels to take a zealous nativistic stand and pass laws against what they call, in racially framed terms, the "Third World Invasion and Conquest of America."[56] Under this organized pressure, at least since 2010, numerous anti-immigrant Republican legislators have even supported legislation to overturn the well-accepted interpretation of the U.S. Constitution's 14th amendment giving citizenship to all babies born in the U.S. whatever their parents' immigration status.[57] Unmistakably, racist theories and their terminology about dangerous "invasions" of immigrants of color and about "the great replacement" of whites have become well-entrenched in white conservative politics in the U.S.

Ordinary Whites' Fear of Demographic Change

Ordinary white Americans, as many surveys and experimental studies find, share many of the elite views and fears about the reality of being or becoming a *white minority*. This is most true now for those in states already with this demographic reality, and will likely increase in many others over the next decade or two. A recent Pew Research Center national survey found that 46 percent of white respondents felt a future majority-minority country would "weaken American culture," and 53 percent thought this white minority condition would bring more racial conflict. Only a quarter said this majority-minority reality would be *good* for the country, as contrasted with the majority of Black and Latina/o respondents who thought that new societal reality would be a good thing.[58]

Around the beginning of Donald Trump's presidency, another national poll found a *substantial majority* of his overwhelmingly white supporters indicated they were disturbed by growing U.S. racial diversity and viewed current immigrants, who are mostly of color, as a societal burden.[59] Yet another national survey found that the respondents most negative in their attitudes toward current immigrants tended to live in rural areas or small towns, to live in southern areas, to have relatively low levels of education, and to be Republicans. Predictably, this very negative group also tended to be in the least racially diverse communities as compared with other subgroups within the poll's total sample.[60]

Other survey research has found that those respondents who most strongly identified as white were also the most likely to support white nationalist political candidates like Trump. Additionally, majorities of whites in several surveys have revealed a strong fear of losing traditional white privilege in the future or shown a strong nostalgia for a time when whites did not face the population changes now diversifying their communities.[61] Moreover, after Trump lost his 2020 reelection attempt, surveys by University of Chicago researchers found that whites' "great replacement" notions in regard to nonwhite immigration and about the decline in white birth rates were central to their white nationalist framing.[62]

In addition to these surveys, experimental studies have discovered that presenting whites with information on their declining population percentage increases their negative feelings for people of color and other negative reactions to them. In one study presenting white college students with projections showing whites becoming a demographic minority made them angrier and more fearful of people of color than white students who had not been shown the projections.[63] In another experiment, reminding white subjects with a strong white identity of the nonwhite demographic growth generated more concern among them about declining white power and more negative views of immigration than for whites not thus reminded.[64] Other recent experiments presenting whites with data on demographic change have found that whites who see a greater white status threat from the browning of America were also more likely to perceive "mixed-race faces as more Latino than white." These researchers conclude from their several experiments that white fear of the coming demographic change even "alters race perception in a manner that *increases* the number of people who are seen as minorities and who are, therefore, more vulnerable to discrimination."[65]

Recently too, other social scientists reported in a *Washington Post* op-ed on a study involving a sample of 2,600 whites. Researchers split these respondents into two groups, each reading different simulated news stories on alternative Census Bureau projections of a U.S. racial future. One hypothetical news story reported just that there was a coming white minority. The second hypothetical news scenario noted that Latina/o and Asian American populations had increased, but also that there were increases in white-other intermarriages and that there was a population forecast of a more diverse future but with a redefined and expanded white majority. A majority of the first group of white respondents expressed anger or anxiety over the first coming-white-minority scenario, but "these negative emotions were far less frequent when participants read the second story about a more inclusive white majority."[66]

As I noted in Chapter 1, given these various findings on white racialized fear and anxiety, some social science and media analysts are concerned that media or scholarly presentations of dry demographic data on the coming white minority that do not accent the possibility of a greatly expanded white group in the future are unnecessarily disturbing whites.[67] Unfortunately, downplaying this probable reality of a majority-minority U.S. is just another form of white racial framing that caters too much to whites' racist framing and fears. Even more seriously, this downplaying ignores the reality and views of nonwhite Americans who frequently see such racial population change more positively and as diversifying or democratizing the U.S. future. In my view, this scholarly and popular appeasement of fearful whites—rather than aggressive and sustained attempts to *reeducate* them on real democratic and justice values—makes the likelihood of a peaceful and successful transition to a white minority nation *and* a more democratic multiracial America far more difficult. As leading U.S. demographers Dudley Poston and Rogelio Sáenz have emphasized, many whites have long viewed terms like "minority" negatively and as "reserved for people of color, just like many see the use of 'welfare' and 'Obamacare' for Blacks and other people of color." And they add a note of societal realism: "The reality is clear. The U.S. is becoming less white. The U.S. is moving toward becoming a majority-minority country."[68]

White Fear of Losing White Status and Privilege

Central to much white fear and anger about becoming a population minority is the ongoing concern about losing significant personal and societal power and privilege. Social psychological studies have suggested that, as one summary put it, whites "will act to defend their position as prototypical and 'All-American' when they feel this position is threatened." Envisioning a racial status threat, many whites also increase their calls for one-way assimilation and hyper-conformity by people of color "to white cultural norms." And they will also "respond to the threatened loss of their prototypicality" with hostility to all types of racial diversity.[69]

Some academic researchers argue that this growing fear and anger among working-class (usually defined as those without college degrees) whites has less to do with U.S. racial matters and more to do with their troubling health and related socioeconomic experiences, including their declining life expectancy and the increase in their "diseases of despair" and "deaths of despair." Such analysis references their high rates of suicide, alcohol or drug overdoses, and associated diseases. In a recent book, *Deaths of Despair and the Future of Capitalism*, scholars Anne Case and Angus Deaton argue this deadly white despair has to do with the decline in good manufacturing jobs for this group of Americans:

> Destroy work and, in the end, working-class life cannot survive. It is the loss of meaning, of dignity, of pride, and of self-respect that comes with the loss of marriage and of community that brings on despair, not just or even primarily the loss of money.[70]

They also link these supposed working-class job problems to the opioid epidemic and the lack of access to good health care in white working class areas.

However, as sociologist Tressie McMillan Cottom has summarized, recent field studies suggest that important parts of this common argument are not supported by empirical data. For example, these working-class white deaths are also substantial in places where whites "have *not* experienced job losses, where they do enjoy access to health care and a certain amount of economic security." In her and other social science critics' view, the increase in whites' diseases and deaths of despair is less about real socioeconomic and health losses than whites' *perceived* loss in their socio-racial status in U.S. society. Reviewing empirical data, they argue that white perception of loss is "enough to undermine positive health outcomes and health-seeking behaviors.... and that that perceived loss is enough for people to not seek out health care or to engage in dangerous health behaviors."[71]

Cottom uses this social psychological explanation to add insight into the actions of the thousands of whites who attacked the U.S. Capitol and members of Congress in January 2021, largely in an attempt to restore their white nationalist champion Donald Trump to power:

> And they engaged in—if you think about self-selecting into a conflict with armed police as a dangerous health behavior, that's one way to think about it.... That's a risky health behavior, and that's about perceived status, and that we haven't thought concretely enough about how dangerous privileged people will become if they just perceive that they have less privilege, not actual loss of privilege, but they perceive they have less privilege.[72]

Note too that numerous political analysts have argued there was, and is, a major class effect determining the votes of Trump's white voters. For instance, Brookings Institution's Richard Reeves contends that many white working-class and lower-middle-class Americans view upper-middle-class professionals with relatively high incomes, and the educational and retirement privileges that go with that, as leaving them and most other Americans behind.[73] He contends that large numbers voted for Trump for that reason. However, what this commonplace class analysis of these Trump era elections typically downplays or leaves out is that a large proportion of Trump's white voters have actually been *advantaged* middle-class and upper-middle-class whites, as well as the majority of wealthy whites who provided huge monetary funding and critical organizing in getting Trump elected. Literally, in his elections race has regularly "trumped" class.

To take another major example of this racialized reality, many whites in all classes still view the 2008 and 2012 elections of Barack Obama negatively, as having reduced their racial dominance and privilege (often called "freedom") and taking "their country" away from them. Social science studies have examined the impact on whites of being reminded about the racial implications of Obama's election. One study found whites who read an article on the societal-change importance of Obama's election demonstrated more white group-threat responses and anti-Black bias than those who had not read it.[74] To the present day, many whites consider the election of a Black president to be a major symbol of negative change in U.S. socio-political matters and, thus, in whites' racial status, privilege, and power.

As I noted in the Introduction, following Obama's terms in presidential office, Donald Trump's "Make America Great Again" slogan was heard by many whites as "Make America White Again." This white racist message and concern, as scholar Brian Rosenwald notes, "went beyond Obama's position on issues, since Obama was arguably the most conservative Democratic candidate in 2008."[75] That is, it was more about Obama's phenotype and whites' sensed loss of racial status and privilege. In fact, after winning the 2016 election, Obama himself underscored this point in an interview with a *New Yorker* journalist:

> A President who looked like me was inevitable at some point in American history. It might have been somebody named Gonzales instead of Obama, but it was coming. And I probably showed up twenty years sooner than the demographics would have anticipated. And, in that sense, it was a little bit more surprising. The country had to do more adjusting and processing of it. It undoubtedly created more anxiety than it will twenty years from now, provoked more reactions in some [white] portion of the population than it will twenty years from now.[76]

In his later 2020 book, Obama further commented about the negative reactions of many whites:

It was as if my very presence in the White House had triggered a deep-seated panic, a sense that the natural order had been disrupted. For millions of Americans spooked by a Black man in the White House, [Trump] promised an elixir for their racial anxiety.[77]

In contrast, analysts at white right-wing think tanks sometimes deny that white fear and panic over the changing U.S. racial demographics are real. Instead, they claim that the rising national intermarriage rate and the election of Barack Obama indicate most whites are accepting of that racial demographic change.[78] Of course, a *substantial majority* of whites actually voted against Obama in the both the 2008 and 2012 elections, and white-Black intermarriages are still the least common among all U.S. intermarriages involving whites and major groups of color. In addition, many whites still oppose such intermarriages, including in their own families.

White Christian Voters: Fetishizing a White Nationalist President

A rather obvious example of white actions reflecting deep concerns and fears about the nonwhite population growth can be seen in white political organizing and voting in the 2016 and 2020 presidential elections. In his successful 2016 presidential campaign, the outspoken white nationalistic and nativistic Donald Trump got a substantial majority of white voters, nearly six in ten. And he got an even larger percentage, about two-thirds, of white voters with no college degree. In contrast, Trump got a much smaller percentage of most nonwhite voting groups.

Significantly, numerous mainstream political analysts have downplayed the centrality of white voters' racist framing in the 2016 or 2020 elections. For instance, analyst John Hibbing has argued that whites' racist framing is not the central motivation for Trump's white voters. What is central is what he calls the "securitarian" orientation of Trump's voter base—that is, the strong belief that the "noblest and most essential task of a human being is to protect person, family, culture, and country from the … threats they believe are posed by outsiders." However, Hibbing contradicts his rejection of these white voters' racist framing as central when he also notes that these insiders are "the historical and numerical core of the country—the dominant race, religion, and language group."[79] Apparently, these core insiders just happen to be white, Christian, and native English speakers.

It is *not* just chance, however, that many of Trump's conservative white Christian voters openly racialize and oppose immigrants of color and their descendants, as well as many government health and other support programs they think provide too much support for them and other Americans of color. Hibbing adds that while sometimes the Trump supporters are moved by fear and anxiety, on the whole they are not pessimists with a low sense of social well-being. For Trump supporters, security is not a tiresome, regrettable burden necessitated by unremitting fear; rather, it is an uplifting mission. Doing one's duty is rewarding in and of itself and creating a secure environment for insiders is a duty.[80]

In his arguments, Hibbing seems to suggest that security for these white Christian insiders includes necessary racial discrimination by them and agreeable government officials to protect white Christian families, culture, and country from troublesome nonwhite "others," even those whose families have longer histories in U.S. society than many white families do.

In contrast, social scientists Richard Fording and Sanford Schram have shown that a sizeable proportion of the Trump voters in 2016 were white nationalist extremists who had not voted in the 2012 election that a Black man won. Trump's overtly racist framing attracted them back into politics and energetically mobilized them to work actively to make him president. This election actually *mainstreamed* extreme white nationalism in the Republican Party.[81] One can add to this the further point that religion scholar Robert P. Jones has made. Many Trump voters were motivated by white *Christian* nationalism. "Through it all," Jones emphasizes, "Trump has retained the support of white Christians." Exit polls for the 2006 election showed that he got *81 percent* of white evangelical Protestant voters. Strikingly too, the Pew Research Center "postelection analysis based on validated voters found that strong majorities of white Catholics (64 percent) and white mainline Protestants (57 percent) also cast their votes for Trump."[82] In contrast, he only got 4 percent of African American Christian voters.

While some are puzzled as to why so many white Christian voters have supported a political candidate like Trump who is infamous for violating many precepts of conventional Christian morality, their commitment to white Christian nationalism provides a clear answer to this puzzle. They voted for him because they believe that he would, and still will, preserve the white Christian dominance of the U.S. they consider to be under attack from the growing numbers and political influence of Americans of color, including non-Christians. As Jones has explained,

> Trump's own racism allowed him to do what other candidates couldn't: solidify the support of a majority of white Christians, not despite, but through appeals to white supremacy. By activating the white supremacy sequence within white Christian DNA, which was primed for receptivity by the perceived external threat of racial and cultural change in the country, Trump was able to convert white evangelicals in the course of a single political campaign from so-called values voters to "nostalgia voters."[83]

Note too that this white Christian nationalism is the contemporary version of a very old white racial framing of this country. For centuries, that framing has emphasized that the country was founded by white Protestant Christians who built it according to their conservative Christian religious views and values. As analyzed by sociologist Phil Gorski, white Christian nationalists (now including Catholics) today see these centuries-old Christian views and values "as under threat from the growing presence of non-whites, non-Christians, and immigrants," essentially the same message articulated by Donald Trump and his followers' Make America Great Again rhetoric in two presidential elections.[84]

We might note too that much of this heavy emphasis on white Christian founders is erroneous and historically illiterate, since many of the leading white founders were actually deists. These included four of the first five presidents—George Washington, Thomas Jefferson, James Madison, and James Monroe. These famous founders generally subscribed to a philosophical perspective accenting human reason over traditional Christian religion. As one summary puts it,

> Deists believe in a supreme being who created the universe to operate solely by natural laws—and after creation, is absent from the world. This belief in reason over dogma helped guide the founders toward a system of government that respected faiths like Christianity, while purposely isolating both from encroaching on one another so as not to dilute the overall purpose and objectives of either.[85]

Ironically, given the insistence of many Americans that the U.S. president be and operate as a Christian, the Article VI, Section III, of the U.S. Constitution specifically says that "no religious test shall ever be required as a qualification to any office or public trust under the United States." This constitutionally excludes a political requirement to be a Christian of any persuasion.

White Mass Shooters: Acting on "Great Replacement Theory"

Yet another white response to becoming a decreasing minority of the population of the U.S. and other white-dominated countries has involved significant individual and collective violence. Individual white terrorists have used murderous violence to express and activate their fear of being replaced as dominant societal powerholders and as their country's population majority. Their stated views are essentially grounded in white nativistic and nationalistic ideas dating back centuries in Western history, but in recent decades they have also used the racist language and narratives of the newer "great replacement" and "white genocide" theories. As one terrorism researcher has put it, "It's the narrative that connects them all."[86]

Some of the online blog posts and manifestos of these white terrorists are quite histrionic and directly linked to their rationalizing of horrific acts of mass violence. For example, in an October 2018 attack on a Jewish synagogue in Pittsburgh, Pennsylvania, a white anti-Semitic terrorist murdered eleven people. The middle-aged gunman falsely asserted in blog posts that scheming Jewish Americans were transporting Latin American "invaders" in immigrant caravans to the southern U.S. border in order to, in his racist conspiratorial mind, help dilute and replace the country's "white race."[87] In online posts before his vicious terrorist attack, he had reposted another white supremacist's message that Western civilization is "headed towards certain extinction within the next 200 years and we're not even aware of it" with his own extremist message that the Hebrew Immigrant Aid Society "likes to bring invaders in that kill our people. I can't sit by and watch my people get slaughtered. Screw your optics. I'm going in."[88]

The great increase in social media on the ever-expanding global internet has accelerated this sharing of these white nativistic and nationalistic ideas. Consider a similar violent event reflecting fear of white demise, this time in another predominantly white country. In March 2019, in the city of Christchurch, New Zealand, a lone white male terrorist attacked a mosque and Islamic center with submachine guns, killing 51 people. Prior to his attack, he too posted a white supremacist manifesto accenting "great replacement" themes, which opened its argument by focusing on declining white birthrates. Yet again, this terrorist's concern was that whites will be sharply reduced in numbers and power by the migration of nonwhite groups to predominantly white countries. His manifesto reflected the online and offline language of white nativists and nationalists in other historically white-dominated countries, language he mindlessly regurgitated.[89]

Another white male terrorist, also influenced by "great replacement" thinking picked up in social media and by previous killings, attacked and killed 23 mostly Latina/o shoppers in El Paso, Texas in August 2019. Referencing the Christchurch mosque shootings months earlier, he too issued a white supremacist manifesto titled "The Inconvenient Truth." Just before his murderous attack, he posted this manifesto on a dark-web online message board, in which he emphasized anti-immigrant themes (e.g., the "Hispanic invasion") and what he viewed as the threat of the white population becoming a statistical and cultural minority ("ethnic replacement"). There he explicitly insists that his "attack is a response to the Hispanic invasion of Texas. They are the instigators, not me. I am simply defending my country from cultural and ethnic replacement brought on by an invasion."[90] His murderous manifesto emphasized, like recurring statements from numerous commentators on right-wing talk shows and cable television channels, that because of this Hispanic immigration, the Democratic Party would soon be in dangerous political control of the country. In his view, this violent attack was an "incentive" for Hispanic Americans to move back to their home countries, again showing the ignorance many whites have in regard to U.S. racial demography. That is, most of these Americans were actually *born* in the U.S., their home country. Both the Pittsburgh and El Paso murderers use racist language similar to that of then President Donald Trump about the "invasion" of Latina/o immigrants from south of the U.S. border. Actually, this contemporary racist framing is a current version of what some scholars have long called the "Latino threat narrative." As I demonstrated previously, white nativists' concerns and fears of being replaced by these and other immigrants of color, those considered racially undesirable, are by no means new in U.S. history.

In May 2022, yet another white male terrorist, also influenced by "great replacement theory" he read about online, killed ten Black shoppers in Buffalo, New York. He too posted a wild-eyed manifesto before his attack and focused it around white supremacist contentions about European Americans being replaced, again using the immigrant "invasion" and "white genocide" language commonplace among white nationalists and nativists in traditional and social media:

> We are experiencing an invasion on a level never seen before in history. Millions of people pouring across our borders, legally. Invited by the state and corporate entities to replace the White people who have failed to reproduce, failed to create the cheap labor, failed to create new consumers and tax base that the corporations and states need to have to thrive.

Yet this white teenager, just off to college, develops a detailed call to arms to white America. His killings are to show the "replacers that as long as the White man lives, our land will never be theirs and they will never be safe from us" and "to spread awareness to my fellow Whites... and to encourage further attacks that will eventually start the war that will save the Western world, save the White race and allow for humanity to progress into more advanced civilizations."[91] Here and at the end of the manifesto he calls for a *white army* to engage in a war to save the Western world. Note too that in his obsessive white mindset African Americans—who have ancestors going back farther in this country's history than a great many white Americans—are the "invaders" and "replacers" he traveled a long distance to seek out and murder.

These recent white terrorist attacks have been, partially or centrally, inspired by national and global commentators in countless white nationalistic and other white supremacist publications and on social media websites. For instance, the explicit language and conceptualization of the "great replacement theory" have been generated and reinforced by the writings and speeches of white far-right European intellectuals, activists, and politicians. One influential version of the "great replacement" language has been developed by the French philosopher and political activist Renaud Camus, who like numerous other white nationalists has ties to the pan-European movement now called Generation Identity. Those currently associated with this white supremacist movement have links going back decades to white French, German, and other European intellectuals who emphasized the territorial and cultural "rights" of white Europeans to countries where they have long lived. These supposed rights include the right to reject nonwhite and non-Christian (especially Islamic) immigrants to their historically white Christian countries. European extreme-right commentators and communities

> use a range of methods to broadcast the Great Replacement theory, including dehumanizing racist memes, distorting and misrepresenting demographic data, and using debunked science.... Proponents of the so-called "Great Replacement" theory argue that white European populations are being deliberately replaced at an ethnic and cultural level through migration and the growth of minority communities.[92]

Their white nationalist and nativistic framing, which ignores the cultural and territorial rights of countries Europeans invaded and colonized, has greatly influenced contemporary white extremists in the U.S.

Insurrectionary Protests against Majority-Minority Change

Many *collective* white protests, violent and nonviolent, have also been motivated by strong white anxiety and fear about the decline in white dominance in population, power, and privilege. Recall from my previous discussions that the fearful language of white replacement was heard repeatedly from the neo-Nazi and other white nationalist demonstrators who flooded Charlottesville, Virginia in summer 2017 to protest removal of a slaveholding Confederate general's statue. A peaceful female counter-demonstrator was killed by a white male activist. And Donald Trump's positive reactions to that white nationalist protest have been cheered by the leaders and other members of white supremacist groups there and since.[93] Over Trump's years in the public spotlight, especially as a Republican politician and president, he has inspired numerous white supremacist and other white far-right actions, both from individuals and groups.

For example, in the week following his 2016 election, there was a significant national increase in racist incidents. According to the Southern Poverty Law Center (SPLC) about 400 bias-related incidents were verified, with 1,000 incidents more in the next few weeks. This was a major increase over those recorded in previous months.[94] The SPLC also reported that the number of white supremacist and other hate groups increased dramatically during the Trump presidential years. In addition, a 2018 national survey found that a majority of respondents agreed that Trump's "statements and behavior have encouraged white supremacist groups."[95] Moreover, one important research study of the events leading up to the January 2021 Capitol insurrection examined in detail his "public rhetoric between 2015–2020 citing tweets, speeches, and news interviews" and found that this rhetoric "created an environment for violence among his supporters prior to and throughout his presidency."[96]

Certainly, the most serious of these violent white reactions so far is this 2021 insurrectionary attack on the U.S. Capitol. It was motivated to a substantial degree by white fear and anger over racial demographic change and its consequences for white power and privilege. The white rioters there made clear their racist framing in shouted slogans and on their signs and flags. As political scientist Hakeem Jefferson has underscored, years of social science research

> make clear that what we witnessed in Washington, D.C., is the violent outgrowth of a belief system that argues that white Americans and leaders who assuage whiteness should have an unlimited hold on the levers of power in this country. And this, unfortunately, is what we should expect from those whose white identity is threatened by an increasingly diverse citizenry. ... They are a dangerous mob of grievous white people worried that their position in the status hierarchy is threatened by a multiracial coalition of Americans who brought [Joe] Biden to power and defeated Trump.[97]

Exactly who were these violent insurrectionists? As I noted briefly in the Introduction, most were white, and most of those were male. Additionally, few were from the youngest (Gen-Z) generation, and relatively few were the next youngest Millennials. Most were middle-aged and older. A major study by social scientist Robert Pape and other University of Chicago researchers examined 380 people arrested for the Capitol attack. Most had come from geographical areas where polling and other data suggested whites were fearful about numerical increases in immigrants and other Americans of color. That is, they disproportionately came from counties with significant *losses* in white populations and *increases* in non-white populations, and mostly places a considerable distance away from the Washington, D.C. site of their insurrection. In an interview, Pape summarized his findings that Capitol insurrectionists "are *mainly middle-class to upper-middle-class whites* who are worried that, as social changes occur around them, they will see a decline in their status in the future."[98] In a *Washington Post* op-ed he further explained:

> The Jan. 6 assault on the Capitol by a violent mob at the behest of for-
> mer president Donald Trump was an act of political violence intended
> to alter the outcome of a legitimate democratic election.... [T]he in-
> surrection was the result of a large, diffuse and new kind of protest
> movement congealing in the United States.... Those involved are, by
> and large, older and more professional than right-wing protesters we
> have surveyed in the past. .... But like earlier protesters, they are 95
> percent White and 85 percent male. [99]

The insurrectionists were mostly middle-class and upper-middle-class
whites obviously anxious about racial status decline at a time of escalating
socio-racial change. They included many business owners, lawyers, doc-
tors, and other middle-class professionals actually fearful of losing some
white privilege and status in an increasingly majority-minority nation.
Unmistakably, this insurrection was mostly not about social class inequality and discontent among whites. Few insurrectionists were like many
U.S. demonstrators in earlier decades who did protest mainly over their
declining socioeconomic conditions. Indeed, few this time were actually
unemployed.

In addition, these white insurrectionists trying to reinstall Donald
Trump as president had significant support in the larger white population.
A few months after the insurrection, researchers did a national survey
and estimated from the respondents' answers that about 47 million adults
agreed the 2020 election was "stolen from Donald Trump and Joe Biden
is an illegitimate president." Additionally, an estimated 21 million felt that
violence was "justified to restore Donald J. Trump to the presidency."
Among these 21 million, they estimated, about 7 million owned a gun,
and at least 3 million had been in the U.S. military. In addition, they
estimated from the survey that about 6 million "supported right-wing
militias and extremist groups."[100] While the researchers did not separate
out the white respondents, it is likely that most of these violence-oriented
Americans are white. About the same time, Democracy Corps researchers
did focus group interviews with Trump-aligned conservative voters in
Georgia, Wisconsin, and Ohio. These mostly white voters were animated
about the federal government destroying their "freedom" and about losing
"their" country to nonwhite Americans. They too were often supportive
of the Capitol insurrectionists and of violent anti-virus-lockdown protestors previously in Michigan, viewing the white "violence and disruption
of the legislature [there] as justified."[101]

The January 2021 Capitol insurrection was not an isolated event. Since
that insurrection the country has seen yet more white aggression and disruption that target government procedures and policies, especially those
with democratizing effects. Increasingly, many whites have sought to control by belligerent and harassing means their local and state governments'

actions, including those of school boards, city councils, and state election agencies. As one journalist recently put it,

> Jan. 6 is every day now, in the words of a recent *New York Times* editorial that noted the growing evidence: election officials harassed by conspiracy theory addicts, death threats issued to politicians who vote their conscience, GOP lawmakers pushing measures to make it harder for citizens to vote and easier for partisans to overturn legitimate voting results.[102]

Summarizing this reality, U.S. terrorism researcher Michael Jensen has noted:

> What I expected or anticipated is what we've seen since January 6— which is local organizing and mobilizing. In the year since January 6… individuals [are] showing up at local board meetings and harassing people or threatening local election officials. You see this not only among lone, isolated actors but among extremist groups as well.[103]

Actually, for some decades now, many whites have actively organized at these various government levels in order to emphasize and protect their racial power and privilege against democratizing change. Unsurprisingly, too, their white right-wing framing has even coded as a racial matter formerly undisputed public health strategies, including wearing a protective anti-virus face mask or getting vaccinated against the deadly COVID-19 virus.[104]

Recent national surveys have found that many Americans support such political harassment and violence, at least to some extent. One American Enterprise Institute survey found that 39 percent of Republicans agreed with the statement that "if elected leaders will not protect America, the people must do it themselves, even if it requires violent actions." Commenting on the results, the survey director noted that "any time you have a significant number of the public saying use of force can be justified in our political system, that's pretty scary."[105] Moreover, a survey of whites by social scientist Justin Gest found that nearly two thirds said they would support a *new* political party committed to a far-right government "stopping mass immigration, providing American jobs to American workers, preserving America's Christian heritage, and stopping the threat of Islam."[106]

Significantly too, many of these white reactionaries have directed their racialized hostility toward the typically peaceful Black Lives Matter (BLM) demonstrators—large proportions of whom were actually younger whites—in U.S. cities over recent years (see Chapter 6). For example, they have falsely blamed the 2021 Capitol insurrection on BLM groups and other progressive organizations. False movement equivalence is also common in racist-right media and among white racist-right politicians. For example, Donald Trump's white right-wing lawyers in his second impeachment trial in 2021 "used a video montage that created a false equivalency between the Capitol riot and Black Lives Matter protests that followed the police killing of George Floyd in Minneapolis last May, invoking race in arguments for the president's innocence."[107]

Conclusion: U.S. Authoritarianism

The U.S. has a long history of antidemocratic and racialized authoritarianism, most conspicuously seen in its centuries of slavery and Jim Crow segregation. The white antidemocratic and authoritarian views and actions assessed in this chapter clearly link to this long history of systemic racism. We see a majority of white Americans still asserting some such views, and they have often acted to enforce them in racially discriminatory practices and undemocratic institutions. Recently examining whites' prejudiced views of cultural, ethnic, or racial others in World Values Surveys for 1995–2011, political scientists Steven Miller and Nicholas Davis found that the greater their anti-others prejudices, the less value a white person places on democracy and the more likely they are to support authoritarian political and military rule.[108]

This authoritarian orientation among North Americans has long been studied by social psychologist Bob Altemeyer. He defines right-wing authoritarianism at the individual level as "the desire to submit to some authority, aggression that is directed against whomever the authority says should be targeted and a desire to have everybody follow the norms and social conventions that the authority says should be followed."[109] Taken together, the major dimensions of this right-wing authoritarianism constitute what might be called the right-wing *authoritarian frame*.

In the U.S. case, operating out of a racist framing of society, white right-wing authoritarians tend to follow uncritically charismatic right-wing demagogues such as the former president Donald Trump. They typically view straight white Christians as the more virtuous Americans and the standard for social desirability, with the negatively framed outsiders being people of color, including immigrants. Most whites learn this right-wing authoritarian frame from socialization at home, school, and church, and from certain conservative media. Their authoritarian perspective links to such emotions as hostility, anger, fear, and sense of threat from Americans of color. Studies of this white American authoritarianism have noted how white authoritarians' sense of nonwhite outsiders as an existential threat frequently links to right-wing political attachments and actions, both nonviolent and violent. One survey by Altemeyer of several U.S. states' legislators found that the mostly white Republican members of state legislatures averaged significantly *higher* scores on an authoritarianism attitude scale than did the more racially diverse Democratic members of the same legislatures.[110]

In addition, a recent Morning Consult survey of numerous people in the U.S. and other English-speaking countries utilized a set of questions from Altemeyer's right-wing authoritarianism scale, questions that again measure their authoritarian tendencies. The Morning Consult report divided respondents into those scoring in the very top 15 percentiles of the right-wing authoritarianism scale (high RWA) and those who scored in the very bottom 15 percentiles (low RWA). Some 26 percent of U.S. respondents fell into the high RWA category, twice or more than the percentage of the Canadian, Australian, or British respondents. Moreover, in the U.S. survey, most high-RWA respondents said they were also right-leaning politically, and most were also over 44 years old. In contrast most low-RWA respondents said they were also left-leaning politically and were under 45 years old.[111]

In addition, the U.S. respondents' views of the people who took part in the violent U.S. Capitol insurrection varied dramatically, with 26 percent of the high-RWA respondents saying the insurrectionists were "protecting the U.S. government," as compared to only 3 percent of low-RWA respondents. The latter were overwhelmingly of the view that the attackers were "undermining the U.S. government."[112] Unsurprisingly, the Morning Consult report on this survey notes that many of former president Trump's supporters demonstrated significant authoritarian characteristics during the 2020–2021 presidential election season. These dangerous authoritarian and antidemocratic characteristics, common among white Americans as we have seen in this chapter, have persisted into the present and, strikingly enough, pose a major threat to the future of U.S. democracy.

Notes

1 Neal A. Lester and Jazmine Z. Lester, "Cheerios and Fear of a Black Planet," *East Valley Tribune*, July 13, 2013, https://www.eastvalleytribune. com/columns/east_valley_voices/lester-cheerios-and-fear-of-a-Black-planet/article_3c0914ba-eb58-11e2-a923-001a4bcf887a.html (accessed April 25, 2022).
2 Julia Manchester, "David Duke: Charlottesville Protests about 'Fulfilling Promises of Donald Trump'" *The Hill*, August 12, 2017, https://thehill. com/blogs/blog-briefing-room/news/346326-david-duke-charlottesville-protests-about-fulfilling-promises/ (accessed March 31, 2022).
3 Franklin D. Roosevelt, "Inaugural Address, March 4, 1933," in *The Public Papers of Franklin D. Roosevelt*, Volume Two: *The Year of Crisis, 1933*, ed. Samuel Rosenman (New York: Random House, 1938), pp. 11–16.
4 Mary Elizabeth Dean, "What Is Denial Psychology and How to Address It," BetterHelp.com, https://www.betterhelp.com/advice/general/what-is-denial-psychology-how-to-address-it/ (accessed May 26, 2021).

5 Woody Holton, *Liberty Is Sweet: The Hidden History of the American Revolution* (New York: Simon & Schuster, 2021), p. 295. See also Bernard Trujillo and Kevin R. Johnson, *Immigration Law and the U.S.–Mexico Border: ¿Sí se puede?* (Tucson: University of Arizona Press, 2011), p. 4.

6 Joe R. Feagin and Clairece B. Feagin, *Racial and Ethnic Relations*, 8th ed. (Upper Saddle River, NJ: Prentice-Hall, 2008), Chapter 3.

7 "Ezra Klein Interviews Woody Holton," *New York Times*, October 19, 2021, https://www.nytimes.com/2021/10/19/podcasts/transcript-ezra-klein-interviews-woody-holton.html (accessed October 21, 2021).

8 Ibid.

9 "Statistics on Slavery," https://faculty.weber.edu/kmackay/statistics_on_slavery.htm (accessed May 11, 2021).

10 Robert A. Rutland, ed., *The Papers of George Mason: 1725–1792*, vol. 3 (Chapel Hill: University of North Carolina Press, 1970), pp. 965–966; and Paul Finkelman, "Slavery and the Constitutional Convention," in *Beyond Confederation: Origins of the Constitution and American National Identity*, eds. Richard Beeman, Stephen Botein, and Edward C. Carter (Chapel Hill: University of North Carolina Press, 1987), p. 225.

11 Donald E. Lively, *The Constitution and Race* (New York: Praeger, 1992), pp. 4–5. Lively draws on research by William M. Wiecek.

12 Cristina Beltrán, *Cruelty as Citizenship* (Minneapolis: University of Minnesota Press, 2020), pp. 41–42.

13 Laura L. Lovett, *Conceiving the Future: Pronatalism, Reproduction, and the Family in the United States, 1890–1938* (Chapel Hill: University of North Carolina Press, 2009), pp. 77–90.

14 Madison Grant, *The Passing of the Great Race* (New York: Charles Scribner's Sons, 1916).

15 Quoted in Jane Coaston, "The Scary Ideology behind Trump's Immigration Instincts," Vox.Com, November 6, 2018, https://www.vox.com/2018/1/18/16897358/racism-donald-trump-immigration (accessed December 3, 2022).

16 Lothrop Stoddard, *The Rising Tide of Color: Against White World-Supremacy* (New York: Scribner's, 1920), Kindle loc.305.

17 Ibid., Kindle loc. 3325.

18 Lothrop Stoddard, *The Revolt against Civilization: The Menace of the Under-Man* (New York: Charles Scribner's Sons, 1922), p. 63.

19 Matthew Guterl, "On Civility," October 3, 2017, https://matthewprattguterl.com/2017/10/03/on-civility/ (accessed June 29, 2022).

20 Ian Frazier, "When W. E. B. Du Bois Made a Laughingstock of a White Supremacist," *New Yorker*, August 19, 2019, https://www.newyorker.com/magazine/2019/08/26/when-w-e-b-du-bois-made-a-laughingstock-of-a-white-supremacist (accessed March 30, 2021).

21 Clint Smith, "Why Confederate Lies Live On," *The Atlantic*, May 10, 2021, https://www.theatlantic.com/magazine/archive/2021/06/confederate-lost-cause-myth/618711/(accessed June 29, 2022).

22 Quoted in Ibid.

23 J. Gerald Kennedy and Liliane Weissberg, eds., *Romancing the Shadow: Poe and Race* (revised edition; New York: Oxford University Press, 2001), p. 196; see also Elise Lemire, *"Miscegenation": Making Race in America* (Philadelphia: University of Pennsylvania Press, 2002).

24 Frazier, "When W. E. B. Du Bois Made a Laughingstock of a White Supremacist."

25 Quoted in William H. Tucker, *The Science and Politics of Racial Research* (Urbana: University of Illinois Press, 1994), p. 93.
26 Ibid.
27 Quoted in Pankaj Mishra, "Watch This Man," *London Review of Books*, November 2011, https://www.lrb.co.uk/the-paper/v33/n21/pankaj-mishra/watch-this-man (accessed May 30, 2022).
28 Feagin and Feagin, *Racial and Ethnic Relations*, Chapter 3.
29 John David Smith, "The Historiographic Rise, Fall, and Resurrection of Ulrich Bonnell Phillips," *The Georgia Historical Quarterly*, 65 (Summer, 1981): 147–148.
30 W. E. B. Du Bois, *Black Reconstruction in America 1860–1880* (New York: Harcourt, Brace and Co., 1935).
31 Quoted in Dan T. Carter, *The Politics of Rage: George Wallace, The Origins of the New Conservatism, and the Transformation of American Politics*, 2nd ed. (Baton Rouge: Louisiana State University Press, 2000), p. 11.
32 I summarize here from Joe R. Feagin, *White Party, White Government: Race, Class, and U.S. Politics* (New York: Routledge, 2012), Chapter 3. See also 1960s polling data in "Poll Shows Whites in City Resent Civil Rights Drive," *New York Times*, September 21, 1964, https://www.nytimes.com/1964/09/21/archives/poll-shows-whites-in-city-resent-civil-rights-drive-majority.html (accessed May 29, 2022).
33 Joe R. Feagin and Kimberley Ducey, *Racist America: Roots, Current Realities, and Future Reparations*, 4th ed. (New York: Routledge, 2019), Chapter 9.
34 Jane Coaston, "The Scary Ideology behind Trump's Immigration Instincts," Vox.Com, November 6, 2018, https://www.vox.com/2018/1/18/16897358/racism-donald-trump-immigration (accessed March 5, 2021).
35 J. M. Berger, "Alt History," *The Atlantic*, September 16, 2016, https://www.theatlantic.com/politics/archive/2016/09/how-the-turner-diaries-changed-white-nationalism/500039/ (accessed June 18, 2021); and Julia Ebner and Jacob Davey, "The Great Replacement," Institute for Strategic Dialogue, 2019, https://www.isdglobal.org/wp-content/uploads/2019/07/The-Great-Replacement-The-Violent-Consequences-of-Mainstreamed-Extremism-by-ISD.pdf (accessed April 2, 2021).
36 Coaston, "The Scary Ideology behind Trump's Immigration Instincts."
37 Patrick Buchanan, as quoted in Clarence Page, "U.S. Media Should Stop Abetting Intolerance," *Toronto Star*, December 27, 1991, p. A27.
38 Patrick Buchanan, as quoted in John Dillin, "Immigration Joins List of 92 Issues," *Christian Science Monitor*, December 17, 1991, p. 6. I expand here on data in Feagin and Ducey, *Racist America*, p. 95.
39 Patrick J. Buchanan, "A Brief for Whitey," March 21, 2008, www.buchanan.org (accessed March 31, 2008).
40 Patrick Buchanan, *Suicide of a Superpower: Will America Survive to 2025?* (New York: St. Martin's, 2011), Introduction and Chapter 1.
41 Peter Brimelow, *Alien Nation: Common Sense about America's Immigration Disaster* (New York: Random House, 1995), pp. 10, 59.
42 Christopher Caldwell, "The Browning of America: A Review of Diversity Explosion: How New Racial Demographics Are Remaking America," *Claremont Review of Books* 14 (Winter 2014/15), https://claremontreviewofbooks.com/the-browning-of-america/ (accessed April 16, 2020)
43 Niall Ferguson, *The War of the World: Twentieth-Century Conflict and the Descent of the West* (New York: Penguin, 2006), p. xvii; and Mark Logan, "White Supremacy Is History and China is the Future," *China Morning Sun Post*, August 27, 2017, http://www.scmp.com/comment/insight-opinion/article/

2108274/white-supremacy-history-and-china-future (accessed December 28, 2017). Italics added.

44 See Joe R. Feagin and Eileen O'Brien, *White Men on Race* (Boston, MA: Beacon, 2003); and Rhonda Levine, "The Souls of Elite White Men: White Racial Identity and the Logic of Thinking on Race," paper presented at annual meeting, Hawaiian Sociological Association, February 14, 1998.

45 Hakeem Jefferson, "Storming the U.S. Capitol Was about Maintaining White Power in America," fivethirtyeight.com, January 8, 2021, 538.org, https://fivethirtyeight.com/features/storming-the-u-s-capitol-was-about-maintaining-white-power-in-america/ (accessed June 22, 2021). Coates is quoted in this article.

46 Bernard E. Harcourt, "The Fight ahead," https://bostonreview.net/race-politics/bernard-e-harcourt-fight-ahead, January 2021, https://bostonreview.net/race-politics/bernard-e-harcourt-fight-ahead (accessed March 12, 2021).

47 Kate Stanhope, "NBC: We Disagree with Donald Trump on 'a Number of Issues,'" *Hollywood Reporter*, June 25, 2015, https://www.hollywoodreporter.com/live-feed/nbc-we-disagree-donald-trump-805198?utm_source=Yahoo&utm_campaign=Syndication&utm_medium=Donald+Trump%27s+Anti-Immigrant+Remarks+Spark+Outrage+in+Mexico (accessed June 26, 2015).

48 Jane Coaston, "The Scary Ideology behind Trump's Immigration Instincts."

49 Ibid.

50 Quoted in Thomas Edsall, "Why Trump Is Still Their Guy," *New York Times*, April 21, 2021, https://www.nytimes.com/2021/04/21/opinion/trump-republicans.html?campaign_id=39&emc=edit_ty_20210421&instance_id=29494&nl=opinion-today&regi_id=54115655&segment_id=56003&te=1&user_id=6a44bcdea3628e8ce52c97f8996a95fe (accessed January 10, 2022).

51 Quoted in Thomas B. Edsall, "The 'Third Rail of American Politics' Is Still Electrifying," *New York Times*, November 3, 2021, https://www.nytimes.com/2021/11/03/opinion/us-immigration-politics.html (accessed December 9, 2022).

52 Quoted in Ibid.

53 Tom McCarthy, "'He's so Openly Racist': Why Does Iowa Keep Electing Steve King to Congress?" *The Guardian*, October 27, 2018, https://www.theguardian.com/us-news/2018/oct/26/hes-so-openly-racist-why-does-iowa-keep-electing-steve-king-to-congress (accessed June 20, 2021). See also Sheryl Gay Stolberg and Brian M. Rosenthal, "Man Charged After White Nationalist Rally in Charlottesville Ends in Deadly Violence," *New York Times*, August 12, 2017, https://www.nytimes.com/2017/08/12/us/charlottesville-protest-white-nationalist.html?action=click&auth=login-email&login=e-mail&module=RelatedCoverage&pgtype=Article&region=Footer (accessed April 2, 2021).

54 Callum Paton, "Florida Senator's 'Racist' Replacement Theory Stance against Abortion Slammed by Reproductive Rights Supporters," May 30, 2019, https://www.newsweek.com/florida-senators-racist-replacement-theory-stance-against-abortion-slammed-1439253 (accessed June 20, 2021); Greg Kesich, "The View from Here: Conspiracy Theory Takes Hold in Maine GOP," 9, June 23, 2019, https://www.pressherald.com/2019/06/23/-greg-kesich-conspiracy-theory-takes-hold-in-maine-gop/ (accessed June 20, 2021).

55 Logan Hullinger, "Rep. Perry Pushes 'Replacement Theory' during Committee Hearing," *York Dispatch*, April 17, 2021, https://www.yorkdispatch.

com/story/news/politics/2021/04/15/rep-perry-pushes-replacement-theory-during-committee-hearing/7229074002/ (accessed June 20, 2021).

56 "The Nativists Are Restless," *New York Times*, January 31, 2009, http://www.nytimes. com/2009/02/01/opinion/01sun1.html (accessed August 4, 2011).

57 "130 Republicans in Congress Want to Consider Ending Birthright Citizen-ship," *ThinkProgress*, October 26, 2010, http://thinkprogress.org/2010/10/26/-gop-birthright-citizenship/ (accessed April 18, 2011).

58 Ryan W. Miller, "46% of Whites Worry becoming a Majority-Minority Nation Will 'Weaken American Culture,' Survey Says," *USA Today*, https://perma.cc/M4H8-HKDR (accessed January 10, 2022).

59 See survey in Ed Kilgore, "Trump Fans Really Want a Less-Diverse America," *New York Magazine*, June 23, 2016, http://nymag.com/daily/intelligencer/2016/06/trump-fans-really-want-a-less-diverse-america.html?mid=twitter_nymag%20percents%20of%20trump%20supports%20who%20don%E2%80%99t%20want%20diversity (accessed September 19, 2016); and Justin Gest, Tyler Reny, and Jeremy Mayer, "Roots of the Radical Right: Nostalgic Deprivation in the United States and Britain," *Comparative Political Studies* (2017), https://doi.org/10.1177/0010414017720705 (accessed November 21, 2017).

60 This diversity was measured as fewer immigrants and people of color in their ZIP codes. Research by Rene Flores and Ariel Azar cited in Thomas B. Edsall, "The 'Third Rail of American Politics' Is Still Electrifying," New York Times, November 3, 2021, https://www.nytimes.com/2021/11/03/opinion/us-immigration-politics.html (accessed March 18, 2022).

61 See surveys in Ed Kilgore, "Trump Fans Really Want a Less-Diverse Amer-ica." See also Justin Gest, Tyler Reny, and Jeremy Mayer, "Roots of the Radical Right: Nostalgic Deprivation in the United States and Britain," *Comparative Political Studies* (2017), https://doi.org/10.1177/0010414017720705 (accessed November 21, 2017).

62 Robert A. Pape, "Opinion: What an Analysis of 377 Americans Arrested or Charged in the Capitol Insurrection Tells Us," *Washington Post*, April 6, 2021, https://www.washingtonpost.com/opinions/2021/04/06/capitol-insurrection-arrests-cpost-analysis/ (accessed April 6, 2021).

63 H. Robert Outten, Michael T. Schmitt, Daniel A. Miller and Amber L. Gar-cia, "Feeling Threatened about the Future: Whites' Emotional Reactions to Anticipated Ethnic Demographic Changes," *Personality and Social Psychology Bulletin* 38 (2012): 14.

64 Brenda Major, Alison Blodorn, and Gregory M. Blascovich, "The Threat of Increasing Diversity," *Group Processes & Intergroup Relations* 21 (2016): 1–10. See also H. R. Outten, M.T. Schmitt, D. A. Miller, and A. L. Garcia, "Feeling Threatened about the Future: Whites' Emotional Reactions to Anticipated Ethnic Demographic Changes," *Personality and Social Psychology Bulletin*, 38 (January 2012): 14–25; and Maureen A. Craig and Jennifer A. Richeson, "On the Precipice of a 'MajorityMinority' America: Perceived Status Threat from the Racial Demographic Shift Affects White Americans' Political Ideology," *Psychological Science* 25 (2014): 1189–1197.

65 Amy R. Krosch, Suzy J. Park, Jesse Walker, and Ari R. Lisner, "The Threat of a Majority-Minority U.S. Alters White Americans' Perception of Race," *Journal of Experimental Social Psychology* 99 (March 2022): Abstract. Italics added.

66 Dowell Myers and Morris Levy, "The Demise of the White Majority Is a Myth," *Washington Post*, https://www.washingtonpost.com/opinions/the-demise-of-

the-white-majority-is-a-myth/2018/05/18/60fc897c-5233-11e8-abd8-
265bd07a9859_story.html (accessed May 25, 2021).

67 See those cited in Sabrina Tavernise, "Why the Announcement of a Loom-
ing White Minority Makes Demographers Nervous," https://www.nytimes.
com/2018/11/22/us/white-americans-minority-population.html (accessed
December 9, 2022).

68 Dudley L. Poston and Rogelio Sáenz, "Young White Children are the
Minority: The Demography of Whiteness Decline in the United States,"
Paper presented to Population Association of America meeting, St. Louis,
Missouri, April 2021. I am indebted here to a discussion with demographer
Dudley Poston.

69 F. Danbold and Y. J. Huo, "No Longer 'All-American'? Whites' Defensive
Reactions to Their Numerical Decline," *Social Psychological and Personality
Science* 6 (2015): 210–218, https://doi.org/10.1177/1948550614546355, as
summarized at CSWAC Blog, https://cswac.org/no-longer-all-american/
(accessed July 1, 2022).

70 Jim Zarroli, "Review of Deaths of Despair," https://www.npr.org/2020/
03/18/817687042/deaths-of-despair-examines-the-steady-erosion-of-u-s-
working-class-life (accessed April 13, 2021).

71 "Interview with Tressie MacMillan Cottom," https://www.nytimes.
com/2021/04/13/podcasts/ezra-klein-podcast-tressie-mcmillan-cottom-
transcript.html (accessed April 13, 2021).

72 Ibid.

73 Richard V. *Reeves, Dream Hoarders: How the American Upper Middle Class Is
Leaving Everyone Else in the Dust, Why That Is a Problem, and What to Do about
It* (Washington, DC: Brookings Institution Press, 2017), p. 3ff.

74 Allison L. Skinner and Jacob E. Cheadle, "The 'Obama Effect'? Priming
Contemporary Racial Milestones Increases Implicit Racial Bias among
Whites," *Social Cognition* 34 (2016): 544–558.

75 Brian Rosenwald, *Talk Radio's America: How an Industry Took over a Political
Party That Took over the United States* (Cambridge, MA: Harvard University
Press, 2019), pp. 157–158.

76 Quoted in Reeves, *Dream Hoarders*, p. 3.

77 Barack Obama, *A Promised Land* (New York: Crown Random House, 2020),
p. 672.

78 See comments of an American Enterprise Institute official in Tyler Kingkade and Nigel Chiwaya, "Schools Facing Critical Race Theory Battles are
Diversifying Rapidly, Analysis Finds," NBC News, September 13, 2021,
https://www.nbcnews.com/news/us-news/schools-facing-critical-race-
theory-battles-are-diversifying-rapidly-analysis-n1278834 (accessed November
4, 2021).

79 John R. Hibbing, *The Securitarian Personality: What Really Motivates Trump's
Base and Why It Matters for the Post-Trump Era* (New York: Oxford University
Press, 2020), Introduction, n.p.

80 Ibid.

81 Richard C. Fording and Sanford F. Schram, *Hard White: The Mainstreaming of Racism in American Politics* (New York: Oxford University Press, 2020), pp. 183–204.

82 Robert P. Jones, *White Too Long: The Legacy of White Supremacy in American
Christianity* (New York: Simon & Schuster, 2020), Introduction, n.p.

83 Ibid.

84 As quoted in Mike Cummings, "Yale Sociologist Phil Gorski on the Threat
of White Christian Nationalism," *YaleNews*, March 15, 2022, https://news.

yale.edu/2022/03/15/yale-sociologist-phil-gorski-threat-white-christian-nationalism (accessed May 5, 2022).

85   "The Founding Fathers' Religious Wisdom," Center for American Progress, January 8, 2008, https://www.americanprogress.org/about-us/ (accessed June 1, 2022).

86   Rick Noack, "Christchurch Endures as Extremist Touchstone, as Investigators Probe Suspected El Paso Manifesto," *Washington Post*, https://www.washingtonpost.com/world/2019/08/06/christchurch-endures-extremist-touchstone-investigators-probe-suspected-el-paso-manifesto/ (accessed April 6, 2021).

87   Dakin I, Jason Hanna, Joe Sterling, and Paul P. Murphy, "Hate Crime Charges Filed in Pittsburgh Synagogue Shooting that Left 11 Dead," CNN, https://www.cnn.com/2018/10/27/us/pittsburgh-synagogue-active-shooter/index.html (accessed June 18, 2021); Brett Barrouquere, "Pennsylvania Man, Robert Bowers, Charged with Federal Hate Crimes, Murder in Shooting at Pittsburgh Synagogue," *Southern Poverty Law Center*, November 1, 2018, https://www.splcenter.org/hatewatch/2018/11/01/pennsylvania-man-robert-bowers-charged-federal-hate-crimes-murder-shooting-pittsburgh (accessed June 18, 2021).

88   Rich Lord, "How Robert Bowers Went from Conservative to White Nationalist," *Pittsburgh Post-Gazette*, November 10, 2018, https://www.post-gazette.com/news/crime-courts/2018/11/10/Robert-Bowers-extremism-Tree-of-Life-massacre-shooting-pittsburgh-Gab-Warroom/stories/201811080165 (accessed July 1, 2022).

89   Julia Ebner and Jacob Davey, "The Great Replacement," *Institute for Strategic Dialogue*, July 2019, https://www.isdglobal.org/wp-content/uploads/2019/07/The-Great-Replacement-The-Violent-Consequences-of-Mainstreamed-Extremism-by-ISD.pdf (accessed April 2, 2021).

90   John Eligon, "The El Paso Screed, and the Racist Doctrine Behind It," *New York Times*, August 7, 2019, https://www.nytimes.com/2019/08/07/us/el-paso-shooting-racism.html (accessed July 1, 2022). In this summary paragraph, I also draw on David Nakamura, "'It had Nothing to Do with Us': Restrictionist Groups Distance Themselves from Accused El Paso Shooter, Who Shared Similar Views on Immigrants," *Washington Post*, August 10, 2019, https://www.washingtonpost.com/politics/it-had-nothing-to-do-with-us-restrictionist-groups-distance-themselves-from-el-paso-shooter-who-shared-similar-views-on-immigrants/2019/08/08/c44dd7f8-b955-11e9-a091-6a96e67d9cce_story.html (accessed June 20, 2021); and "2019 El Paso shooting," Wikipedia, https://en.wikipedia.org/wiki/2019_El_Paso_shooting#cite_note-Eligon-2 (accessed June 20, 2021).

91   Peyton Gendron, "What You Need to Know," Scrib.com, https://www.scribd.com/document/574156945/Payton-Gendron-Manifestom (accessed May 16, 2022).

92   Julia Ebner and Jacob Davey, "The Great Replacement."

93   SPLC, "Organizers and Leaders of Charlottesville's Deadly Rally Raised Money With PayPal," August 8, 2015, https://www.splcenter.org/hatewatch/2017/08/15/organizers-and-leaders-charlottesvilles-deadly-rally-raised-money-paypal (December 12, 2017); and Rosie Gray, "Trump Defends White-Nationalist Protesters: 'Some Very Fine People on Both Sides'" *The Atlantic*, August 15, 2017, https://www.theatlantic.com/politics/archive/2017/08/trump-defends-white-nationalist-protesters-some-very-fine-people-on-both-sides/537012/ (accessed December 12, 2017).

94 Heather Alaniz, Kimberly D. Dodson, and Jared R. Dmello, "Race, Rallies, and Rhetoric: How Trump's Political Discourse Contributed to the Capitol Riot," *Journal of Criminal Justice and Law*, December 31, 2021, https://jcjl. pubpub.org/pub/9c82zhyh/release/1 (accessed May 10, 2022).

95 Jones, *White Too Long*.

96 Alaniz, Dodson, and Dmello, "Race, Rallies, and Rhetoric."

97 Jefferson, "Storming the U.S. Capitol Was about Maintaining White Power In America."

98 Alan Feuer, "Fears of White People Losing Out Permeate Capitol Rioters' Towns, Study Finds," *New York Times*, April 6, 2021, https://www. nytimes.com/2021/04/06/us/politics/capitol-riot-study.html (accessed April 6, 2021) Italics added.

99 Robert A. Pape, "Opinion: What an Analysis of 377 Americans Arrested or Charged in the Capitol Insurrection Tells Us," *Washington Post*, April 6, 2021, https://www.washingtonpost.com/opinions/2021/04/06/capitol-insurrection-arrests-cpost-analysis/ (accessed April 6, 2021).

100 Robert A. Pape, "21 Million Americans say Biden is 'Illegitimate' and Trump Should Be Restored by Violence: Survey," *The Conversation*, https://www.alternet.org/2021/09/biden-trump/ (accessed September 28, 2021).

101 Alex Henderson, "Angry, Despondent, and Powerless: New Report Reveals How Loyal Trump Voters are Coping with His Loss, *Alternet*, April 2, 2021, https://www.alternet.org/2021/04/trump-voters/?utm_campaign=Rebel Mouse&share_id=6381506&utm_medium=social&utm_source=twitter &utm_content=AlterNet (accessed April 2, 2021); see also Stanley Greenberg, Christopher Parker, and Chad Arthur, "What Will Trump Loyalists' Sensed Powerlessness Mean for Politics?" *Democracy Corps*, March 24, 2021.

102 Margaret Sullivan, "If American Democracy Is Going to Survive, the Media Must Make This Crucial Shift," *Washington Post*, January 3, 2022, https:// www.washingtonpost.com/media/2022/01/03/media-democracy-jan6-atlantic-npr/ (accessed January 3, 2022).

103 David Rosen, "Who Are Trump's Committed Insurrectionists? *The Progressive*, January 14, 2022, https://progressive.org/latest/trump-committed-insurrectionists-rosen-220114/ (accessed February 4, 2022).

104 I am indebted to discussions here with sociologist Randolph Hohle.

105 Tom Gjelten, "'Scary' Survey Finding: 4 In 10 Republicans Say Political Violence May Be Necessary," NPR, February 11, 2021, https://www.npr. org/2021/02/11/966498544/a-scary-survey-finding-4-in-10-republicans-say-political-violence-may-be-necessa (accessed March 12, 2021).

106 Justin Gest, "Why Trumpism Will Outlast Donald Trump," *politico.com*, August 16, 2016, http://www.politico.com/magazine/story/2016/08/why-trumpism-will-outlast-donald-trump-214166#ixzz4N4wM4lsr (accessed July 1, 2022).

107 Del Plaskett Questions Trump Defense Team's Clips of People of Color, PBS.org, February 12, 2021, https://www.pbs.org/newshour/politics/-watch-democrat-questions-trump-defense-teams-clips-of-people-of-color (accessed June 22, 2021).

108 Steven V. Miller and Nicholas T. Davis, "The Effect of White Social Prejudice on Support for American Democracy," *The Journal of Race, Ethnicity, and Politics* 6 (2020): 334–351. doi:10.1017/rep.2019.55.

109 Cameron Easley, "U.S. Conservatives are Uniquely Inclined toward Right-Wing Authoritarianism Compared to Western Peers," morningconsult.

com, June 28, 2021, https://morningconsult.com/2021/06/28/global-right-wing-authoritarian-test/ (accessed June 28, 2021).

110 Bob Altemeyer, *The Authoritarians* (Winnipeg: University of Manitoba, 2006), pp. 200–204.

111 Easley, "U.S. Conservatives Are Uniquely Inclined toward Right-Wing Authoritarianism Compared to Western Peers."

112 Ibid.

Chapter 3

Manufacturing White Racism, Ignorance, and Fear

Elite Conning of Ordinary Whites

Most white Americans have long assumed that white racial dominance is a natural and untroubling U.S. state of affairs. That view is not true. It is not natural to the human state of affairs, but historically has been crafted at the top of this society by elite whites, mostly men, and by their millions of acolytes over centuries. That white-crafted societal order is certainly problematical for a great many Americans, especially Americans of color. For four-plus centuries, these powerful and wealthy whites have operated in their white organizational networks, both concealed and well-known, to wield great political, economic, media, and other institutional power.

Unsurprisingly, the dominant white framing of U.S. racial matters has been substantially created, codified, and maintained by this white elite, although its construction and perpetuation operate in routine interaction with the views and usages of ordinary white Americans. As social analysts Karl Marx and Friedrich Engels long ago pointed out, "the ideas of the ruling class are in every epoch the ruling ideas: i.e. the class, which is the ruling material force of society, is at the same time its ruling intellectual force."[1] The white elite has dominated the creation, discussion, and dissemination of a system-rationalizing racist frame in all major institutional arenas. For instance, research on the racist ideas and actions of many U.S. presidents has demonstrated that these very powerful white men controlling major sociopolitical institutions have worked hard "to nurture and support the nation's racism."[2] This country's dominant white racial framing did not arise naturally or accidentally.

Today, as in the past, the white elite's majority often frame the likelihood of a white minority nation negatively—as probably reducing and otherwise impacting their central role and power in this white-dominated society.[3] As I demonstrated in previous chapters, whites' fear over becoming a population and power minority means different things depending on their class level. While that fear is to some degree part of white racist rhetoric and framing in all white social classes, it is enhanced for the elite

DOI: 10.4324/9781003359883-4

whites who are very concerned about preservation of their centuries-old class *and* racial dominance in U.S. society. Indeed, no matter what happens to the white population's numerical majority, this white elite will likely press very hard to maintain its great societal power.

Unsurprisingly, this powerful white elite, or a major faction within it, often creates or uses major societal crises to assert or expand its societal power and protect its interests. In large-scale societal conflicts, such as those during the 1960s civil rights movements or those over nonwhite immigration before, during, and after the Donald Trump administration, a major faction in this powerful white elite usually mobilizes the country's racial or class identities to their advantage. Elite white political actors, such as former president Donald Trump and his major advisors and backers, have consciously emphasized one of these identities (e.g., whiteness) by accenting another identity (e.g., outgroup non-whiteness). We observe this racist strategy in Trump's frequent commentaries on supposedly threatening nonwhite immigrants, both before and after the January 2021 Capitol insurrection that he helped to generate. As that overwhelmingly white insurrection revealed, many in Trump's base of ordinary whites are willing to engage in violence on behalf of the sociopolitical interests of the right wing of this country's dominant elite (see Chapter 4).

Significantly, that large white base has often been conned into supporting elite interests in societal power battles by the "wage of whiteness," a recurring socio-racial reward they have received over centuries now. Indeed, by the early 18th century, a shrewd white male elite, many of them major slaveholders, had enhanced its societal dominance over ordinary whites with this conning socio-racial reward that African American sociologist W. E. B. du Bois aptly labeled the "public and psychological wage of whiteness."[4] That is, for centuries that ruling elite has provided almost all whites with some racial power and privilege over African Americans and other Americans of color.

Today, as in the past, the white elite knows well the power of this racialized conning of the general white population. The elite utilizes deception and deflection in white-controlled political and other institutions that often sets mostly working and middle class whites against mostly working class people of color. As a result, most ordinary whites generally accept racially framed ideas that they are superior in many ways to people of color and that the federal government is too biased in numerous government programs toward people of color.[5]

Strikingly too, the dominant racial frame of most white Americans, including most elite corporate leaders, has long centered an anti-Black perspective. My colleagues and I have demonstrated this centuries-old empirical reality in numerous research studies.[6] Today, that dominant white frame frequently accents Black Americans in duplicitous white politicians' attacks on so-called critical race theory, on supposed excessive "wokeness," and on the well-researched *1619* Project accenting foundational U.S. racism—all terms and concepts principally or substantially created by Black American activists and scholars over many decades. Demonstrably, from the first decades of its existence, this country's elite white leaders have been committed to and obsessed with defending and legitimating the societal subordination of Black Americans, as well as other Americans of color.

Unmistakably, the dominant white elite often cultivates socio-political ignorance in the general population. Referencing his supporters, ex-president Donald Trump once boasted, "I love the poorly educated." Recent polling research by Richard Fording and Sanford Schram has demonstrated empirically that low information white voters, those with a low level of political knowledge and who resist critical thinking about racial framing, were much more likely to be supportive of Donald Trump than other white voters. They supported him "on the basis of social and economic anxieties about refugees, immigrants, African Americans, and the presidency of Barack Obama."[7] In addition, a research study by sociologist Darren Sherkat examined the general cognitive sophistication of voters in a national 2018 survey. Using a ten-item vocabulary exam to measure cognitive sophistication, and controlling for formal education and other relevant social factors, his model accurately predicted that nearly three quarters of the white respondents who did not know the meaning of any of these mostly common vocabulary words voted for Trump. About 51 percent with average scores on the vocabulary exam were predicted to have supported Trump, but only 35 percent of those with a perfect ten score on the exam were predicted to have done so. Strikingly too, this voting relationship link to cognitive sophistication was similar for those with *and* without college degrees. Additionally, Sherkat notes that only half of all the white respondents actually knew six or more of the ten words on the relatively easy vocabulary exam. He concludes:

> If you are that deficient, it would be a struggle to read a single article in the *New York Times*. To try to get your information from print media would be impossible. Hence, most [white] Americans get most of their information from television news or talk radio. No big words, just easy explanations.[8]

Today, as in the past, relatively low information whites have been a substantial part of the base of right-wing political organization.

Far-Right Activism: White Suburbs and Beyond

The rise of the white far-right political movement occurred well before the current growth of a more openly white-nationalist Republican Party.

In her book *Suburban Warriors*, Lisa McGirr terms the early version of the contemporary far-right movement as the "New Right" and argues that it mostly emerged during the 1950s–1960s civil rights era among conservative white suburbanites. A mostly grass-roots movement of affluent white men and women, it centrally developed in conservative suburbs of big Sunbelt cities like Los Angeles, Atlanta, Charlotte, and Phoenix. However, these suburban right-wing activists were *not* a random sample of ordinary whites, for most were relatively well-off white middle- and upper-class male professionals and business leaders, and their supportive white wives. In the Sunbelt and elsewhere, these early far-right activists were motivated by Christian, anti-Communist, anti-union, and/or libertarian conservatism. Supported by wealthy white conservatives and right-wing magazines like *National Review*, they gradually took over a then more moderate and diverse Republican Party and recreated it as a right-wing, predominantly white conservative Christian party. This growing far-right faction in the Republican Party aggressively opposed the progressivism of the 1960s racial and gender rights movements and of moderate Democratic Presidents John Kennedy and Lyndon Johnson, especially their increased efforts at racial desegregation and multiracial democracy.[9]

These early white Republican extremists played an important role in the unsuccessful 1964 presidential campaign of Republican Barry Goldwater, which included his and their active opposition to 1960s civil rights laws. This new racist-right Republican Party was further grounded in the racist "southern strategy" of the late 1960s' Republican presidential candidate Richard Nixon (1969–1974), the active political strategy noted in Chapter 2 that was very successful in moving many white voters fearing racial change from the Democratic Party to the Republican Party, a strategy adopted by all subsequent Republican presidential candidates.

Later far-right movements and organizations, such as the Tea Party movement (2009–2016) within the Republican Party and numerous new right-wing think tanks, are the direct heirs of this earlier New Right movement. Today, they make up a much more extensive set of arch-conservative groups and organizations. As McGirr summarizes, the U.S. right-wing currently "enjoys the full backing of powerful right-wing media outfits such as Fox News and the support of the panoply of well-heeled conservative foundations and rightwing advocacy organizations."[10] Moreover, she emphasizes that the extensive array of contemporary racist-right media and organizations is more top-down in creation and construction than the earlier grassroots conservative movement charted in her investigative book.

White Christian Nationalism: Religious Manipulation of White Fears

A very important example of these top-down right-wing advocacy organizations is the Council for National Policy (CNP). It was created in the 1980s by the white minister and wealthy apocalyptic fiction author Tim LaHaye. The politically successful CNP has networked an array of powerful religious-right activists from the country's most powerful Protestant Christian organization, the heavily white evangelical Southern Baptist Convention, with Republican political operatives and independent evangelical ministers with their own radio and television media. This far-right organization has had lasting impacts. As journalist Jonathan Wilson-Hartgrove has summarized, major political figures who have aggressively defended former president Donald Trump "from the White House—Steve Bannon, Mike Pence, Kellyanne Conway—have in fact been connected through the CNP for decades to the white evangelicals... who have been most eager to praise Trump as a champion of 'religious values.'"[11] Researcher Anne Nelson, who has studied these long-existing, often shadowy right-wing networks, notes that in them there are "many echoes of Civil War-era resentment of federal authority." Furthermore, this very influential networking movement

> has devoted major resources and energy to winning state-level elections, including many state legislatures. It is common for them to pilot bills in certain states, to leverage them to others through organizations such as the State Policy Network and the American Legislative Exchange Council.[12]

In a famous 1980 speech to white evangelical leaders another early leader of the white Christian nationalist movement, Paul Weyrich, laid out their antidemocratic goals:

> Now many of our Christians have what I call the goo-goo syndrome—good government. They want everybody to vote. I don't want everybody to vote. Elections are not won by a majority of people, they never have been from the beginning of our country and they are not now. As a matter of fact, our leverage in the elections quite candidly goes up as the voting populace goes down.[13]

That is, if all people vote, and here he especially meant voters of color, that significantly reduces the political power of arch-conservative white Christians. Indeed, Weyrich was an early activist who helped to create new political organizations to further Christian nationalist goals. In 1973, he was a cofounder of the American Legislative Exchange Council (ALEC). As journalist Andrew Whitehead has emphasized, this ALEC organization has long supported voting policies "that disproportionately affect people of color: strict voter ID laws, automated purging of registration lists, limiting mail-in or early voting, or slashing the number of polling places."[14] Moreover, as I show in Chapter 4, the ALEC organization has become centrally important in linking a broad array of political organizations, leading corporations, and politicians seeking to achieve numerous far-right political goals at state and federal government levels.

Another far-right coalition that is shaping much contemporary state legislation is the theocratic Christian Right coalition called Project Blitz, which was organized in 2015. Such Christian Right groups seek to make the U.S. a country ruled by evangelical Christians and guided by their interpretation of biblical law. Project Blitz has developed a package of model bills they have been successful in getting right-wing state legislators to pass. The prominent religion scholar Frederick Clarkson notes that their model Christian nationalist bills range "from requiring public schools to display the national motto, 'In God We Trust' (IGWT); to legalizing discrimination against LGBTQ people; to religious exemptions regarding women's reproductive health."[15] Moreover, since 2019, this coalition has sought yet other far-right legislation from state legislatures, including laws restricting what books public libraries can include. Still, "the Dominionism-driven Christian nationalist agenda remains the same. The playbooks advise legislators to cloak their religious mission in the guise of more secular intentions and they've renamed several bills to make them sound more appealing."[16] The Project Blitz group has also gotten many state legislators to attend state "Prayer Caucuses," which often imbed various arch-conservative religious and political goals.

This contemporary white Christian nationalism has had a variety of other political impacts. For example, in June 2022, the right-wing majority of the U.S. Supreme Court issued an opinion substantially written by the white arch-conservative Catholic Justice Samuel Alito. In that blockbuster opinion, Justice Alito, quoting among others the 17th-century English judge Sir Matthew Hale who once sentenced women "witches" to death, argued that the 1970s *Roe v. Wade* Supreme Court decision supporting a woman's right to abortion and other personal bodily control was wrongly decided. The decision rules that "the Constitution does not confer a right to abortion; *Roe* and *Casey* are overruled; and the authority to regulate abortion is returned to the people and their elected representatives [in the states]."[17] Religion researcher and expert Robert P. Jones has argued that this radical judicial action is the

> legal equivalent of a time machine that threatens to transport American jurisprudence back to the 1950s. It is part of a gambit—seen in attacks on LGBTQ rights, immigrants, the separation of church and state, and critical race theory—to hold onto a particular conservative vision of white Christian America and impose it upon a more religiously and racially diverse nation that is increasingly supportive of this set of rights grounded in a Constitutional right to privacy.[18]

Drawing on recent national survey data, Jones adds that the *only* major U.S. religious group wherein a majority hold the view that abortion should be illegal in all or most cases is white evangelical Protestants. For a half century or more, the national attack on legal abortion has been disproportionately rooted in white evangelical Christian thought, a perspective spurring organized political action to make the U.S. centrally a white evangelical Christian nation.

This white evangelical Christian movement is behind numerous other "culture war" attacks, such as those on public schools for restricting Christian religious rituals there or for teaching honestly about U.S. racism, human sexuality, and LGBTQ realities.[19] Unmistakably, the misnamed "culture wars" are actually a united *religious war* seeking to impose white right-wing Christian views and values on all Americans and to make the U.S. a much more politically authoritarian society. Since at least the 1970s, many white Republican politicians, including most recently Donald Trump at the presidential level, have successfully adopted this white archconservative Christian framing in their own major political campaigns.

Media Control: Manufacturing White Framing

For centuries, the dominant white elite has imposed its white racial framing of society and exercised its other elite power not only in U.S. political, educational, and religious institutions but also in and through major radio and television networks—and, most recently, in an array of social media. As of this writing, some 200-plus executives in just *five* huge media corporations control at least 90 percent of major U.S. media outlets: radio and television stations, newspapers and magazines, book publishers, music videos, satellite transmissions, and motion picture studios. This number is down significantly from the 50 or so media corporations with this shared media control as recently as the 1980s. Currently, these mega-corporations are AT&T (Time Warner, CNN), Comcast (NBC, Telemundo, Universal), Disney (ABC, ESPN), ViacomCBS (CBS, Paramount), and News Corp (Fox News, *Wall Street Journal*). They also act as collaborative corporate units. That is, they have joint corporate ventures and their corporate boards have numerous shared directors.[20] These media conglomerates are still mostly controlled by whites, and disproportionately elite white men. In addition, a substantial majority of full-time news reporters, supervisors, and editors at most mainstream newspapers, news magazines, and news websites are white. At major television networks whites are generally over-represented in major managerial jobs. Additionally, Federal Communications Commission (FCC) data indicate that less than 6 percent of full power television stations are owned by Americans of color. This latter group is significantly underrepresented among owners of major commercial radio stations as well.[21] Of course, this white, mostly male domination is true for major corporations generally. Currently, whites make up about 93 percent of the powerful Fortune 500 CEOs, and *86 percent* of all those CEOs are white men. Yet this country's workforce is now about 77 percent white, and only about 38 percent white male.[22]

Additionally, major social media companies, which also spread white racial framing of society widely, have rather modest percentages of Black and Latino employees—for example, in 2021, just 11.2 percent of Twitter's "leadership roles" and just 9.8 percent in such Facebook (Meta-Platforms, Inc.) positions. Most in these top decisionmaking positions are white, with a significant percentage in some companies being Asian American.[23]

Media analysts Edward Herman and Noam Chomsky have argued from empirical data that these major media corporations are controlled by a capitalist elite that runs them primarily in terms of their corporate profit-making interests. Furthermore, this mostly white elite has long viewed the general public as ill-informed outsiders who "need to be placated with necessary illusions in order to keep them from challenging the material interests of the elite. The media is crucial in providing these illusions."[24] Powerful white top executives and other high-level white employees in various branches of these dominant media corporations shape, rework, or block important news and other information for U.S. televisions, radios, smartphones, newspapers, computers, and other media devices. A good example of their recurring racist framing can be seen in how they tend to view Black boys as men. Associated Press coverage of the shooting of a Black teen-aged male victim referred to him as a "black man," but their coverage of the white male, 18-year-old mass killer in the Buffalo mass killing listed him as a "white teen."[25] These powerful corporate decision-makers typically operate from a social propaganda model of newsmaking and broadcasting. That is, their major task is to *manufacture* public consent to the operations of the usually white-run and racially inegalitarian local and national political, economic, educational, law enforcement, and other important institutions.

Several key organizational filters in shaping this public consent are clear in what this decisionmaking elite does, or does not do. One important filter involves the large size, concentration, and elite ownership of the profitseeking media companies they firmly control. Another screening filter involves the heavy dependence of these media executives on corporate advertisers for their own profitmaking. Directly or indirectly, these big advertisers have significant command over much media news and other informational programming. Also important in this information filtering process is these media corporations' reliance on getting much input from a powerful cadre of very disproportionately white government officials, business executives, and other official experts. The scholar Alan MacLeod notes that

> By relying on official sources like politicians, think tanks and PR companies, sources that make sure their point of view is always

represented, what they say becomes a story and news is written in a light that is favourable to them and their interests.[26]

MacLeod further notes that Herman and Chomsky underscore how powerful officials and organizations can successfully protest unwanted mainstream media presentations with "boycotts, lawsuits, smear campaigns, letter-writing campaigns and more... making sure the media report stories in a certain way (or do not report them at all)."[27]

In addition, over the past few decades, huge internet-based tech companies such as Facebook (Meta), Twitter, and Google have come to play a dominant national role in the distribution of news and other programming generated by the mainstream media giants. Facebook (Meta) and Google together currently account for the *substantial majority* of U.S. news viewers, in most age groups, who are directed to major news websites. Together with the media mega-corporations, they have immense power over the character and slant of the political-economic and other societal information presented (or not presented) to Americans, as well as to hundreds of millions of people beyond U.S. borders. Their great societal power extends to shaping or blocking much of what local, state, and federal legislators and other government officials seek to do in terms of important government safety regulations, tax laws, and other legislation affecting corporate operations and profitmaking.[28] In this way, contemporary media corporations and allied tech conglomerates buttress the U.S. capitalistic order in a necessary system–reinforcing manner. They thereby manufacture much of what the public knows, and does not know, about contemporary U.S. society and its frequently oppressive capitalistic class structure.

Critically considering the powerful online media, Noam Chomsky has recently noted that a person who reads the *New York Times* or the *Washington Post* or listens to the more liberal television news channels can get a fairly good "range of opinion, not very broad ... but at least there is some discussion and occasionally you get a critical voice here and there." However, in regard to major online social media, he continues, "People tend to go to things that just reinforce their own opinions, so you end up with bubbles." He adds that Google and Facebook (Meta) "are doing it by monitoring everything about you so that somehow advertisers will be able to make more money approaching you."[29] In addition to shaping consumer buying, this and other informational microtargeting greatly helps to manufacture popular support for a still very inegalitarian political and economic system.

Additionally, in a further analysis of this Herman-Chomsky propaganda model, the scholar Florian Zollmann has pointed out that the powerful organizational filters that shape and censor much mainstream media news and other public information include the important racial and gender biases of those people who are doing the filtering—and not just their social class framing and interests. Most major media gatekeepers are "members of a male- and white-dominated elite and this has consequences for news access and outcomes."[30] That is, this elite is very influential in shaping and maintaining society's dominant racist and sexist framing and the consequent, well-institutionalized racist and sexist discrimination in society. Indeed, extensive Western imperialism over several centuries now has been implemented, framed, and defended from these dominant white racist and male sexist frames. Seen from these controlling frames, to take a major example, numerous U.S. and European military interventions have been "a necessary component of 'enlightening' and 'civilizing' primitive, unruly (feminized) 'others.' Europeans thus positioned their alleged rationality" firmly against the racial and gender inferiority of hundreds of millions of colonized "others."[31] Unquestionably, a critical media propaganda model must consider seriously the commanding role of these white racist and male sexist frames as regular news and information filters in Western societies and beyond.

As I underscored previously, this white racist framing is especially important because it is riddled with *strong emotions* supportive of the inegalitarian status quo. Manufacturing such racialized emotions is as important as manufacturing the racist ideas. As a result, a great many whites at all class levels are quite emotional about the reality of a white minority nation resulting from the extensive browning of America. As we have previously seen, many are fearful, angry, even raging against this likely societal change.

One key reason for this is that the elite, mostly white decisionmakers and their implementing acolytes in the mainstream media, social media, and political sphere have generated and fostered these white emotions, most especially by manufacturing an array of commonplace racist narratives and other misinformation about present and coming racial change. Legal analyst Brittany Farr has accented the role of the mostly white controlled media's problematical coverage of the racial demographic change in accelerating white fear about a majority-minority nation. Much of that media coverage has used language and arguments that have created a "moral panic" in the white population. By moral panic she means "a widespread reaction to a social problem.... It is an incident, set of conditions, or turn of events that threatens core values."[32] From her review of the mainstream media, she argues that these media invoke "longstanding [white] fears about racial difference and white political power in the United States."[33]

As I show throughout this book, these elite white decisionmakers have long controlled major media and manipulated ordinary whites using elements of the dominant white racial framing in educational, religious, political, and media institutions. That dominant framing's concepts, narratives, and emotions not only generate *consent* to the country's current racial inequalities but also create people, especially white men, who are willing to *violently attack* targets that threaten racially egalitarian change and to risk their lives to sustain those traditional societal inequalities and the major institutions that imbed them. This white framing periodically generates violent "soldiers for the status quo," as in the case of the January 2021 Capitol insurrection (see Chapter 6).

Right-Wing Talk Radio: Propagating Racist Framing

As I noted previously, much of the Republican Party has shifted significantly to the far right since the Richard Nixon presidential administration, substantially in response to actual and threatened racial desegregation of formerly segregated public and private institutions. Indeed, that Party's so-called southern strategy has appealed not only to the racist framing of that desegregation by white southern voters but also to that of many white northern voters. In addition to this influential Republican Party political strategy, from the 1970s to the present a substantial array of right-wing talk radio shows, cable television channels like Fox News, and newspapers like the *Wall Street Journal* have been important in influencing and manipulating white racial views in a much more white nationalist and nativist direction.

Indeed, politically conservative Americans, and especially white Americans, have come to view these old and new right-wing media outlets as normal and unbiased, thereby giving them significant power to shape their viewers and listeners' socio-political views. For the most part, these right-wing media have evolved outside mainstream media networks like ABC, CBS, NBC, PBS, and NPR, and they have often generated much societal misinformation—including false political and racial conspiracies—that intensifies many whites' anxiety or fear about the future of white population dominance, power, and privilege.

Unmistakably, in recent decades, the development and expansion of far-right talk radio has been central to reinvigorating or intensifying right-wing U.S. politics. Far-right talk radio hosts have helped to generate a political process "through which increasing numbers of Americans came to live in echo chambers, receiving news only from sources sharing their political perspective."[34] For example, until his death in February 2021, talk radio's Rush Limbaugh had spoken to the largest radio audience of any such radio host. For more than 200 days each year he held forth for hours with his right-wing, often extremist, and politically polarizing views. His audience was estimated at 20 million a week in the 1990s and at 13–14 million a week not long before he died.[35]

Commonplace in Limbaugh's right-wing presentations was a constant barrage of explicitly and implicitly racist commentaries on an array of political and social issues. For instance, he regularly mocked and described in blatantly racist terms Black athletes in the National Basketball Association and the National Football League, as well as Black political and civil rights figures such the Reverend Jesse Jackson. When Barack Obama appeared on the national political scene in the 2000s, Limbaugh regularly attacked him in racist terms, with the clear purpose of heightening

> his older, overwhelmingly white audience's identification with their white identity by scaring them about the black president who—the host reminded them repeatedly—wanted to take what they had earned and give it to black people as part of a radical plan to transform the traditional America they knew and loved.[36]

Limbaugh constantly reminded his mostly white listeners of fictitious nonwhite threats to their families or their white power and privilege. In this way, he helped to generate, or make even wilder, white political conspiracies about the "browning of America." He paved the way for the emergence of Donald Trump as a successful race-baiting, white nationalist Republican presidential candidate and president.

Soon after the January 6, 2021 Capitol insurrection, Limbaugh made belligerently supportive comments praising the angry and violent Trump-supporting attackers there. Like other right-wing commentators, he portrayed them as white "patriots" similar to the 1776 American revolutionaries. However, he then went a step farther, suggesting that a lot of timid conservatives "say that any violence or aggression at all is unacceptable, regardless of the circumstances. I am glad Sam Adams, Thomas Paine, the actual tea party guys, the men at Lexington and Concord didn't feel that way."[37]

Significantly, Limbaugh's death soon after he made these provocative comments has helped to accelerate the decline in right-wing talk radio. Over the last decade or so, the corporate owners of many talk radio stations, which are increasingly publicly traded and visible firms, have put pressure on right-wing radio hosts to tone down their extreme sociopolitical commentaries so as to not lose important advertisers. There has also been a decline in the percentage of certain age groups, especially younger groups, listening to the far-right talk radio shows. Nonetheless, these changes in talk radio have not resulted in less far-right political propaganda and misinformation being spread, but a movement of that to yet other outlets such as online social media.[38]

We should note that another central feature of far-right influence in shaping the thought of ordinary whites is the extensive reach of white Christian-fundamentalist talk radio and television networks such as the Christian Broadcasting and Trinity Broadcasting networks. These are especially impactful in rural and small-town areas and in the midwestern and southwestern regions. Shows on these networks frequently link far-right racial and political views to certain Christian fundamentalist perspectives, and they too are frequently filled with societal misinformation.

As progressive Christian analyst Jonathan Wilson-Hartgrove has pointed out, powerful groups like the right-wing Family Research Council have a major role in getting racial and political propaganda spread across the country's more conservative white Christian churches. They send out far-right publications like *Watchmen on the Wall*, videos for church services, draft sermons, and voter guides for church bulletins to tens of thousands of conservative religious leaders. In many places, this right-wing information network is much more important than the traditional sources of local news because of the financial demise of many local newspapers and other local media sources in recent decades. Wilson-Hartgrove argues that these religious-right efforts are substantially driven by right-wing corporate interests unconcerned with the actual socioeconomic and public program needs of these local communities: That is, they frequently manipulate local "people to support candidates who work against their interests once they take office—cutting corporate taxes, then slashing budgets for public education, public health, environmental protections, and public infrastructure." [39]

Fox Network Impacts: Manufacturing Racist Framing

Generally speaking, the contemporary polarized cable and social media information environments in the U.S. have made it difficult to get the mostly right-wing Republican voters to accept much accurate information about politics and policymaking from mainstream media sources such as the long-established broadcast television networks. The commitment of such voters to an arch-conservative Republican Party has been very hard to change.

In the mid-1990s, the Australian-born, naturalized U.S. citizen, and media capitalist Rupert Murdoch founded the arch-conservative Fox News Channel. Since then, the constant daily barrage of Fox News cable broadcasts, much of it filled with political and other societal misinformation, has had significant impacts on the U.S. political scene. Indeed, President Joe Biden himself commented on the danger to democracy that Murdoch's extensive media empire has created. According to Jonathan Martin and Alexander Burns, Biden asserted that Fox News "is one of the most destructive forces in the United States" and that Murdoch is "the most dangerous man in the world." [40] Interestingly, Biden is not alone among Western officials in this view, as New Zealand's Green Party Head of Policy and Communications, David Cormack, has commented that "A huge reason that our politics is not so extremely polarised and so far out there is because we no longer have Murdoch-owned press in New Zealand, and it's never taken a foothold." [41]

One significant study of Fox News's political effects on U.S. elections by Gregory Martin and Ali Yurukoglu found that in the election years

2004 and 2008, the Republican share of the total U.S. presidential vote would have been about 3.6–6.3 points less but for the strong impact of Fox News on these presidential voters.[42] Additionally, a recent U.S. media study by David Broockman and Joshua Kalla incentivized (with modest payments) 304 regular Fox News viewers to watch CNN news for a month in 2020 to see if their views about various political matters might change. They also did a content analysis of Fox and CNN news coverage (e.g., their agenda setting and information framing) and also of actual information provided (i.e., partisan coverage filtering) in that month to document what turned out to be dramatic differences in news coverage. Soon after the viewing month, they did a survey of the mostly conservative participants and found a major impact on their views from watching the CNN news more frequently. The participants' "factual perceptions of current events… and knowledge about the 2020 presidential candidates' positions" had shifted toward the broader CNN presentations. They found that these Fox viewers were persuaded to new views "by viewing opposition partisan media instead of their own." That is, the Fox News's right-wing political bias affected these conservative voters' choices "at least in part because it hides information about aligned incumbents' failures and distorts perceptions of political rivals."[43]

In addition, another survey of these respondents some weeks later found that the CNN news impacts had receded as they went back to their old Fox News viewing pattern and their previous political attitudes. Broockman and Kalla conclude that this shifting back and forth in these mostly conservative respondents' attitudes was not so much a matter of them having unchangeable political views and preferences as that they get very conservative views replenished repeatedly over their lives of watching Fox News and other arch-conservative media without much countering information and in acquaintance networks that mostly share these views. Those constant repetitions are what make such conservative Americans' views so hard to change.[44]

Unsurprisingly, this is an intentional goal of the white Fox News corporate elite—to constantly present national and international news and commentary from politically right-wing and white racially framed perspectives. For example, in his many weekly commentaries, the Fox channel's influential political commentator Tucker Carlson, has frequently accented the ongoing U.S. shift from a more white to a less white population as problematical. In his recurring white-racist framing, this population change is brought on by what he terms dangerous "Third World" immigration, the white supremacist code for undesirable immigrants of color.[45] He has used the extremist language of white demographic "replacement" in characterizing what he alleges is the Democratic Party's *intentional* goal to get more voters by actively encouraging more immigrants of color.[46] For example, at one point in spring 2021, he summarized his own view: the U.S. left has become literally hysterical if you use the term "replacement," if you suggest that the Democratic Party is trying to replace the current electorate, the voters now casting ballots, with new people, more obedient voters from the Third World.... Demographic change is the key to the Democratic Party's political ambitions. In order to win and maintain power. Democrats plan to change the population of the country.[47]

As he often has done, Carlson references here ongoing U.S. demographic change that for the most part does *not* result from recent immigration, but instead from past decades of nonwhite immigrants coming largely for *economic* reasons, especially to support their families, and encouraged then by many white politicians and employers in both national parties to do so. Moreover, if these current immigrants were mostly whites from Europe, Carlson and similar right-wing media analysts would likely never make such conspiratorial assertions about them or seek to ban them.

Significantly, a *New York Times* analysis of Tucker Carlson's Fox show in this recent period revealed that he had made commentaries like this about the Democratic Party and its leaders more than 400 times. His recurring commentary has reproduced white supremacist misinformation and conspiracies, and it intentionally does so to anger and get more white viewers—and thus has sharply increased Fox's profits. As one *Times* reporter has also noted,

> Carlson's producers often trawl the web for supporting material. In the show's early years, clips would sometimes be sent to the network's fact checkers, who would occasionally discover that a story had actually originated farther afield, on a racist or neo-Nazi site like Stormfront.[48]

Sadly, Carlson's focus on "great replacement theory" also echoes the manifestos of the aforementioned white mass murderers in El Paso, Buffalo, and elsewhere.

Not long after the January 2021 Capitol insurrection, Carlson singled out women of color in the U.S. Congress who were emphasizing the voting choices and democratic rights of Americans of color. He quoted Democratic Representative Cori Bush of Missouri, who said this about the insurrection:

> Let's be clear, this was a racist attempt to overturn an election. This was more about trying to disenfranchise the voices of the Black, brown, indigenous people's voices, trying to invalidate our vote.... So I'm speaking up. You are going to hear that we are not going to let this go because this is a racist attempt, we have to call it what it is, it's White supremacy at its finest.

Assessing these critical comments from his own white racist framing, Carlson insisted that "What the Democrats really have in mind is a new version of Reconstruction. Look up 'Reconstruction' if you're not familiar with that story."[49] The reactionary Carlson clearly did not have a positive view of this remarkable Reconstruction period of *expanding* U.S. democracy, one where African Americans were freed from enslavement and got their *first* constitutional rights. Besides, as he should know, this was true only for a short period until white Klan-type groups, created or aided by former white slaveholders, used extreme anti-Black violence to end most of that era's brief democratic gains.

Furthermore, several white members of Congress, including the far-right member Matt Gaetz, have insisted that Fox's Tucker Carlson is "correct about Replacement Theory as he explains what is happening to America." In his obviously uninformed commentary, Gaetz added the white extremist argument that the Anti-Defamation League (ADL) "is a racist organization" for its accurate critique of Tucker Carlson.[50] Sadly too, even the former Republican speaker of the U.S. House, Newt Gingrich, openly expressed support for the "great replacement theory" of ardent white supremacists on the Fox cable channel: "The anti-American left would love to drown traditional, classic Americans with as many people as they can who know nothing of American history, nothing of American tradition, nothing of the rule of law," Gingrich said, parroting "great replacement theory" similar to that of Carlson. He further alleged that, "When you go and look at the radical left, this is their ideal model. It's to get rid of the rest of us because we believe in George Washington or we believe in the Constitution."[51] Operating from a white racist frame targeting immigrant Americans, the nativistic and nationalistic Gingrich meant white people when he emphasized "traditional, classic Americans" are being replaced by immigrants of color.

Heidi Beirich, the head of the Southern Poverty Law Center's Intelligence Project, has noted that Tucker Carlson

> probably has been the No. 1 commentator mainstreaming bedrock principles of white nationalism in this country, which is fear of immigrants, fear of Muslims, keeping them out and arguing that whites are under attack.... What white supremacy is about is keeping this country white.[52]

Indeed, Carlson has been celebrated by white nationalist and supremacist organization leaders and websites (e.g., the influential white supremacist blog Stormfront).

Recently, the head of the U.S. Anti-Defamation League, Jonathan Greenblatt, sent a letter to Fox's right-wing chief executive, Lachlan Murdoch, in which he explained that Tucker Carlson was regularly propagating a "foundational theory of white supremacy." In return, the younger Murdoch actively defended Carlson's racist views about the "great replacement theory," signaling that at its top corporate level the Fox network thinking remains overtly white supremacist. In his follow-up letter to Murdoch, Greenblatt detailed the many white supremacist views commonly articulated by Fox channel commentators. "Great replacement theory" is being "promoted by the white supremacist movement as it fits in with their wider belief about the impending destruction of the white race." And in the U.S. case, many of these white supremacists "blame Jews for non-white immigration," and their

> theory in more recent years has morphed into a toxic conspiracy theory that claims that Jews are trying to "replace" the white race with non-white immigrants. Carlson did not accidentally echo these talking points; he knowingly escalated this well-worn racist rhetoric.

By doing this, Greenblatt concluded, Carlson "galvanizes extremists and lights the fire of violence."[53]

Indeed, this indictment includes the actions of the white nationalist former president, Donald Trump. Demonstrably influenced by such far-right media presentations, Trump has periodically retweeted and thereby spread these white supremacist myths, including aspects of white replacement theories. For example, on August 23, 2018, after Fox's host Tucker Carlson did a negative broadcast on South African land reform—reform redressing earlier white land theft from indigenous Black populations in apartheid South Africa—Trump tweeted that he had asked the U.S. Secretary of State to investigate white-alleged "land and farm seizures and expropriations and the large scale killing of [white] farmers."[54] Here Trump was referencing false white supremacist claims about South Africa that had spread widely on the major online social media.

One puzzle in thinking about the commonplace white replacement theory's extraordinary fearfulness about white population replacement in the U.S. case is that these white theorists often downplay—and some do not even seem to realize—just how much power whites, especially the white elite, still have in U.S. society. In this regard they appear to be out of touch with the empirical reality of overwhelming white dominance in most major U.S. institutions. Actually, it is this white population *dominance* that is often at the forefront for these white extremists, for clearly that current numerical superiority is an essential part of their racial framing of themselves as dominant white people as well as of U.S. society generally.

Note too that these contemporary conspiratorial racist assertions signal a growing white replacement framing with a new name but *old* pedigree. Recall from Chapter 2 that early 20th-century white supremacists like influential authors Madison Grant, a Columbia University law graduate, and

Lothrop Stoddard, a Harvard University history Ph.D., published books titled *The Passing of the Great Race* and *The Rising Tide of Color Against White World-Supremacy*, respectively. More than a century ago, both these foremost white intellectuals had aggressively articulated a view of a "great white race" being replaced by people of color.

Significantly, the role of Fox News and other right-wing media outlets manufacturing these contemporary white racist theories and fears has been criticized by knowledgeable insiders. Referencing the central role of the Fox News channel in mainstreaming and spreading white supremacist views, former Fox executive Preston Padden has described how that channel and the Fox network generally have moved dramatically over the years from center-right to extremist right. In his informed insider view the current Fox network's racist-right programming has intentionally contributed in major ways to

> divisions in our society by stoking racial animus and fueling the totally false impression that Black Lives Matter and Antifa are engaged in nightly, life-threatening riots across the country; ... former President Trump's "Big Lie" that the election was stolen from him by providing a continuous platform for wild and false claims about the election...; and the Jan. 6, 2021, violent assault on the U.S. Capitol by continually promoting former President Trump's "Stop The Steal" rally. Fox News has caused many millions of Americans... to believe things that *simply are not true*.[55]

Unmistakably, well beyond the influence of traditional political news discussions in mainstream media, the arch-conservative talk radio and television channels like Fox News have regularly created or accentuated a large-scale political divide. This relatively new and intensified political *polarization* is conspicuous in many opinion polls. For instance, one 2020 national Pew Research survey found that 77 percent of those who supported then presidential candidate Donald Trump and 80 percent of respondents who supported then presidential candidate Joe Biden said that they disagreed with the other group on "core values," not just on political issues.[56]

In recent years, this polarization has been so great that far-right Republican politicians in Congress—very disproportionately white and male— rarely will compromise on major legislative matters with moderate and liberal Democratic Party politicians. Their mostly white voter base often penalizes them for departing from an arch-conservative "party line." Indeed, these politically and racially extremist Republicans have often been backed or featured in the conservative talk radio and television commentary programs. This intentional, and frequently profitable, political polarization has resulted in the near extinction of moderate Republicans and has brought about legislative paralysis or arch-conservative legislative domination at numerous local, state, and federal government levels over the past few decades. Researcher Brian Rosenwald has concluded that in their political quest these extremist Republicans "fed a beast that, over time, destroyed their party."[57]

Digital Media Impacts: Manufacturing Racist Framing and Action

In addition to examining the propagation of white racist framing on right-wing radio stations and television networks, we need to assess the similar impact of other social-talk media, including internet media like Facebook (Meta), Twitter, YouTube, Instagram, and Reddit. Increasing greatly since the early 2000s, these social media provide a public square for widespread circulation of right-wing framing, including strong white supremacist and nationalist framing. Numerous white tech entrepreneurs and some other tech entrepreneurs who developed these media have a socially libertarian perspective, typically one grounded in a white-Western framing of society. This perspective has kept these platforms relatively unrestricted, including for the extensive distribution of racist-right messaging.[58]

As scholar Jen Schradie concludes from her case study of North Carolina politics, racist and other extreme right-wing framing has generally been better amplified across the digital social media than liberal framing messages. Right-wing groups

> turned the internet into a digital bullhorn which projected information favorable to their cause across a web of sympathetic organizations.... I can't say absolutely that the rise of these conservative groups and their ferocious embrace of digital media was the definitive factor that led to the Republican takeover of state government [in North Carolina]. But the correlation is a strong one.[59]

Undeniably, this aggressive right-wing use of digital social media, sometimes assisted by politicized interference there from overseas sources (e.g., from Russia), has significantly facilitated the takeover of numerous state governments by arch-conservative Republicans and their ability, via gerrymandering and other voter suppression, to expand their significant control over the U.S. Congress, Supreme Court, and presidency.

The online mechanisms of this right-wing success are important to assess. For instance, automated right-wing messages (e.g., bots) and intentionally generated fake news on the internet have played an important role in numerous right-wing Republican government takeovers. In the North Carolina case such internet posting was about more than just putting online (e.g., on Facebook and Twitter) some propaganda using white nationalist and other far-right themes in order to manipulate the minds of gullible white readers and voters in local elections. It was much broader than that, because these mostly white posters and media users were part of a growing national and international social media ecosystem, one with a large integrated set of white nationalist and other far-right messages, messengers, and users. Significantly, too, in this North Carolina case, it was *not* working-class whites who were the most active in these well-organized online efforts, but yet again it was *middle-class and upper-class whites*. This racialized right-wing ecosystem was also much better supported financially than the digital efforts on the political left in North Carolina, though the latter did have the state's important Moral Monday movement and NAACP organizations to help narrow the digital gap somewhat there. Schradie concludes that in North Carolina the right-wing Republican groups "aligned with powerful media and other resource-rich institutions to create a digital hegemony." They were also well-integrated at the national level with wealthy white funders who helped finance these digital right-wing political efforts there and in other states.[60]

Moreover, at the national level, the political rise of Donald Trump was greatly facilitated by effective use of these digital media by the right-wing Republican Party and other right-wing political groups. This use of digital media accelerated once Trump was in the presidential office. Indeed, right-wing online attacks on mainstream media and progressive media journalists accelerated before, during, and after Donald Trump's presidency. As media analyst Silvio Waisbord summarizes,

> Female, minority reporters and journalists who cover issues interwoven with right-wing identity anchors have been primary targets. This trend reflects growing forms of mob censorship linked to the demonization of journalists and the press by [white right-wing] populist leaders.... [M]ob censorship as bottom-up, citizen vigilantism aimed at disciplining journalism.

Countering this demonization and other hate speech targeting journalists is very difficult, given how widespread it is across multiple online outlets.[61]

Evidence of the great political power of this digital social media use can be seen in what happened when some major online sites suspended Donald Trump and his white right-wing associates in January 2021 for false election theft assertations. This suspension resulted in a major decline in online media misinformation spread about the 2020 election. Among other examples, online social media conversations of ordinary users about the false allegations of U.S. national election fraud were found to have dropped sharply.[62]

Using Digital Media to Enact Racialized Violence

We should underscore another digital social media area that is critically important in spreading white supremacist and other far-right ideas—the great array of image boards and forums, encrypted chat channels, and other alternative media platforms. Media analysts Julia Ebner and Jacob Davey term this a weaponized "dark social ecosystem."[63] White far-right posters and viewers there have aggressively weaponized significant segments of these online media to radicalize and manipulate various white age groups, especially younger generations. This is very problematic because the U.S. government and human rights media monitors are very limited in their ability to respond to the online spread of extreme-right propaganda and terrorist plots there. This is a national policy failure with long-term, anti-democratic consequences. "Although major online platforms have introduced some voluntary measures to counter white nationalist and supremacist content, many of the fringe platforms frequented by extreme-right groups use free speech and libertarian arguments as the baseline for their dangerous policies."[64]

Growing social science evidence links extremist discussions and exhortations in these far-right social media to various white crimes targeting Americans of color and liberal white Americans. One analysis of U.S. counties found that an increase in just one month's right-wing extremist discussions on the arch-conservative social media site Parler in a county was linked in the next month to an increase in right-wing violence and other extremist actions there.[65]

How and why do these online extremist discussions shape extremist actions offline? Researchers working on impacts of right-wing social media argue that a change in manipulated viewers' ideological preferences is less important than a change in their perceived view of current societal *norms*. That is, as social scientist Daniel Karell puts it, participating in extremist social media can change a person's view of the restraining social norms and as a result "those who are already ideologically right-wing and who have been considering engaging in contentious action will become *more likely* to do so."[66] The negative impact of right-wing online communities often stems from people being exposed to extremist rhetoric targeting outgroups that leads them to believe these hostile "ideas and behaviors are more pervasive than they are" and that countering societal norms are weak or equivocal.[67] Online extremist discussions allow right-wing listeners to resurrect formerly unthinkable social norms "that facilitate violence—not because of (newfound) belief or ideology, but simply because they saw it online."[68]

For some years now, both the dark social media websites and the more mainstream social media websites, including Facebook (Meta), have allowed white supremacist and other far-right groups to use their websites to organize violent and other aggressive group protests, including the planned pro-Trump protests before, during, and after the violent January 6, 2021 Capitol insurrection. While Facebook's top corporate executive claimed this Capitol attack was organized mostly on other social media, the Tech Transparency Project (TTP) research showed that Facebook, for some time before the Capitol insurrection, had permitted white far-right militias and other white supremacist organizations to organize on their platform, to spread extremist conspiracies, and to facilitate their rallies. These Facebook efforts laid the "groundwork for the broader radicalization that fueled the Capitol insurrection."[69] The TTP research found many Facebook examples of far-right extremists talking about weapons, violent anti-government actions (e.g., calls to "occupy Congress"), and coordination of their criminal activities. They did much organizing in limited-access Facebook groups, the "insulated communities that allow people to organize out of the public eye while still having access to a large online following."[70] One such Facebook group even asked its prospective members if they were "willing to die for their country" as a requirement to join.[71]

Strikingly, white groups organizing for political violence did not end with that violent January 2021 Capitol insurrection. A follow-up TTP study months after that unprecedented event found yet more Facebook discussions by white-racist militia and other extremist groups about organizing yet more anti-government violence. The online Facebook algorithm even helped these radical white militias to grow membership by auto-generating Facebook pages for them and helping them better connect with each other. It also provided ads for lethal weapons and body armor near the online insurrection discussions in militia and other "patriot" groups. Facebook was not alone in facilitating these white-racist militia and other far-right conspiracy groups (e.g., advocates of QAnon), for the latter have also had a large right-wing audience for their online Apple and Google podcasts.[72]

White Myths about Racism and Politics

For centuries now, using various media and other institutional outlets, the conservative majority of this country's white elite has worked aggressively to whitewash and mythologize the racial, class, and gender history of the country. Such efforts at generating historical ignorance and misunderstanding are essential to their great success in preserving elite white political and other societal dominance. Unsurprisingly, this widespread historical ignorance and misunderstanding among voters, and often the propagandistic right-wing media making good use of that, have regularly made the election of covertly or openly white supremacist political candidates possible.

To take a major example, throughout his active political life, the former president Donald Trump has operated as a major media influencer whose racial, gender, class, and related political commentaries have frequently been unconcerned with the historical or contemporary societal truths.

Interacting with supportive right-wing media like Fox News and talk show hosts, he has helped to shape and manipulate the societal mythology and extremist political thinking of much of the white population since at least the 1990s. This has long been graphically clear in Trump's disturbing speeches about people of color when he was a presidential candidate and then president, and since he lost the 2020 presidential election. In political speeches and conferences with members of Congress, Trump not only negatively stereotyped immigrants of color—especially from what he once called "shithole" countries in the Caribbean and Latin America—but also wished for more white immigrants from European countries like Norway.[73] He also used the made-up term "Kung-flu" as an ethnocentric mocking label for the COVID-19 pandemic, which he often blamed on Chinese officials.

As president, Trump surrounded himself with mostly white advisors and appointed officials who pressed for, or at least acquiesced in, a white nativistic or nationalistic presidential perspective and policy agenda. Such racist policy ideas have included building a large wall (only) on the southern U.S. border, encouraging armed private groups to block nonwhite immigrants from coming across that border, and implementing inhumane immigrant detainment policies along that border. Additionally, since his 2020 election loss, Donald Trump and his mostly white political allies have further developed and spread a mythological and whitewashed history of that major election being stolen from him.

Reflecting on Trump and his supporters' antidemocratic actions after this 2020 election loss, the prominent historian David Blight has noted that Trump's presidency reinvigorated far-right organizations and exposed the numerous undemocratic or otherwise problematical U.S. institutions—ranging from "the Senate to the Electoral College to our media environment, to a lack of support for public education." He underscores the important point that Trump and his supporters' equivalent of the old bitter Confederate "Lost Cause" mythology (after the Civil War) is

> a set of beliefs in search of a history and a story…. The stolen election is the biggest of their beliefs, but they've got a lot of others: the liberals are coming for your guns, and liberals are coming for your taxes, and the liberals want to plow all your tax money into those cities for the Black and brown people, and liberals are going to open up the border and continue this browning of America….[74]

Indeed, that 19th-century Lost Cause myth of white southerners still exists and foregrounds the false idea that, if the federal government had not pushed so fast for real democracy during the Reconstruction era after the Civil War, the U.S. would have been better off, to the present day. A somewhat similar anti-government perspective has aggressively developed in recent decades, principally in white right-wing circles across all regions and especially since the 1960s federal civil rights laws officially ended legal segregation. Indeed, by the 1980s the reactionary Ronald Reagan administration intentionally generated white hostility to numerous federal non-military programs, often stereotyped inaccurately as mainly for Americans of color, and actually weakened enforcement of those pathbreaking civil rights laws (see Chapter 4).[75]

Conclusion

In spite of the harsh realities of this country's still systemic racism, a grand societal myth of great racial progress has been articulated for at least five decades now by many whites, especially by the white elite and its immediate acolytes who have successfully manufactured and fostered this widespread myth. Social scientist Jennifer Richeson argues the myth of racial progress provides whites

> a reason to blame the victim: If we're converging on equality, then those left behind must not be trying. And it diffuses moral responsibility for actively and significantly reforming the American system: If we're converging on equality anyway, then why do we need laws and other measures to promote it?[76]

Even a majority of U.S. Supreme Court justices explicitly cited this "progress" myth in holding that a key provision of the 1965 Voting Rights Act need not be enforced in their *Shelby County v. Holder* (2013) ruling.[77] They invalidated a major section of that Act which is still much needed to protect African American voters and other voters of color, who have been shown to still face numerous white voter suppression strategies. Indeed, white voter suppression efforts disproportionately affecting voters of color have increased in numerous states *after* that reactionary court decision.[78] In Richeson's accurate view, this commonplace mythology of racial progress has officially absolved the top, mostly white, decisionmakers from taking action against continuing racial oppression across the country:

> It is obviously true that many of the conditions of life for Black Americans have gotten better over time…. But many areas never saw much progress, or what progress was made has been halted or even reversed. The mythology of racial progress often rings hollow when it comes to, for instance, racial gaps in education. Or health outcomes. Or voting rights. Or criminal justice. Or personal wealth. History is not a ratchet that turns in one direction only.[79]

Indeed, the recent years of violent racist events across the U.S., ranging from many unwarranted police killings of people of color to overt white insurrectionist attacks like that in 2021 on the U.S. Capitol, have dramatically shown that this white-crafted racial progress narrative is quite mythical and often anti-democratic in its effects.

Notes

1 Karl Marx and Friedrich Engels, *The German Ideology*, ed. R. Pascal (New York: International Publishers, 1947), p. 39.
2 Kenneth O'Reilly, *Nixon's Piano: Presidents and Racial Politics from Washington to Clinton* (New York: Free Press, 1995), p. 11.
3 See Joe R. Feagin and Eileen O'Brien, *White Men on Race* (Boston, MA: Beacon, 2003); and Joe R. Feagin and Kimberley Ducey, *Elite White Men Ruling: Who, What, When, Where, and How* (New York: Routledge, 2017).
4 W. E. B. Du Bois, *Black Reconstruction in America 1860–1880* (New York: Harcourt, Brace and Co., 1935).
5 See Peter Temin, *The Vanishing Middle Class: Prejudice and Power in a Dual Economy* (Cambridge, MA: MIT Press, 2017).
6 See studies cited in Joe R. Feagin and Kimberley Ducey, *Racist America: Roots, Current Realities, and Future Reparations*, 4th ed. (New York: Routledge, 2019).
7 Richard C. Fording and Sanford F. Schram, *Hard White: The Mainstreaming of Racism in American Politics* (New York: Oxford University Press, 2020), p. 153.
8 Darren E. Sherkat, "Cognitive Sophistication, Religion, and the Trump Vote," *Social Science Quarterly* 102 (2021): 179. DOI: 10.1111/ssqu.12906; Darren Sherkat, "How Can We Be So Sure That Most Trump Voters Are Morons?" *Down with Tyranny*, https://www.downwithtyranny.com/post/guest-post-how-can-we-be-so-sure-that-most-trump-voters-are-morons (accessed April 26, 2022).
9 Lisa McGirr, *Suburban Warriors: The Origins of the New American Right* (Princeton, NJ: Princeton University Press, 2015), Preface.
10 Ibid.
11 Jonathan Wilson-Hartgrove, "Who Poisoned Talk Radio?" Sojourners, May 2020, https://sojo.net/magazine/may-2020/who-poisoned-talk radio (accessed January 12, 2021).
12 As quoted in Wilson-Hartgrove, "Who Poisoned Talk Radio?"
13 Quoted in Andrew Whitehead, "The Growing Antidemocratic Threat of Christian Nationalism in the U.S.," *Time.com*, May 27, 2021, https://time.com/6052051/antidemocratic-threat-christian-nationalism/ (accessed May 5, 2022).
14 Ibid.
15 Frederick Clarkson, "Project Blitz' Seeks to Do for Christian Nationalism What ALEC Does for Big Business," *Religion Dispatches*, April 27, 2018, https://religiondispatches.org/project-blitz-seeks-to-do-for-christian-nationalism-what-alec-does-for-big-business/ (accessed March 21, 2021).
16 Frederick Clarkson, "Christian Right Bill Mill, Project Blitz, Hasn't Gone Away, It's Just Gotten More Secretive," *Religion Dispatches*, July 12, 2021, https://religiondispatches.org/exclusive-christian-right-bill-mill-project-blitz-hasnt-gone-away-its-just-gotten-more-secretive/ (accessed April 25, 2022).
17 *Dobbs v. Jackson Women's Health Organization*, 945 F. 3d 265.
18 Robert P. Jones, "Alito and Public Opinion Reveal the Link between Roe and a Broader White Christian Nationalist Agenda," May 3, 2022, https://

robertpjones.substack.com/p/alito-and-public-opinion-reveal-the?s=racial (accessed May 5, 2022).

19 Ibid.
20 Helen Johnson, "The Unprecedented Consolidation of the Modern Media Industry Has Severe Consequences," *Miscellany News*, April 29, 2021, https://miscellanynews.org/2021/04/29/opinions/the-unprecedented-consolidation-of-the-modern-media-industry-has-severe-consequences/ (accessed July 9, 2021).
21 For more detail, see Feagin and Ducey, *Racist America*, Chapter 7.
22 Richard L. Zweigenhaft, "Diversity among Fortune 500 CEOs from 2000 to 2020: White Women, Hi-Tech South Asians, and Economically Privileged Multilingual Immigrants from around the World," January 2021, *Who Rules America?* website, https://whorulesamerica.ucsc.edu/power/diversity_update_2020.html (accessed May 11, 2022). See also Gillian B. White, "There Are Currently 4 Black CEOs in the Fortune 500," *The Atlantic*, October 26, 2017, https://www.theatlantic.com/business/archive/2017/10/Black-ceos-fortune-500/543960/ (accessed January 10, 2018); and Burns, Barton, and Kerby, *The State of Diversity in Today's Workforce*, p. 4.
23 Twitter, "Diversity and Inclusion Report 2020," https://careers.twitter.com/en/diversity/annual-report-2020.html (accessed July 25, 2021); Facebook, "Diversity and Inclusion Report 2021," https://about.fb.com/wp-content/uploads/2021/07/Facebook-Annual-Diversity-Report-July-2021.pdf (accessed July 25, 2021).
24 Alan MacLeod, "Introduction," in *Propaganda in the Information Age*, ed. Alan MacLeod, (New York: Routledge, 2019), p. 1. See also Edward S Herman and North America Chomsky, *Manufacturing Consent* (New York: Pantheon Books, 1988).
25 K. Stewart, "NABJ Disturbed by Unconscious Bias Displayed in Buffalo Shooting Coverage," NABJ Online, https://nabjonline.org/blog/nabj-disturbed-by-unconscious-bias-displayed-in-buffalo-shooting-coverage/ (accessed June 27, 2022).
26 MacLeod, "Introduction," p. 5.
27 Ibid.
28 Johnson, "The Unprecedented Consolidation of the Modern Media Industry Has Severe Consequences."
29 Alan MacLeod, "Interview with Noam Chomsky," in *Propaganda in the Information Age*, ed. Alan MacLeod (New York: Routledge, 2019), p. 15. See Herman and Chomsky, *Manufacturing Consent*.
30 Florian Zollmann, "A Propaganda Model for the Twenty-First Century," in *Propaganda in the Information Age*, ed. Alan Macleod (New York: Routledge, 2019), p. 40.
31 Ibid.
32 Brittany Farr, "A Demographic Moral Panic: Fears of a Majority-Minority Future and the Depreciating Value of Whiteness," *Law Review Blog*, August 16, 2021, https://lawreviewblog.uchicago.edu/2021/08/16/rrs-farr-demographic/ (accessed January 12, 2022).
33 Ibid.
34 Brian Rosenwald, *Talk Radio's America: How an Industry Took over a Political Party That Took over the United States* (Cambridge, MA: Harvard University Press, 2019), p. 265.
35 Ian Reifowitz, *The Tribalization of Politics: How Rush Limbaugh's Race-Baiting Rhetoric on the Obama Presidency Paved the Way for Trump* (New York: Ig Publishing, 2019), pp. 35–36.

36 Ibid., p. 35.
37 Jeremy Blum, "Rush Limbaugh Compares Violent Trump Mob to American Revolutionaries," *HuffPost*, January 7, 2021, https://www.huffpost.com/entry/rush-limbaugh-trump-mob-american-revolutionaries_n_5ff773c1c5b6 214c5518bb86 (accessed March 12, 2021). Trump is quoted in this article.
38 Rosenwald, *Talk Radio's America*, p. 264.
39 Wilson-Hartgrove, "Who Poisoned Talk Radio?"
40 Jonathan Martin and Alexander Burns, *This Will Not Pass: Trump, Biden, and the Battle for America's Future* (New York: Simon & Schuster, 2022). I draw the quote from the review by Brian Stelter, "Biden called Murdoch the 'Most Dangerous Man in the World,' New Book Alleges," CNN Business, April 4, 2022, https://www.cnn.com/2022/04/03/media/reliable-sources-biden-murdoch-fox-news/index.html (accessed April 5, 2022).
41 Charlotte Graham-McLay, "Why New Zealand Rejected Populist Ideas Other Nations Have Embraced," *The Guardian*, https://www.theguardian.com/world/2020/oct/19/why-new-zealand-rejected-populist-ideas-other-nations-have-embraced (accessed July 2, 2022).
42 Gregory J. Martin and Ali Yurukoglu, "Bias in Cable News: Persuasion and Polarization," *American Economic Review* 107 (2017): 2565–2599.
43 David Broockman and Joshua Kalla, "The Manifold Effects of Partisan Media on Viewers' Beliefs and Attitudes: A Field Experiment with Fox News Viewers," *OSF Preprints*, April 1, 2022, pp. 3–4. DOI: 10.31219/osf.io/jrw26.
44 Ibid.
45 Tali Arbel, "Fox Stands behind Tucker Carlson after Anti-Defamation League Urges His Firing," *Chicago Sun-Times*, April 12, 2021, https://chicago.suntimes.com/entertainment-and-culture/2021/4/12/22381091/tucker-carlson-fox-news-anti-defamation-league-urges-his-firing (accessed April 13, 2021).
46 Nathan Place, "'Antisemitic, Racist and Toxic': Tucker Carlson Faces Calls to Resign after Promoting White Supremacist 'Replacement' Theory," *The Independent*, April 9, 2021, https://www.independent.co.uk/news/world/americas/us-politics/tucker-carlson-fox-white-supremacist-b1829366.html (accessed June 30, 2021).
47 Tucker Carlson, "The Truth about Demographic Change and Why Democrats Want It," https://www.foxnews.com/opinion/tucker-carlson-immigration-demographic-change-democrats-elections (accessed April 13, 2021).
48 Nicholas Confessore, "What to Know about Tucker Carlson's Rise," *New York Times*, April 30, 2022, https://www.nytimes.com/2022/04/30/business/media/tucker-carlson-fox-news-takeaways.html (accessed May 16, 2022).
49 Both the Bush and Carlson quotes are from Tucker Carlson, "Democrats Pushing Unity through Domination of Their Opponents," FoxNews.com, https://www.foxnews.com/opinion/tucker-carlson-on-joe-biden-and-forced-unity (accessed July 6, 2021). See also Zack Stanton, "How Trumpism Is Becoming America's New 'Lost Cause,'" *Politico*, January 21, 2021, https://www.politico.com/news/magazine/2021/01/21/trump-civil-war-reconstruction-biden-lost-cause-461161 (accessed July 1, 2022).
50 Matt Gaetz (@mattgaetz), *Twitter* feed, September 25, 2021, https://twitter.com/search?q=ADL%20%40mattgaetz&src=typed_query (accessed September 27, 2021).
51 Zack Linly, "Newt Gingrich Is Afraid 'The Left' Will Replace 'Classic Americans' with Immigrants, and I Struggle to See the Problem," *The Root*, https://www.theroot.com/newt-gingrich-is-afraid-the-left-will-replace-classic-a-1847431320 (accessed August 6, 2021).

52 Quoted in Amanda Marcotte, "Tucker Carlson Claims There's No White Nationalism," Salon.com, August 15, 2018, https://www.salon.com/2018/08/15/tucker-carlson-claims-theres-no-white-nationalism-his-shows-obsessive-racism-suggests-otherwise/ (accessed June 30, 2021).
53 Jonathan A. Greenblatt, "ADL Response to Lachlan Murdoch, Chairman and CEO of Fox News, on Tucker Carlson," https://www.adl.org/news/media-watch/adl-response-to-lachlan-murdoch-chairman-and-ceo-of-fox-news-on-tucker-carlson (accessed April 13, 2021).
54 JTA, "ADL Condemns Trump for Tweeting South Africa White Nationalist Conspiracy Theory," *Forward*, August 23, 2018, https://forward.com/fast-forward/408782/adl-condemns-trump-for-tweeting-south-africa-white-nationalist-conspiracy/ (accessed May 4, 2022).
55 Preston Padden, "Former Murdoch Exec: Fox News Is Poison for America," https://www.thedailybeast.com/former-murdoch-exec-says-fox-news-is-poison-for-america?ref=home (accessed July 5, 2021). Italics added.
56 "Amid Campaign Turmoil, Biden Holds Wide Leads on Coronavirus, Unifying the Country," *Pew Research Center*, October 9, 2020, https://www.Pewresearch.org/politics/2020/10/09/amid-campaign-turmoil-biden-holds-wide-leads-on-coronavirus-unifying-the-country/ (accessed January 5, 2021).
57 Rosenwald, *Talk Radio's America*, p. 262.
58 I am indebted here to discussions with sociologist Randy Hohle.
59 Jen Schradie, *The Revolution That Wasn't: How Digital Activism Favors Conservatives* (Cambridge, MA: Harvard University Press, 2019), p. 272.
60 Ibid.
61 Silvio Waisbord, "Mob Censorship: Online Harassment of U.S. Journalists in Times of Digital Hate and Populism," *Digital Journalism* 8 (2020): 1030–1046.
62 Elizabeth Dwoskin and Craig Timberg, "Misinformation Dropped Dramatically the Week after Twitter Banned Trump and Some Allies," *Washington Post*, January 16, 2021, https://www.washingtonpost.com/technology/2021/01/16/misinformation-trump-twitter/ (accessed July 1, 2022).
63 Julia Ebner and Jacob Davey, "The Great Replacement," *Institute for Strategic Dialogue*, July 2019, https://www.isdglobal.org/wp-content/uploads/2019/07/The-Great-Replacement-The-Violent-Consequences-of-Mainstreamed-Extremism-by-ISD.pdf, p. 24 (accessed April 2, 2021).
64 Ibid., p. 30.
65 Daniel Karell, "Online Extremism and Offline Harm," SSRC, June 1, 2021, https://items.ssrc.org/extremism-online/online-extremism-and-offline-harm (accessed July 1, 2021).
66 Ibid. Italics added.
67 Ibid.
68 Ibid.
69 Tech Transparency Project, "Capitol Attack Was Months in the Making on Facebook," January 19, 2021, https://www.techtransparencyproject.org/articles/capitol-attack-was-months-making-facebook (accessed July 6, 2021).
70 Ibid.
71 Ibid.
72 Ibid.
73 Jen Kirby, "Trump Wants Fewer Immigrants from 'Shithole Countries' and More from Places like Norway," vox.com, January 11, 2018, https://www.vox.com/2018/1/11/16880750/trump-immigrants-shithole-countries-norway (accessed July 12, 2021).
74 Quoted in Stanton, "How Trumpism Is Becoming America's New 'Lost Cause.'"

75 See Stanton, "How Trumpism Is Becoming America's New "Lost Cause.'"

76 Jennifer Richeson, "Americans Are Determined to Believe in Black Progress,"
    The Atlantic, August 2020, https://www.theatlantic.com/magazine/archive/
    2020/09/the-mythology-of-racial-progress/614173/ (accessed May 5, 2021).

77 *Shelby County v. Holder*, 570 U.S. 529 (2013).

78 Vann R. Newkirk II, "Politics: How *Shelby County v. Holder* Broke America,"
    The Atlantic, July 2018, https://www.theatlantic.com/politics/archive/2018/
    07/how-shelby-county-broke-america/564707/ (accessed May 2, 2020).

79 Richeson, "Americans Are Determined to Believe in Black Progress."

Chapter 4

Browning of America
Economic and Educational Impacts

One of the ironies of contemporary elite and ordinary whites showing substantial surprise or fear about current demographic change and the coming reality of a majority-minority U.S. population is that historically many areas of North America have had very large populations of color, even majority-minorities. This has been typical for centuries. As I discussed in Chapter 1, great white profitmaking, major white community development, and major white family prosperity have involved many generations of whites oppressing and exploiting workers of color. During the 80 percent of this country's history when it was structured as a totalitarian slavery or totalitarian Jim Crow society, elite and ordinary whites developed extensive arrangements for armed and other aggressive enforcement of that massive racial oppression. Unsurprisingly, large concentrations of rebellious Indigenous, Black, and other nonwhite Americans did regularly push back against this oppression and thus generate significant racial anxiety and fear in whites, yet not enough for a majority of them to support racially democratizing the country and liberating those groups of color from that extensive oppression. Indeed, the white repressive reaction to these rebellions is seen in the famous Second Amendment to the U.S. Constitution, one major purpose of which is often forgotten today—that is, to buttress armed white state militias that would put down with force the nonwhite rebellions *for their freedom.*[1]

Generations later, the major civil rights movement for freedom and social justice, and consequent civil rights laws, of the 1950s–1970s era did finally bring partial liberation from extreme racial oppression for Americans of color, yet today the latter still have to organize and press for full racial equality for themselves and their oppressed communities. Meanwhile, as I documented previously, a great number of whites have continued to harbor much fear and anger about becoming a white minority country, and they have engaged in much active pushback, some of it violent, against major changes in the direction of significantly greater racial equality and multiracial democracy.

DOI: 10.4324/9781003359883-5

Thus, even today one can cogently ask, just how realistic is this persisting or increasing white fear of a coming white minority nation? Just what significant racial changes have occurred so far in U.S. economic, educational, and political institutions, and what significant changes in these areas are likely in the future? In this chapter, I mostly examine some real and expected economic and educational changes and their societal impacts, as well as the continuing white hostility and opposition to them. Then, in the next chapter, I give more attention to numerous significant political impacts and political resistance to them. In both chapters, I accent the long historical contexts for these very important if often variable contemporary impacts.

The Economic Browning of America

Persisting Economic Concentration and Control

Certain major economic and educational aspects of U.S. society seem very likely to persist for decades to come, even with the national majority-minority reality emerging in the 2040s. In numerous historical and contemporary field studies, my colleagues and I have shown that the most important societal context for this racial demographic change is what can be termed the elite-white-male dominance system.[2]

In the Declaration of Independence year of 1776, near the beginning of the American revolution, the famous Scottish economist long celebrated by white conservatives, Adam Smith, actually problematized the great power and profitmaking greed of the leading economic actors of that day—the large landowners, merchants, and manufacturers who were then the leading capitalists. In Great Britain and North America, virtually all were elite white men. As Smith put it in his famous book *The Wealth of Nations,*

> All for ourselves and nothing for other people, seems, in every age of the world, to have been the vile maxim of the masters of mankind. As soon, therefore, as they could find a method of consuming the whole value of their rent [i.e., income] themselves, they had no disposition to share them with any other persons.[3]

When the collection of North American colonies became a nation named the U.S., its elite-white-male dominance system was already foundational, a dominance system that has for centuries insured that whites, especially the powerful white men, have very disproportionate political, economic, and educational power.

Conspicuous among these mostly white "masters of mankind" today are ultrawealthy capitalists like the billionaire Koch brothers and their powerful networks of similarly wealthy whites. Since at least the 1990s, Charles and (the late) David Koch—powerful capitalists heading up major oil, chemical, lumber, and paper companies—have made very successful efforts to move the U.S. in much more economically concentrated, politically reactionary, and socially inegalitarian directions. Making use of numerous far-right organizations they have heavily funded, Charles Koch and numerous other ultrawealthy whites have worked together with right-wing corporate lobbies, conservative university institutes, and white evangelical groups to effectively gain control over the Republican Party, and thereby many local, state, and federal governing systems in the U.S. This extensive right-wing networking and the resulting political organizations have elected numerous right-wing local, state, and federal legislators who have successfully reduced government funding for, and other involvement in, an array of necessary public programs such as those affecting the health, education, and general welfare of the country's population (see below and Chapter 5). Not unexpectedly, these efforts have featured the centrally important economic goals of corporate America, including major reductions in government regulation and in government taxation of corporate America. For example, over recent years, the corporate income tax revenues of numerous state governments have been greatly reduced, and "in seven states, more than 60% of corporations pay no state corporate income tax."[4] These societally destructive political-economic actions from the increasingly monopolistic and greedy "masters of mankind" are the very ones that Adam Smith warned about in *The Wealth of Nations*.

Generally, the names and operations of these right-wing networked organizations—for example, Americans for Prosperity (AFP), the State Policy Network (SPN), and the American Legislative Exchange (ALEC)—and their antidemocratic legislative goals are mostly hidden from the general public. They collaborate with yet other right-wing organizations advocating for corporate economic interests such as the U.S. Chamber of Commerce, the Club for Growth, and Americans for Tax Reform, as well as with right-wing think tanks such as the Manhattan Institute, Cato Institute, and Heritage Foundation.[5]

This ALEC organization, founded by a white Christian nationalist discussed in Chapter 3, has become centrally important in the linking together of these and other right-wing groups and associated corporations. As community activist Jim Freeman summarizes, ALEC "has a reported three hundred–plus corporate members and two thousand legislative members who work together—usually secretively—on legislation that advances those corporations' common agenda."[6] This coordinating right-wing organization has been behind the introduction of thousands of reactionary "model bills" in state legislatures across the country, including those further deregulating businesses, cutting corporate taxes, and defunding or otherwise restricting public support efforts like public health and education agencies. Many such reactionary laws have actually been passed, mainly in Republican-controlled state legislatures.

Freeman underlines the reality that this legislation covers many right-wing economic and political goals, but suggests too that one major underlying goal is to protect the white power and benefits gained from the country's still foundational and systemic racism. Indeed,

> perhaps the most powerful force advancing strategic racism in the United States is an organization [ALEC] whose current and recent members represent a "Who's Who" of U.S. corporations, including Walmart, Google, Home Depot, AT&T, General Electric, Coca-Cola, Ford, ExxonMobil, Johnson & Johnson, Kraft Foods, Verizon, Pfizer, Chevron, Bank of America, Microsoft, Visa, Coors, General Motors, American Express, Koch Industries, Facebook, UPS, Eli Lilly, Time Warner Cable, Comcast News Corporation, Dell, Amway, IBM, FedEx, Anheuser-Busch, Dow Chemical, McDonald's, State Farm, Northrop Grumman, Procter & Gamble, and Wells Fargo, along with hundreds of others.[7]

Note too that as ALEC and related right-wing networking have gotten some public attention in recent years, numerous corporations have publicly severed official ties with them, even as their top executives' commitments to reactionary corporate goals and systemic racial inequalities in the economy and society largely remain in effect.

In his recent book *Evil Geniuses*, the investigative journalist Kurt Andersen notes that before he did his field research on corporations' arch-conservative political efforts, he "didn't know how long and concerted and strategic the project by the political right and the rich and big business had been"[8] In a summary comment, Andersen references the pivotal 1980s era when this right-wing elite used former actor and President Ronald Reagan as a front man in beginning the aggressive effort to weaken or end many of the country's more progressive laws and programs developed since the 1930s New Deal era. This reactionary political-economic reality sought by arch-conservatives has gradually been implemented. Its substantially successful agenda has included these goals:

> profit and market values would override all other American values;… that many millions of middle-class jobs and careers would vanish: along with fixed private pensions and reliable healthcare; that a college degree would simultaneously become unaffordable and almost essential to earning a good income; that enforcement of antimonopoly laws would end; that meaningful control of political contributions by big business and the rich would be declared unconstitutional…; that our revived and practically religious deference to business would

enable… absolute refusal to treat the climate crisis as a crisis; that after doubling the share of the nation's income that it took for itself, a deregulated Wall Street would nearly bring down the financial system, ravage the economy, and pay no price for its recklessness.[9]

As of now, even in the face of a major browning of America, this dominant economic power and the associated political power seem likely to persist for this country's mostly white top decisionmakers for many decades to come. Optimism about major racial-group changes in future arrangements of societal power and privilege must be tempered with a recognition that elite white men still run this country's major institutions, have the greatest socioeconomic resources to utilize daily, and generally act in their own elite economic and political interests.

Corporate Diversifying and the Browning of America

White male dominance at the top of the U.S. economic system remains conspicuous in current statistics indicating white men make up 86 percent of Fortune 500 corporate CEOs, with white women making up half of the remaining 14 percent. These most powerful of our economic decision-makers, together with the decisionmakers heading up other major societal institutions, are now mostly white baby boomers and Gen-Xers. It is likely that these top decisionmakers in most U.S. economic and political institutions over the next decade or two will increasingly be white Gen-Xers and older white millennials, with perhaps some from the younger white Gen-Z generation. As of today, it appears that those at the top of the decisionmaking pyramid will still be very disproportionately white, and very disproportionately male.

Recent analyses by sociologist Richard Zweigenhaft have detailed the limited increases in nonwhite and woman CEOs at Fortune 500 companies now over several decades of the browning of America, yet these numbers have become stagnant or declined in the most recent years. Future corporate diversity will likely come slowly at best. Drawing on data on corporate CEOs who were not white male for the years 2000–2020, on data indicating few such candidates for corporate CEO positions now in the elite pipeline, and on studies indicating that corporate CEOs who are not white men have faced "more daunting challenges than their white male counterparts, and … have shorter tenures as CEOs than do their white male counterparts," Zweigenhaft concludes that the "future does not look bright when it comes to diversity among Fortune 500 CEOs." He further suggests that those *few* such CEOs who do emerge are likely to be "men and women with multicultural backgrounds, who are multilingual, and who can move comfortably in the global elite."[10]

Nonetheless, in recent years some major CEOs and their boards have made mostly modest efforts toward diversifying their corporate boards, workforces, and racial climates, in large part as a response to recurring pressures from civil rights groups, their consumers, or employees of color. These actions have improved with the increased browning of America. For a time, after the nationwide protests against police brutality and other systemic racism in summer 2020, numerous corporate CEOs did come out in favor of some efforts by corporations to meet some needs of the racially diverse communities they serve (see Chapter 6).[11] Interestingly, Darren Walker, the Ford Foundation's top executive and member of several corporate boards himself, has noted how the browning of America at the level of corporate boards *might* eventually change their commitment toward more workforce diversity and more positive community involvement: "If 20 years from now the Fortune 500 has dozens of people of color and women as CEOs, if there are boards and committees that are diverse, I think it's a resounding yes that corporations will be more engaged."[12] He is of course talking about the distant 2040s, and using rather vague language for this diversity change.

One result of even these modest CEO and corporate board actions on diversity has been the creation of significant tensions between important segments of the U.S. business community, including the national Chamber of Commerce, and much of the right-wing Republican Party leadership and associated media pundits. Unsurprisingly, the top executives and corporate organizations critical of racist-right Republicanism have been strongly chastised for speaking out by some leading Republican politicians, including those in the U.S. House and Senate, and by right-wing media commentators. Some of these influential politicians have even threatened political retaliation. As journalist Molly Ball summarizes,

> Fox News anchors and conservative firebrands rant about "woke capital" and call for punitive, anti-free-market policies in retaliation. Many of the companies and business groups that implacably resisted Barack Obama have proved surprisingly friendly to Biden, backing portions of his big-spending domestic agenda and supporting his COVID-19 mandates for private companies.[13]

Why did these modest CEO diversity actions and other corporate diversity changes take place? Important academic analysts such as Harvard's Jeffrey Sonnenfeld emphasize that numerous CEOs are now a bit younger, more broad-minded on some social issues, and more likely to reject the most polarizing Republicans like former president Donald Trump.[14] Another explanation accents the more diverse consumer and employee pressures these CEOs and their corporations face today. Opinion surveys indicate that a majority of the general public, including corporate workers, want top executives to be frank about their views on important societal issues. Indeed, a Global Strategy survey of 1,000 white-collar workers in large companies found that more than two thirds were opposed to the January 2021 Capitol insurrection, and that 54 percent were supportive of company officials "speaking out on social or political issues that impact the companies' values." Most white-collar respondents also indicated their company's values had "played a role in them deciding to work for them."[15]

An additional source of increased pressure on top corporate executives and their boards has been international. In 2004, the racially and nationally diverse United Nations leadership began a movement to pressure these corporate executives to go beyond short term profits in making decisions about financial assets to seriously consider long-term environmental, social, and governance (termed ESG) criteria in making corporate decisions about financial and other resources they control. Ever since, several rating agencies have emerged that evaluate companies on their ESG performance. Increasingly, and especially with protests over racial justice developing in the U.S. and internationally since the 2010s, these ESG ratings have been used in making investment decisions by many company executives and other investors in the U.S. and elsewhere. Prior to those global protests by millions of people, corporate America was already, as one general review puts it, "facing pressures from investors, consumers, and regulators to consider a broader range of stakeholders."[16] These include significant pressures for top executives to make meaningful racial and gender diversity improvements in corporate boards, middle management, and their white-collar and blue-collar workforces.

This general review of corporate actions underscores data showing these moderately progressive ESG criteria have sometimes affected a company's economic performance:

> Socially conscious stakeholders use ESG to measure the sustainability and societal impact of a company.... While ESG factors can affect a company's bottom line directly, they can also affect a company's reputation, and investors and business leaders are increasingly applying these nonfinancial factors in their analysis to identify the material risks and growth opportunities of a company.[17]

Increasing numbers of company executives are now accenting at least some ESG goals in their operations, in spite of conventional economists' and most wealthy shareholders' emphasis on company profits and shareholder concerns as the *only* appropriate company goals. If corporations' top decisionmakers do not take into serious consideration yet other important stakeholders, such as people in the communities their operations impact, they increasingly face serious public flak and other visible pushback that can sometimes affect reputations and profits.[18]

Still, much aggressive opposition against significant corporate commitments to ESG principles has come from major right-wing organizations such as the ALEC and their wealthy white funders. These link up with hundreds of right-wing corporate and legislative officials and groups to work, usually off the public radar, against ESG goals and, as in the past, to get reactionary laws passed by conservative state legislatures that deregulate businesses, cut business taxes, and defund important social welfare programs. From the beginning, these right-wing organizations' leaders and members have seen fictional "free markets" as under threat from the increased ESG efforts and have resisted them in many ways, including in assertively right-wing presentations at an array of important business conferences.[19]

In addition, one disturbing and revealing example of how powerful white men can implement what appears to be a "major" diversity effort, and yet remain mostly in control even as the country's racial demography changes, can be seen in how the National Football League's (NFL) white elite set up a supposedly progressive hiring process called the "Rooney Rule." Since 2003, this hiring rule has required each NFL team, which mostly operate as independent semi-corporate entities, to interview at least one nonwhite person when hiring a new head football coach. (The rule was revised in 2022 to require future interviews for top positions to include two women and/or people of color.) However, although in place for nearly two decades, this required procedure has so far brought modest changes in actual NFL hiring decisions. As of early 2023, for example, there were just three Black head coaches among the 32 NFL teams, even though about 60 percent of their players were Black (70 percent are nonwhite). Unmistakably, the Rooney rule has been routinely implemented to leave the powerful, mostly white male, top executives and owners with the most decisionmaking power. Leading sports scholars recently concluded that:

> Such policies have been designed by whites and for whites (particularly males). Moreover, these policies help maintain the notion of diversity, and the effective management of it as the neoliberal project it was constructed to be. Policies such as the Rooney Rule allow sport organizations to give the impression of being socially responsible, while also capitalizing on the benefits of diversity (e.g., hiring talented African American head football coaches). But these policies often do not require these organizations to deconstruct their cultures of similarity (i.e., white supremacy), and ultimately reconstruct them into truly equitable environments.[20]

Additionally, those people of color who do finally make it into their major decisionmaking positions will for the most part have to conform servilely to already established white male norms and folkways of their historically white institutions. Changes in racial representation do not necessarily lessen white normative dominance in these institutions.

Centuries of Browning Labor for Profit

The browning of this country's working population has been a central feature since the importation of enslaved African workers in 1619 by English colonists in Jamestown, Virginia. Unmistakably, the white economic elite and most ordinary whites have greatly benefited from every era of this white-engineered browning of workers, going back more than four centuries. Without centuries of whites' intentional browning of labor, the white population would likely be far less developed and affluent today. Whites made trillions of dollars in profits off of enslaved Black labor from the early 17th century to the mid-19th century. As the scholar Nancy Fraser has noted, "Not machinery, not land, but slaves constituted the single most valuable form of capital in early nineteenth-century United States."[21] One detailed analysis of this valuable labor explains that

> Enslaved people plowed and sowed fields; harvested and packaged crops; and raised, milked, and butchered livestock. They cooked and served food, cleaned houses, weaved and mended clothing, and provided child care services. They cut hair, carried luggage, and drove wagons, carts, and carriages.[22]

Many famous white Americans, including early white "founders," became wealthy substantially because of the large number of enslaved workers that they "owned." For instance, in the 1780s, the much celebrated first U.S. president, George Washington, held in bondage about 216 African American workers, whom he often viewed and treated in inhuman terms as essential economic investments. One detailed summary of their work, enforced by violent flogging, makes clear the significant luxury and wealth they created for Washington and his family:

> Slaves washed his linens, sewed his shirts, polished his boots, saddled his horse, chopped the wood for his fireplaces, powdered his wig, drove his carriage, cooked his meals, served his table, poured his wine, posted his letters, lit the lamps, swept the porch, looked after the guests, planted the flowers in his gardens, trimmed the hedges, dusted the furniture, cleaned the windows, made the beds, and performed the myriad domestic chores.[23]

A great many elite and ordinary whites in the South and the North were unjustly enriched, directly or indirectly, by this enslaved African American labor. Ordinary whites held jobs policing enslaved workers, growing foodstuffs for enslaved workforces, transporting and trading products produced by enslaved workers, working in plantation-related skilled trades, and operating as officials in numerous government and private institutions of a slavery-based society.[24] Without the highly exploited labor of millions of enslaved African Americans there would not have been such economic support for these ordinary white individuals and their families.[25]

Then, during the long Jim Crow era (circa 1877–1969), white employers again made huge profits off of very underpaid "free" Black labor. For these Black workers, whites perpetuated an internal racial colony "by transforming recently emancipated slaves into debt peons through the sharecropping system," as well as into very low-wage workers in newly emerging industries.[26] By the mid- to late-19th century, white employers also made major profits off of the very underpaid labor of Latina/o and Asian American laborers, most of them immigrants and their immediate descendants. These Latina/o and Asian American workers also became internal racial colonies of mostly low-wage agricultural, construction, and service workers. Since the early 17th century, this country's systemic racism has been developed on, and grounded in, extreme white economic exploitation of many millions of workers of color. Whites in the elite and other social classes have unjustly enriched themselves at the expense of these unjustly impoverished Americans of color.[27]

Contemporary Browning of Workers

This highly racialized process of unjust enrichment and unjust impoverishment continues today. Much of corporate America still *requires*, and makes substantial profits from, an array of racially exploitative labor programs their mostly white top executives have been central to creating, supporting, and maintaining. This extensive exploitation has included many millions of blue-collar workers of color, men and women, who are often underpaid relative to their white counterparts. For example, over many decades up to the present, this corporate labor exploitation has included extremely underpaid prison laborers, with many of these being men and women of color incarcerated as part of the operation of a racially unjust criminal justice system.[28] Additionally, over these same decades, large corporations and small businesses in many geographical areas have made great profits off of the labor of millions of documented and undocumented immigrants of color, many of whom are very underpaid. Estimates are that low-paid undocumented immigrants, mostly workers of color, have long made up *at least half* of U.S. agricultural field and crop workers—without whom much of the U.S. food system would stop functioning well.[29]

Now as in the past, these and other modestly paid workers of color are essential to keeping the U.S. economy afloat. They are the majority of workers in the 25 lowest-paying job categories that have workers of color. As one recent report summarizes, "Black workers are most dramatically overrepresented among home health aides, nursing assistants, security guards, taxi drivers, and truck and tractor operators. Latinx workers are particularly concentrated among farm workers, cleaners, construction workers, landscapers, and packagers."[30] Clearly, a continuing problem facing these workers involves their relatively low wages—i.e., wage exploitation—and chronic wage stagnation. As researcher Valerie Wilson has emphasized,

> Wage stagnation can be directly traced to a number of intentional policy decisions on behalf of those with the most income, wealth, and power—decisions that have eroded the leverage of the vast majority of workers while directing most of the gains to the top. Two of the ways this has played out are through declining unionization and an economy for which genuinely full employment has been a rare occurrence.[31]

Much change in this essential workforce is expected in the near future. In addition to the development of a nonwhite majority in the U.S. population by the mid-2040s, a significant change will take place in the country's population of workers much sooner. That is, there is now in some states, and soon will be nationally, a dramatic shift in the composition of the majority of workers in the critical working-age cohorts. Presently, the U.S. working class, defined as workers without a college degree, constitutes about two-thirds of country's primary labor force (18-year-old to 64-year-old workers). If current rates of college completion stay relatively constant for key U.S. demographics, workers of color will make up a majority of this working class very soon, by about 2032 according to a Census Bureau projection.[32]

Millions of working class jobs are opening up now, and will be in the near future, because of retiring white workers, and many will necessarily be taken by younger workers of color. The great irony in this current and coming economic reality is that these often racially exploited workers of color will likely save the U.S. from the severe economic distress and decline that is now threatening rapidly aging Japan and European countries where there is a much smaller young worker replacement cohort. Moreover, beyond replacement of aging white workers, these younger workers of color will provide the necessary federal taxpayers who can keep supporting the country's important Social Security and Medicare programs. These programs, in another major societal irony, mainly serve the oldest segment of the U.S. population, a segment that will for some time into the future be very disproportionately white. As demographer William Frey summarizes, a "growing diverse, globally connected minority population will be absolutely necessary to infuse the aging American labor force with vitality and to sustain populations in many parts of the country that are facing population declines."[33]

However, we should strongly emphasize another critical aspect of this young nonwhite worker and family cohort—the matter of social justice and equity in educational and other socioeconomic resources. One scholarly assessment of the future U.S. workplace notes the continuing role of systemic racism as the country continues to racially diversify:

> The workers, innovators, and community leaders who will take up the economic mantle of the future are the babies, youth, and students of today—most of them people of color, and far too many growing up in or near poverty, living in neighborhoods and attending schools deprived of vital resources, and systematically cut off from opportunities to thrive.[34]

Without equitable and substantial individual and family resources, these Americans of color will be much less likely to thrive and fulfill the major societal role they otherwise need and deserve to hold. I will return to this critical resources issue later in this chapter.

Increasing Racial and Class Inequality

Achieving equity and societal justice in access to socioeconomic resources for the younger generations of color is a democratizing goal facing major racial and class barriers. Perhaps the most significant of these is the great racial inequality that is foundational and systemic in U.S. society, today as in the past. Over the decades since the 1980s, the country's mostly white and conservative top capitalists and associated politicians they fund have created a society that has become significantly more unequal in racial and class terms. The national economic impact on ordinary Americans of this conservative political backtracking is detailed in a striking RAND research report:

> The three decades following the Second World War saw a period of economic growth that was shared across the income distribution, but inequality in taxable income has increased substantially over the last four decades. We document the cumulative effect of four decades of income growth... and estimate that aggregate income for the population below the 90th percentile over this time period would have been $2.5 trillion (67 percent) higher in 2018 had income growth since 1975 remained as equitable as it was in the first two post-War decades.[35]

One analysis of this RAND study underscores a key finding:

> The median full-time worker in America today earns about $50,000 a year. If they had been held harmless by the last 45 years of neoliberal [and racist] economic policy ... instead of earning $50,000 a year, they would earn between $92,000 and $100,000 a year.

This reality does not explain "every pathology in our society, but a huge proportion of them, from our budget deficits to our surreally polarized politics."[36]

Today, this highly oppressive and inegalitarian reality is still in place, for most ordinary American workers but especially for those of color. Recently, Census Bureau data revealed that there is great household income inequality across major racial groups. White median household income was $74, 912, while that of Black households was much less at $45, 870 and that of Latina/o households was much less at $55,321.[37] Other data show a similar pattern for members of the country's oldest racial group, Native Americans.[38] Today, as in the past, households of workers of color typically face very substantial income inequality.

Consider too the huge racial wealth gap. Government Consumer Finance surveys have found huge differentials in median family wealth between white families and Black and Latino families. In one recent survey white median wealth was nearly eight times that of Black families and more than five times that of Latina/o families.[39]

The most conspicuous aspect of wealth inequality is the great and growing wealth of the mostly white national elite. In the last quarter of 2021 the Federal Reserve System estimated that the *top one percent* of U.S. households (an overwhelmingly white group) held *32.3 percent* of the country's wealth, up significantly from 23.5 percent in 1989. In comparison the *bottom 50 percent* of all households (much more racially diverse) held just *2.6 percent* of the country's wealth in 2021, down from its 3.7 percent in 1989.[40] Even more dramatic is the fact that the country's wealthiest one tenth of one percent of households (the top of the ruling elite, with average household wealth of $116 million, again overwhelmingly white) has almost as much wealth as the bottom 90 percent of all households, a top elite percentage up sharply from the 1970s.[41]

This racial and class inequality plays out in major U.S. geographical and educational patterns. The economist Robert Reich has noted how numerous cities have become more economically segregated between a "fortunate fifth," most of whom are white and well-off Americans "whose symbolic and analytic services are linked to the world economy," and a four fifths of that is low or modest income and "consists of local service workers—custodians, security guards, taxi drivers, clerical aides, parking attendants, sales people, restaurant employees—whose jobs are dependent on the symbolic analysts."[42] Many in the four fifths, in large cities especially, are people of color. Moreover, the more affluent towns and cities do better under these divisive circumstances, while less affluent ones do poorly and the gap between the two has become much wider over time. Indeed, Reich contends that the fortunate, heavily white fifth has largely seceded from the rest of their cities and of this country, and now seek lower taxes for affluent people like them, less public educational and other public welfare spending, and more policing and prisons to provide them security against the rest of the population. Given this geopolitical reality, over recent decades, and especially under arch-conservative Republican control, the federal government has responded to the fortunate fifth by actually reducing its contribution to state and local government spending for numerous public support programs, including public education, health, and environmental efforts, and especially those facilitating the welfare and mobility of Americans of color.

Intergenerational Transmission of Wealth

Consider too that below the ultrawealthy white elite in the racial-class hierarchy, most ordinary whites, especially in the upper-working-class and middle-class majority, in generation after generation have also benefitted from societal transmission processes that pass along their white ancestors' unjustly gained economic and sociocultural capital from the slavery, Jim Crow, and/or contemporary eras (see Chapter 1). This persists today, and will likely do so in the foreseeable future. Each white generation's own discriminatory actions targeting people of color create new opportunities for further unjust enrichment for their families, which can also be passed to later white generations. For approximately 21 generations now, the country's large-scale racial oppression has created extensive inequalities in resources and life chances between whites as a group and numerous groups of color.

Rooted in white-controlled legal, political, and economic institutions, this intergenerational reproduction of white economic and social capital remains central to U.S. society. At some point in their histories, the substantial majority of white families have secured important family assets because of what some call "white affirmative action" programs. For example, in the 19th and early 20th centuries, an array of white-run government giveaways, including land for farming by federal and state homestead acts, provided many socioeconomic opportunities and resources mostly for white families. These resource-providing programs usually came from land, labor, and other thefts from Indigenous Americans, African Americans, and other Americans of color. White families typically have passed these unjust enrichments along to successive generations, to the present day.

Later on, in the decades before, during, and after World War II, another array of federal programs provided very discriminatory access for whites

to yet more socioeconomic resources. Major federal programs were sub-
sidized mostly or very disproportionately for whites, such as the Federal
Housing Administration's loan programs and the federal veterans' housing
and educational programs. Enabled to buy homes, whites passed wealth
accumulated from home equities to assist descendants in developing businesses, funding college educations, and generally being able to at least have
middle class lives. Yet other federal programs provided significant socioeconomic assistance to (mainly white) farmers, bankers, and other businesspeople, enabling them to survive the 1930s Great Depression and for them
and their descendants to thrive thereafter. Political scientist Ira Katznelson
wrote a book with much documentation of this long resource provision
era, one when aggressive government "affirmative action was white."[43]

The consequences of these and other white affirmative action programs
have been dramatic. Government-subsidized housing, highway, and urban development programs helped greatly in increasing the movement of
white middle-income families to the suburbs, further sharpening and ra-
cializing the urban-suburban divide in metropolitan areas. This suburban
migration has been stimulated and aided by racialized investment decisions of mostly white-run corporations, banks, and developers. Furthermore, many white-controlled suburban communities have developed laws
or regulations to block or restrict housing developments for moderate-
income residents, especially those of color.[44]

Much government-assisted affirmative action for whites has persisted to
the present, and social science research shows white families still are able
to pass along much unjust enrichment from one generation to the next.
Pathbreaking research by sociologist Jennifer Mueller has examined the
differential transmission of wealth between white families and families
of color in a southwestern area, as recorded in student histories of their
families. They reported huge racial differences in acquisition and transfer
of family wealth and social capital over several family generations, to the
present day:

> White families reported *more than six times* as many transfers of mon-
> etary assets across generations in these families' histories—216 trans-
> fers of monetary assets reported in the 105 white families' histories,
> compared to a paltry 13 such transfers reported among 39 families
> of color. Intergenerational inheritances of land, home and businesses
> were similarly disproportionate.[45]

Equally as revealing in the student diaries was how often these white families had benefited from the aforementioned government affirmative action programs disproportionately advantaging whites.

Today, most white Americans inherit at least some economic or cultural
wealth from their ancestors, including those who profited significantly

from the slavery and Jim Crow systems. Economists Lawrence Kotlikoff and Lawrence Summers used historical data on longitudinal age-earnings and age-consumption to examine in detail the importance of the inter-generational transfers of wealth in U.S. families. They found that most family wealth formation (about 80 percent) comes from these transfers of wealth across family generations and that a *negligible fraction* of this family capital accumulation is accounted by the savings of individual workers. In their view, economic models accenting worker retirement savings as a critical form of U.S. capital accumulation are wrongheaded and should be replaced by models emphasizing intergenerational wealth transfers.[46] Of course, whites vary by class and gender in the scale and type of their inherited wealth, yet the majority do benefit thus to a significant degree.

Additionally, most whites benefit from white racial privilege in the form of persisting subtle, covert, or overt racial *favoritism* in jobs, housing, education, and other societal areas. Today, as in the past, social network-ing capital is racially differentiated and generally privileges whites, again intergenerationally. Sociologist Nancy DiTomaso interviewed 200 whites about how they secured jobs over their lives. They reported that they had mostly gotten jobs through white networks of acquaintances, friends, and family, not just because of personal skills and qualifications (that is, their job-related "merit"). Over their lifetimes, they had avoided much job market competition and gotten jobs by using racially segregated networks that greatly favor whites. Strikingly, *not one* respondent expressed concern about this unjust job hunting system. Such "opportunity hoarding" is es-sential to the intergenerational transmission of white wealth, yet is rarely seen by whites as racially discriminatory.[47]

Given these massive racial inequalities and their ongoing intergenera-tional transmission, when whites become a statistical minority in the U.S. population in the 2040s, they are still likely to maintain dominant politi-cal, economic, and other societal power. That intergenerational transmis-sion routinely maintains their white group status at the top of the U.S. racial hierarchy. Periodically, they may be joined in that upper echelon of the racial hierarchy by modest numbers of families of color who con-form to the white normative structure there, but they are unlikely to be displaced as the most powerful racial group in US society anytime soon.

The Educational Browning of America

Defunding and Privatizing Public Education

Students of color currently account for a little more than half of all stu-dents in the country's public elementary and secondary schools, and that percentage is growing because of the decline in the population of white schoolchildren. One consequence of this growth in children of color is increased demand from their parents and other relatives for large improvements, especially in government funding, in a broad range of educational programs and opportunities at all levels.[48]

However, for decades, a substantial government defunding of the public educational system, especially at local and state government levels, has been shaped by white conservative decisionmakers committed to the continuation of significant racial segregation and inequality. Many primary, secondary, and post-secondary systems are poorly funded in regard to actual educational need, and thus cannot provide a substantial mobility boost to most young people of color. As community activist and lawyer Jim Freeman notes, the funding for public schools is "in many communities, being reduced, resulting in fewer resources for instruction, student support services, extracurricular activities, and other vital wraparound supports."[49] Public educational programs are often heavily dependent on funding by predominantly white local and state officials who have to please white taxpayers. Today, many whites, including many state legislators, do not want to pay the necessary and substantial local and state taxes to support essential educational programs for children of color.

Strikingly, this white conservative opposition, including among legislators, to major public school funding contrasts with major educational commitments white government officials have made to white children and their parents from the late 1800s to the present. For example, in the decades right after World War II, these white officials sharply increased government funding for public schools, including for colleges and universities. This large-scale funding very disproportionately went for the public schooling of returning white veterans and other white youth, and it played a key role in creating a large middle class among whites for the first time in U.S. history.

Linked to the contemporary public funding problem is the *privatization* of much public education. Over recent decades many conservative white government officials, pressured or influenced by groups like ALEC and major corporate executives, have assisted the latter in making significant profits off the privatization of numerous public programs. Thus, we have seen extensive privatization of public schools in the form of charter and other private schools since the 1960s–1970s racial desegregation era. Sociologist Randolph Hohle argues with much evidence that conservative local, state, and federal government actions have often adopted a strong ideological "language of privatization that degraded all things public as 'black' and inferior and all things private as 'white' and superior."[50] Furthermore, some white far-right think tanks and their political operatives have made clear their desire to *destroy* public education. One operative put it this way to a *New York Times* columnist: "We are right now preparing a strategy of laying siege to the [public] institutions." Elsewhere he also said that "to get universal school choice you really need to operate from a premise of universal public school distrust."[51]

Clearly too, the contemporary attacks on public education, including major defunding and privatization, need to be understood in the larger context of this country's elite-white-male dominance system. White right-wing think tanks and policy organizations like the ALEC organization are key parts of this dominance system and have for decades played an important role in shaping state and federal policies on education at all levels. Like other critical analysts, community activist and lawyer Jim Freeman has emphasized how these right-wing organizations have stealthily become well-organized in a quest for what are the goals of *greater* racial inequality and segregation in U.S. society, including in the public school system. He notes that

> every day the communities I was working with were fighting back against racial inequities—in many cases, they were fighting for their very lives—and at the same time a group of ultra-wealthy Corporate America and Wall Street executives was investing in organizations that were actively opposing those communities' efforts. They were, in effect, promoting the perpetuation of racial injustice.[52]

Of course, the centuries-old societal problem underlying this contemporary white commitment to little or no change in racial injustice is that it is a very old condition whites created and greatly benefit from. That is, most communities of color, and the large majority of families within them, have already suffered *generations* of inequality, of unjust impoverishment from whites' direct and indirect racial discrimination, especially in regard to government-funded opportunity resources like first-rate public education. From an equity and democratic standpoint, Americans of color deserve the same substantial level of public investments—e.g., excellent public schools, college funding programs, government home financing—that whites have had for generations.[53] Until these Americans are provided the same means of getting first-rate educations for their youth and the associated build-up of individual and family wealth, this situation of great racial inequality will undoubtedly persist for yet more generations.

Nonetheless, while it does mean more taxes for better-off whites, a renewed and aggressive funding of public education for the increasing numbers of youth of color will not only bring major increases in resource accumulation for families of color but also should redound to the interests of most Americans. For instance, the whites greatly benefitting from more educated workers of color include, as noted previously, retired whites who depend on government programs like Social Security and also whites who currently live in geographical areas with seriously declining populations and thus deteriorating local economies.

Censoring K-12 Schooling: Fearful Whites in Diversifying Areas

In spite of widespread white efforts since the 1960s civil rights era to preserve significant school segregation, many public (and some private) K-12 school systems are becoming more demographically diverse generally and in terms of some schools within them. Government data indicate that the Gen-Z youth, those Americans born from about 1997 to 2012, are the most racially diverse of all contemporary completed generations, as well as of all such youngest societal cohorts over previous U.S. centuries. This racial diversity will likely be greater for the even younger, only partially completed Generation Alpha, those born after 2012.

Unsurprisingly, these increasingly diverse younger generations seem the most likely to want to know more about this country's racial history. Yet many whites, especially in the older generations, have been persuaded to resist an honest teaching of that problematic U.S. history. We have seen this hard-nosed perspective on contemporary racial education explode in white protests at numerous heated school board and city or county council meetings across the country. For instance, one NBC study examined 33 school districts where school board debates over racial diversity initiatives, including over how U.S. racial history should be taught, were most intense and recurring. The study found that these school districts were generally high on a metric of increasing white student exposure to racial diversity—a quantitative measure of "how likely white students are to have classmates of a different race—not just in their district overall, but in their school."[54] Relevant government data showed that from 1994 to 2020 the exposure of white students to those of color had increased nationally, but in two thirds of these school districts with major diversity controversies this exposure metric was above that national average.[55]

Many white parents have been stimulated to protest educational diversity efforts at these local government meetings by white right-wing media, politicians, and extremist organizations pursuing white-racist political goals. One such organization is the right-wing ALEC organization mentioned previously. Its extremist operatives have worked with others to stir up white political opposition to accurate teaching about U.S. racism (often mislabeled as "critical race theory") and to get conservative state legislators to pass laws that ban that honest history from being taught in K-12 schools and in colleges.[56] Indeed, as of early 2023, at least 25 state legislatures have considered or passed laws that "restrict or ban what students can learn and what teachers can teach about our nation's history."[57]

Significantly, these contemporary right-wing political efforts at local and state educational censorship include much misinformation and intentional distortions. For example, the right-wing political activists and legislators have falsely claimed that many K-12 public school teachers actually teach "critical race theory," even though none of them has provided empirical evidence for this absurd contention. Indeed, education scholars and educators who have routinely reviewed what is taught in thousands of school classes in school systems across the country report *never* having seen K-12 teachers teach actual critical race theory.[58]

Moreover, when asked about their right-wing sloganeering on what they term "critical race theory," these white right-wing political activists and the conservative legislators they influence almost never demonstrate concrete knowledge of the extensive legal research and peer-reviewed law journal publications to which that term refers. To be factually accurate, "critical race theory" was created in the 1980s as a term for research examining institutionalized racism in the U.S. legal system, a perspective developed initially by professors of color in law journals and now mostly taught in law schools and other graduate schools.

Unsurprisingly, the general population is also mostly illiterate in regard to actual critical race theory. A 2021 Reuters poll found that a majority of Americans (57 percent) had heard the term "critical race theory," doubtless from right-wing and mainstream media, but few who said they were familiar with it indicated significant *accurate* knowledge about it. One fifth of these respondents said it is "taught in most public high schools," which is empirically false. On this and six other simple true-false questions about actual critical race theory (CRT), *95 percent* of those who had heard of it could not answer all the questions correctly. Just a third answered more than four of the seven correctly. Citing social scientist Paula Ioanide, the Reuters poll report concludes that the general public is "being fed bad information about the CRT from conservative activists hoping to invigorate the Republican base and dissuade teachers from talking about racism in schools."[59]

Even a brief examination of the local and national white extremist attacks on so-called critical race theory suggests they are really interested in stopping K-12 teachers from teaching an accurate history of U.S. racism and from encouraging younger Americans to think critically about it. Over recent decades, with increased racial diversity in our K-12 students and teachers, there has been some increase in teaching accurately about that history in many school systems. Most importantly, one can easily demonstrate that such instruction is highly relevant and necessary for a country which had 246 years of slavery and 90 years of Jim Crow's near-slavery, altogether most of its history. Indeed, much more of this actual history needs to be taught at all levels of public and private education, especially given this country's increasingly diverse demographic future.

Even now, we are not quite two human lifetimes away from our very oppressive slavery system, and we are far less than one human lifetime from the very oppressive Jim Crow segregation system. Writing recently, historian Charles King noted that this country has so far

> had only one president who came of age when full racial equality was the law of the land. Eighty-one of the 100 current U.S. senators were born in an era when people could be arrested for marrying across racial lines.[60]

No other advanced industrialized country has such a long history of extreme white-racist oppression, most of which was fully legal at the time. Unmistakably, too, this long history of slavery and Jim Crow has had many negative legacies to the present day, legacies that include constant white pressure to move backwards to a more extreme white-dominant racist reality.[61] Indeed, today many elite and ordinary whites appear to want a ban on the teaching of an accurate history of centuries of white racism because they are fearful such instruction will contribute to their losing the dominant racial position in society, especially as the country becomes majority-minority.

We should note too that white conservative-led battles over accurate U.S. history-telling in public school curricula and textbooks are decades old. Conservative white activists and officials in Florida, Texas, and other states have long claimed, inaccurately, that much of the public school curriculum and its textbooks' historical discussions shows a "liberal bias." They have made extremist arguments that a truthful discussion in K-12 textbooks of U.S. slavery, of the 1960s civil rights movements, or of the social programs of the 1930s New Deal era reflects "left-wing indoctrination." For many years conservative white officials have policed the language of K-12 instruction in extreme ways, including the suggestion by some that the discussions of African American slavery and Jim Crow oppression should be watered down dramatically. A more recent example of this old censorship is some Texas educators' view that second-graders be taught about slavery only with the euphemistic term of "involuntary relocation."[62] Thus, because of reactionary political pressure, school and other government officials in larger states like Texas make decisions on public school curricula and textbooks that take the course of least political resistance and make or allow deletions from curricula or textbooks of an honest history of U.S. racism. One unfortunate result is that these white-sanitized textbooks are then used in many smaller states in all regions, since there are only a few large textbook publishers and they typically wish to sell the same books in all states.[63]

Note too what should be an obvious point in this public discussion—that the First Amendment to the U.S. Constitution stipulates that "Congress

shall make no law... abridging the freedom of speech, or of the press."
This important U.S. right of free speech unhampered by federal government lawmaking is likewise protected from similarly restrictive local and
state government actions, as was mandated by major 1920s–1930s Supreme
Court decisions.

However, that Supreme Court has also ruled that what public school
teachers teach children is not fully protected by the First Amendment
and can be officially regulated to some degree by local and state politicians and school officials. Alice O'Brien, general counsel of the National
Education Association, to which millions of public school teachers be-
long, has argued that the new state laws restricting what K-12 and college teachers can teach about U.S. racial history will be fully challenged
in the courts. They will probably be challenged on the grounds that
they violate not only the First Amendment but also the Fourteenth
amendment to the Constitution. In court, teachers' legal representatives
can show that these censorship laws have been implemented mostly by
white right-wing politicians with a clear *white racial bias* lying behind
them, including a desire to restrict presentations of historical data on
systemic racism, much of which data has been generated by scholars of
color. Such white racialized censorship legislation does violate the First
Amendment right of K-12 teachers to teach accurate historical information about their country. This white-framed legislation also violates
the Fourteenth Amendment's "equal protection of the laws" provision
by not respecting nonwhite students desire and need to learn accurately
the history of oppressive white racism and the history of resistance to it
by Americans of color. Indeed, one conservative Republican-generated
Arizona law blocked the Tucson public school system from implementing a Mexican American Studies program, even though its schools had
many Mexican American children craving such honest societal information. That law was challenged in court as racially biased, and a federal district judge struck it down as violating the First and Fourteenth
Amendments.[64]

College Students of Color: Defunding Higher Education

Just as students of color are increasingly a majority in elementary and
secondary schools across the country, they are also increasing significantly
at numerous historically white colleges and universities. Here too public
education faces a crisis not only from conservative state defunding but also
from white conservative attempts to censor teaching about historical and
contemporary white racism.

As Edna Chun and I demonstrate in *Who Killed Higher Education?*,
large-scale state defunding of public higher education by mostly white
conservative legislators has also been influenced by right-wing political

organizations like ALEC. Recall that these legislators are bankrolled politically by right-wing donors and influenced by their political operatives, with their legislative goals being lower taxes, fewer business regulations, and less political democracy. Surprisingly, this intentional and well-organized effort to defund public higher education has received little mainstream media attention. It has mostly happened gradually and surreptitiously. As with the K-12 education, this large-scale state defunding has sharply reduced the access to and quality of higher education opportunities for students of color across the country—those who would prosper like earlier white generations.[65]

Consequently, this defunding has major implications for the socioeconomic future of this country as a whole, especially given the shortages of skilled workers in several major areas of the present and future U.S. economy. Well-educated young Americans of color could help fill employers' job requirements for millions of new jobs in the increasingly advanced economy of the U.S. present and future. Today, however, many professional and technical job openings are not being filled by U.S.-educated workers but by educated workers (e.g., H-1B visa workers) from other countries. Since 2010, the largest numbers of legally documented immigrants have come from the countries of India, China, Mexico, and Cuba, each year about 800,000.[66] About half of these already have college degrees. That is, much legal immigration selectively creams off better educated workers from countries across the globe, including less developed areas that badly need these workers. Well-educated immigrant workers from less developed countries also help U.S. capitalists unfairly contend against U.S. unions and native-born workers seeking better wages and working conditions in this country.

Some conservative economists argue that native-born U.S. workers, white and nonwhite, are not affected by these highly skilled immigrant workers because the U.S. does not currently have an adequate supply of highly skilled workers. However, this is disingenuous, for these mostly white economists know that the main reason for this is because of the failure of conservative white state and local legislators and their corporate elite funders to support adequate funding of public higher education—funding that would sharply increase needed skilled workers, including from historically oppressed U.S. populations of color.[67] Peter Cappelli, a Wharton School management scholar, has underscored this contemporary labor reality: "Foreign workers on H-1B visas offer employers many advantages: they cannot typically quit the employer who hires them without losing their status, their opportunities in their home country often are substantially worse than these U.S. opportunities, and so forth." Because of this substantial importation of skilled labor, both U.S. labor market conditions (e.g., increased wages) and U.S. educational institutions do not have to shift aggressively to meet the native-born educated labor shortfall. Thus,

"U.S. employees do not pursue these fields because of that, and employers then become completely dependent on H-1B workers to fill them."[68]

Censoring Colleges and Universities

Additionally, even as the numbers of college students of color are growing, numerous efforts have been made by right-wing political organizations and legislators to make the teaching climate and curriculum at colleges and universities more whitewashed and less conducive to accurate teaching about this country's systemic racism, as well as its systemic classism and sexism. The previously mentioned ALEC organization has proposed model legislation that right-wing state legislators should pursue to make teaching and research at public colleges and universities less diverse, model legislation with the intentionally misleading title of "Intellectual Diversity in Higher Education Act." If implemented, this vague law would force administrators at public universities to report regularly on their "intellectual diversity."[69] The real goal of such a law is to increase the already significant number of conservative college instructors, courses, and programs, such as by adding more that emphasize uncritically the virtues of market capitalism and those that mythologize or whitewash U.S. racial history. Indeed, a number of the state laws mentioned previously that ban critical teaching about U.S. racist history (i.e., "critical race theory") in K-12 grades have been extended to cover such teaching at the college level. Clearly, in many areas of higher education, these right-wing educational efforts intend to *reduce* intellectual diversity.

Actually, our historically white colleges and universities have a more important diversity problem never addressed by these right-wing legislators and associated right-wing groups—the largely white-normed character of these historically white institutions. Much research demonstrates that college students of color commonly face an array of problematical white norms and white-framed curricula in these educational institutions. This is true for most such students, those who are middle class and especially those who are working class.[70] Sociologist Anthony Jack has recently studied working class students of color as they enter elite educational institutions like Amherst College or Harvard University. For most of them such institutions are a whole new world with hidden normative hurdles that can cause them serious interactive and learning problems, often to the point of their dropping out.[71] Eliminating racially problematical college climates, reforming white-oriented teaching and learning structures, and restructuring curricula at historically white colleges and universities constitute the most important set of academic reforms needed today at historically white educational institutions.

Currently, few of the country's historically white colleges and universities *require* their students to get a substantial education in the country's long history of systemic racism and of civil rights movements working against that antidemocratic racial reality. Indeed, reducing or eliminating the elective courses offered at colleges and universities that inform students about that systemic racism is one goal of the right-wing legislative attacks on academic instruction they misname as "critical race theory."

In national surveys, the white population frequently shows why such critical education is very important, especially as the country moves toward a majority-minority reality. When asked in a recent national poll if giving more attention to U.S. racial history is a good or bad thing for this society, *less than half* (46 percent) of white respondents said that was a good thing, as compared to 75 percent of Black respondents, 64 percent of Asian American respondents, and 59 percent of Latina/o respondents. In addition, less than half of whites thought that much more effort needs to go into creating racial equality in the country, and less than a fifth agreed that to do that "most laws and institutions need to be completely rebuilt." In another national survey, a significant majority of the Black respondents thought it is "very important for people in the U.S. to have conversations about race with people who are not the same race as them," while a majority of whites disagreed.[72]

These and other data on the actual racial views and understandings of this country's white majority indicate an enduring problem in their educations about U.S. history and society. For instance, rarely have white educators in white-controlled educational institutions—from grade school to graduate school—taught a critical and thorough history of our brutal slavery system (about 60 percent of this country's history), our oppressive Jim Crow segregation (about 20 percent of that history), and our still oppressive contemporary racism.[73] Actually, few of these educators themselves have been taught that critical and thorough history of our systemic racism and of the centuries of antiracist resistance of Americans of color. Undeniably, this miseducation of white (and other) Americans is intentional. A powerful white elite has long controlled the process of U.S. knowledge creation and dissemination about racial matters through all levels of public and private schooling. To correct most whites' extensive ignorance and misinformation about U.S. racial history, and to affect whites' strong racist emotions about these matters, will require major changes in our educational system, across all grade levels and in public and private school settings over a significant span of years.[74]

Undoubtedly, one other major change that is very necessary for countering this ignorance and misinformation in our historically white educational system involves a vigorous expansion of faculty and staff of color therein. According to U.S. Department of Education data, among full-time faculty in U.S. colleges and universities, the substantial majority (75 percent) are white. The nonwhite segment (25 percent) includes Asian/Pacific Islander, Black, Latina/o, and Native American faculty, with the latter three groups being seriously underrepresented.[75] One can ask who best advocates for the major diversity changes needed in most of our colleges and universities. Research on college faculty leadership on diversity matters has found that faculty of color are much more likely to be advocates for racial diversity than are white faculty. Higher education scholars Julie Park and Nida Denton conclude that their research on faculty views on racial diversity

> is consistent with past research that faculty of color can enhance the overall quality of education at higher education institutions, for example, by serving as role models, advisors, and leaders.... The presence of faculty of color also impresses upon students of color the institution's commitment to equity and diversity issues.[76]

A Note on the Browning of Elite Schooling

We might note too that the browning of America has affected private schooling for children of this country's elite. For centuries the elite private K–12 schools and colleges have been central to the reproduction, generation after generation, of the country's elite white dominance system. They play an important role in grooming well each new cohort of children from elite families. In a recent ethnographic study of the elite private St. Paul's School in New Hampshire, a former nonwhite student and now Ivy League professor Shamus Khan shows how privileged, disproportionately white students learn to embody, perform, and maintain their upper-class racial and class privileges in a more racially diverse society. In response to the browning of America, this famous private school, which has long served well the moderate/liberal wing of the country's dominant elite, has in recent years significantly increased the racial diversity of its students and faculty. Developing their talents and knowledge to live in, and preside over, a racially diverse society clearly matters for the education of this younger elite generation, but so does maintaining their inherited wealth, top societal status, and great socio-racial privileges.[77] That is, in contrast to the conservative wing of the dominant white elite, parents in the more moderate/liberal wing seem committed to preparing their children for positions of traditional class power, yet in a much more diverse and multiracially democratic U.S.

Conclusion

In this country's communities of color, one does find substantial hope that a future majority-minority society will democratize and finally open up a wider range of socioeconomic opportunities. Consider the relatively new marketing company, EthniFacts. The company's mostly Latina/o leadership is enthusiastic about the positive impacts of the current and future racial diversifying of America. In a very optimistic statement entitled "The Expanding Flag," they open by insisting that

> the unprecedented speed and scope of demographic and social change in the United States has turned us all into immigrants in a teeming terra nova that is being reimagined and reinvented in countless ways all around us, transforming the way we see ourselves and each other, and how we work, play, learn, love and dream.... [T]he time has come for a belated but inevitable recognition that the energy and optimism of America's emerging interethnic majority is one of its greatest assets in a socially-networked, culturally-connected world. The reimagining of America also alerts us to how the cultural and economic contributions of Hispanics, African Americans, Asian and other groups are breathing new life into the traditional values of hard work, faith, family and community that bind us all together....[78]

They then argue that the pace of demographic change is especially accelerated by increased Latina/o growth and political-economic power. They also assert that there is now, and will be in the future, a mutual "culture exchange" that transforms the country's numerous racial and ethnic groups into a truly multicultural society. Latina/os are said to be both "fully American" and "fully Latino"—thereby trying to counter the commonplace white idea of required one-way acculturation to white norms and folkways for immigrants and other Americans of color. Then they conclude that "Inclusion and innovation go hand in hand. The pioneers of the reimagined American frontier are black, brown, red, yellow and white, gay and straight, female and male.... When America bets on its own people, everybody wins."[79] Unmistakably, they envision a country where racial change, diversity, and intergroup tolerance are celebrated, especially given the more inclusive attitudes of the younger and more diverse American generations.

Notes

1 See Carol Anderson, *The Second: Race and Guns in a Fatally Unequal America* (New York: Bloomsbury, 2021).
2 See Joe Feagin and Kimberley Ducey, *Elite White Men Ruling: Who, What, When, Where, and How* (New York: Routledge, 2017).
3 Adam Smith, *An Inquiry into the Nature and Causes of the Wealth of Nations* (Gutenberg Ebook Project, 2001 [1776]), Kindle loc. 6424.
4 Josh Bivens, "Reclaiming Corporate Tax Revenues," *Economic Policy Institute*, April 14, 2022, https://www.epi.org/publication/reclaiming-corporate-tax-revenues (accessed April 14, 2022).
5 Jane Mayer, *Dark Money: The Hidden History of the Billionaires behind the Rise of the Radical Right* (New York: Anchor Books, 2017).

6 Jim Freeman, *Rich Thanks to Racism* (New York: ILR Press, 2021), pp. 24–25.
7 Ibid. See also Edna Chun and Joe Feagin, *Who Killed Higher Education?* (New York: Routledge, 2021).
8 Kurt Andersen, *Evil Geniuses: The Unmaking of America* (New York: Random House, 2020), p. xx.
9 Ibid., p. xxii.
10 Richard L. Zweigenhaft, "Diversity among Fortune 500 CEOs from 2000 to 2020: White Women, Hi-Tech South Asians, and Economically Privileged Multilingual Immigrants from Around the World," *Who Rules America?* website, January 2021, https://whorulesamerica.ucsc.edu/power/diversity_update_2020.html (accessed May 11, 2022).
11 David Gelles, "Red Brands and Blue Brands: Is Hyper-Partisanship Coming for Corporate America?" *New York Times*, https://www.nytimes.com/2021/11/23/business/dealbook/companies-politics-partisan.html (accessed December 20, 2021).
12 Quoted in ibid.
13 Molly Ball, "How Big Business Got Woke and Dumped Trump," *Time*, November 1, 2021, https://time.com/6111845/woke-big-business-dumps-trump/ (accessed December 21, 2021).
14 Ibid. This assertion about age is an exaggeration because current data on top CEOs shows that their average age has increased a little over the last decade to about 58 years. Few are under 50. See Chip Cutter, "CEOs Under 50 Are a Rare Find in the S&P 500," *Wall Street Journal*, May 22, 2019, https://www.wsj.com/articles/ceos-under-50-are-a-rare-find-in-the-s-p-500-11558517401 (accessed December 31, 2021).
15 "Corporations Risk Employee Backlash by Dismissing January 6 Insurrection," *Accountable.US*, December 16, 2021, https://www.accountable.us/news/new-poll-corporations-risk-employee-backlash-by-dismissing-january-6-insurrection/ (accessed December 20, 2021).
16 Ellen Holloman and Hyungjoo Han, "How ESG and Social Movements are Affecting Corporate Governance," *LexisNexis*, https://www.lexisnexis.com/authorcenter/the-journal/b/pa/posts/how-esg-and-social-movements-are-affecting-corporate-governance (accessed January 5, 2022).
17 Ibid.
18 Ibid.
19 See Mayer, *Dark Money;* and Freeman, *Rich Thanks to Racism.*
20 A. J. Weems, J. R. Garner, K. Oshiro, and J. N. Singer, "Corporate Social Responsibility: Considerations for Sport Management in the Age of Neoliberalism," *International Journal of Exercise Science* 10 (2017): 904. I am indebted here to discussions with social scientist Anthony Weems.
21 Nancy Fraser, "Expropriation and Exploitation in Racialized Capitalism: A Reply to Michael Dawson," *Critical Historical Studies* 3 (2016): 174.
22 Center for American Progress, "Systematic Inequality and Economic Opportunity," August 7, 2019, https://www.americanprogress.org/article/-systematic-inequality-economic-opportunity/ (accessed March 29, 2022).
23 Fritz Hirschfeld, *George Washington and Slavery: A Documentary Portrayal* (Columbia: University of Missouri Press, 1997), p. 236. See also pp. 16, 37, 68–69.
24 Peter J. Parish, *Slavery: History and Historians* (New York: Harper and Row, 1989), pp. 126–132.
25 Seth Rockman, *Scraping By: Wage Labor, Slavery, and Survival in Early Baltimore* (Baltimore, MD: Johns Hopkins University Press, 2009), Kindle loc. 231–235; and Joe Feagin, *How Blacks Built America* (New York: Routledge, 2016), passim.

26 Fraser, "Expropriation and Exploitation in Racialized Capitalism," p. 174ff.
27 See Joe R. Feagin and Clairece B. Feagin, *Racial and Ethnic Relations*, 8th ed. (Upper Saddle River, NJ: Prentice-Hall, 2008), Chapters 8–11.
28 Freeman, *Rich Thanks to Racism*, p. 8. See also Nicole G. Van Cleve, *Crook County: Racism and Injustice in America's Largest Criminal Court* (Palo Alto, CA: Stanford University Press, 2016).
29 Thomas Hertz and Steven Zahniser, *Immigration and the Rural Workforce* (Washington, DC: U.S. Department of Agriculture Economic Research Service, 2013).
30 Abbie Langston, Justin Scoggins, and Matthew Walsh, *Race and the Work of the Future: Advancing Workforce Equity in the United States* (Los Angeles, CA: PolicyLink and USC Equity Research Institute, 2020), https://nationalfund. org/wp-ontent/uploads/2020/11/Race_and_the_Work_of_the_Future_ United_States_FINAL.pdf (accessed April 1, 2022).
31 Valerie Wilson, "People of Color Will Be a Majority of the American Working Class in 2032," *Economic Policy Institute*, June 9, 2016, https://www.epi. org/publication/the-changing-demographics-of-americas-working-class/ (accessed March 31, 2022).
32 Ibid.
33 William Frey, *Diversity Explosion* (Washington, DC: Brookings Institution, 2015), Kindle loc. 107.
34 Langston, Scoggins, and Walsh, *Race and the Work of the Future*, n.p.
35 C. C. Price, and K. A. Edwards, *Trends in Income from 1975 to 2018*, RAND Education and Labor Working Paper, WR-A516-1, September 2020, https:// www.rand.org/pubs/working_papers/WRA516-1.htm Italics added (accessed December 22, 2020) Italics added.
36 D. Brancaccio and D. Shin, *New RAND Study Quantifies Cost of Rising U.S. Inequality*, https://www.marketplace.org/2020/12/08/new-rand-study-quantifies-cost-of-rising-us-inequality/ (accessed December 8, 2020).
37 U.S. Census Bureau, Current Population Survey, "Real Median Household Income by Race and Hispanic Origin," 2021, https://www.census.gov/ content/dam/Census/library/visualizations/2021/demo/p60-273/figure2. pdf (accessed March 31, 2022).
38 Dedrick Asante-Muhammad, Esha Kamra, Connor Sanchez, Kathy Ramirez, and Rogelio Tec, "Racial Wealth Snapshot: Native Americans. 2022," NCRC. org, https://ncrc.org/racial-wealth-snapshot-native-americans/ (accessed March 31, 2022).
39 Neil Bhutta, Andrew C. Chang, Lisa J. Dettling, and Joanne W. Hsu, "Disparities in Wealth by Race and Ethnicity in the 2019 Survey of Consumer Finances," *The Fed*, 2020, https://www.federalreserve.gov/econres/notes/feds-notes/ disparities-in-wealth-by-race-and-ethnicity-in-the-2019-survey-of-consumer-finances-20200928.htm (accessed April 16, 2022).
40 Board of Governors, Federal Reserve System, "Distribution of Household Wealth in the U.S. since 1989," https://www.federalreserve.gov/releases/z1/ dataviz/dfa/distribute/table/#quarter:129;series:Net%20worth;demographic: networth;population:all;units:shares (accessed June 7, 2022).
41 Emmanuel Saez and Gabriel Zucman, "Letter to Senator Elizabeth Warren," https://www.warren.senate.gov/imo/media/doc/saez-zucman-wealthtax.pdf (accessed June 7, 2022).
42 Robert B. Reich, "Secession of the Successful," *New York Times*, January 20, 1991, Section 6, p. 16.
43 Ira Katznelson, *When Affirmative Action Was White: An Untold History of Racial Inequality in Twentieth-Century America* (New York: W. W. Norton, 2005),

pp. 38ff. I also draw here from Joe R. Feagin and Kimberley Ducey, *Racist America: Roots, Current Realities, and Future Reparations*, 4th ed. (New York: Routledge, 2019), Chapter 7.

44 See Feagin and Ducey, *Racist America*, Chapters 7–8.

45 Jennifer C. Mueller, "The Social Reproduction of Systemic Racial Inequality," unpublished PhD dissertation, Texas A&M University, 2013. Italics added.

46 Lawrence J. Kotlikoff and Lawrence H. Summers, "The Role of Intergenerational Transfers in Aggregate Capital Accumulation," *Journal of Political Economy* 89 (1981): 707–732.

47 Nancy DiTomaso, *The American Non-Dilemma: Racial Inequality without Racism* (New York: Russell Sage, 2013), pp. 64–66; and Nancy DiTomaso, "How Social Networks Drive Black Unemployment," *New York Times* blog, May 5, 2013, http://opinionator.blogs.nytimes.com/2013/05/05/how-social-networks-drive-Black-unemployment/?nl=today sheadlines&emc=edit_th_20130506 (accessed May 6, 2013). See also Nancy DiTomaso, "Racism and Discrimination versus Advantage and Favoritism: Bias for versus Bias against," *Research in Organizational Behavior* 35 (2015): 57–77.

48 "Voters across Demographics Support Increasing Funding for Public Schools by Wide Margins—Especially Voters of Color and Democrats," *National School Boards Action Center*, https://nsbac.org/2021-poll/ (accessed July 3, 2022).

49 Freeman, *Rich Thanks to Racism*, pp. 54–55.

50 Randolph Hohle, "The Color of Neoliberalism: The 'Modern Southern Businessman' and Post-War Alabama's Challenge to Racial Desegregation," *Sociological Forum* 27 (2012): 142–162.

51 Jamelle Bouie, "Democrats, You Can't Ignore the Culture Wars Any Longer," *New York Times*, April 22, 2022, https://www.nytimes.com/2022/04/22/opinion/red-scare-culture-wars.html (accessed April 22, 2022).

52 Freeman, *Rich Thanks to Racism*, p. 8.

53 For details, see Chun and Feagin, *Who Killed Higher Education?*

54 Tyler Kingkade and Nigel Chiwaya, *NBC News*, September 13, 2021, "Schools Facing Critical Race Theory Battles are Diversifying Rapidly, Analysis Finds," https://www.nbcnews.com/news/us-news/schools-facing-critical-race-theory-battles-are-diversifying-rapidly-analysis-n1278834 (accessed November 4, 2021).

55 Ibid.

56 David Armiak, "ALEC Claims Credit for Voter Suppression and Anti-Critical Race Theory Laws at Secret Meeting," Center for Media and Democracy, September 7, 2021, https://www.exposedbycmd.org/2021/09/07/alec-claims-credit-for-voter-suppression-and-anti-critical-race-theory-laws-at-secret-meeting/ (accessed November 29, 2021).

57 "Critical Race Theory," NAACP Legal Defense and Educational Fund, https://www.naacpldf.org/critical-race-theory-faq/ (accessed April 11, 2022).

58 I am indebted here to discussions with Texas A&M University education researcher Dr. Mimi Young. As a scholar in this area, I have never met a K-12 teacher who teaches from this legal research perspective in their classes.

59 Chris Kahn, "Many Americans Embrace Falsehoods about Critical Race Theory," *Reuters*, Summer 2021, https://www.reuters.com/world/us/many-americans-embrace-falsehoods-about-critical-race-theory-2021-07-15/ (accessed November 5, 2021).

60 Charles King, "The Fulbright Paradox: Race and the Road to a New American Internationalism," *Foreign Affairs*, July/August 2021, https://www.

foreignaffairs.com/articles/united-states/2021-06-18/fulbright-paradox (accessed June 20, 2021).

61 See Feagin and Ducey, *Racist America*.

62 Brian Lopez, "Texas Educators Want to Change 'Slavery' to 'Involuntary Relocation' after GOP Bans," *The Texas Tribune,* June 30, 2022, https://www.rawstory.com/texas-slavery/ (accessed July 3, 2022).

63 Bob Peterson, "Whitewashing Our Past: A Proposal for a National Campaign to Rethink Textbooks," Zinn Education Project, https://www.zinnedproject.org/materials/whitewashing-our-past/ (accessed September 21, 2021).

64 Mark Walsh, "If Critical Race Theory Is Banned, Are Teachers Protected by the First Amendment?" *Education Week*, https://www.edweek.org/policy-politics/does-academic-freedom-shield-teachers-as-states-take-aim-at-critical-race-theory/2021 (accessed July 25, 2021).

65 Chun and Feagin, *Who Killed Higher Education?*.

66 "Could Increased Immigration Improve the U.S. Economy?" *Knowledge@Wharton,* September 10, 2019, https://knowledge.wharton.upenn.edu/article/-us-immigration-policy/ (accessed February 9, 2021).

67 I draw here on discussions with sociologist Mark Fossett.

68 "Could Increased Immigration Improve the U.S. Economy?"

69 "Intellectual Diversity in Higher Education Act," Center for Media and Democracy, www.alecexposed.org/w/images/f/f6/2B12-Intellectual_Diversity_in_Higher_Education_Act_Exposed.pdf (accessed July 3, 2022).

70 See Joe Feagin, Hernan Vera, and Nikitah Imani, *The Agony of Education: Black Students in White Colleges and Universities* (New York: Routledge, 1996).

71 Hilary Burns, "Harvard Professor Sheds Light on the 'Hidden Curriculum' on Elite Campuses," *Boston Business Journal*, https://www.bizjournals.com/boston/news/2021/04/22/harvard-university-anthony-abraham-jack-interview.html?b=1619095870 (accessed July 3, 2022).

72 "Deep Divisions in Americans' Views of Nation's Racial History—and How to Address It," *Pew Research Center,* August 12, 2021, https://www.Pewresearch.org/politics/2021/08/12/deep-divisions-in-americans-views-of-nations-racial-history-and-how-to-address-it/ (accessed August 12, 2021).

73 Kate Shuster, "Teaching Hard History," Southern Poverty Law Center, https://www.splcenter.org/20180131/teaching-hard-history (accessed June 27, 2022).

74 See Chun and Feagin, *Who Killed Higher Education?*

75 U.S. Department of Education, National Center for Education Statistics, "The Condition of Education 2020," NCES document 2020-144.

76 Julie J. Park and Nida Denson, "Attitudes and Advocacy: Understanding Faculty Views on Racial/Ethnic Diversity," *Journal of Higher Education* 80 (2009): 415–438. DOI: 10.1080/00221546.2009.11779023.

77 Shamus Khan, *Privilege: The Making of an Adolescent Elite at St. Paul's School* (Princeton, NJ: Princeton University Press, 2010), p. 19ff.

78 "Home," *Ethnifacts*, https://www.ethnifacts.com/ (accessed September 26, 2021).

79 Ibid.

Chapter 5

Browning of America

Political Impacts

Numerous scholars and popular analysts have explained how, pressured by union and civic organizations and 1930s Great Depression economic conditions, a moderate segment of the white ruling elite shifted over time to support the new social welfare state that emerged from the 1930s–1940s New Deal era and lasted well into the 1970s. During this same period, however, many elite white conservatives were working overtly or covertly to shift the federal government away from these social welfare programs benefitting the general population.

Republican Backtracking on Civil Rights

As I explained previously, by the Richard Nixon years (1969–1974), and soon thereafter, this powerful conservative segment of the elite was expanding and working hard to roll back not only governmental reforms in regard to social welfare programs but also in regard to programs encouraging labor union organization and regulating businesses. They also sought to weaken or end the expanded federal civil rights programs. Central to this reactionary political shift was the racialized fear among elite and ordinary whites about the growing population, economic power, and political power of Americans of color, developments boosted by 1960s–1970s elimination of racist quotas in the U.S. immigration system and racial desegregation of historically white institutions.

Then, in the 1980s, the Republican Ronald Reagan administration accelerated this white rollback of desegregation and other racial justice achievements of the 1950s–1960s. In his own campaign speeches and pronouncements from the White House, Reagan often made subtle and blatant racist appeals to whites. He even began his first presidential campaign by asserting strongly the southern states' rights doctrine in Philadelphia, Mississippi, a place where whites had lynched civil rights workers in the 1960s. Once elected, at the White House, he allowed and participated in an openly racist climate there. To take just one of numerous examples,

DOI: 10.4324/9781003359883-6

Michael Deaver, a major Reagan adviser, famously had a "penchant for telling racist jokes about blacks."[1]

Reagan and his acolytes regularly collaborated with white right-wing political organizations and think tanks committed to weakening or eliminating antidiscrimination programs, affirmative action programs for Americans of color, and other government programs designed to improve conditions for those racially oppressed. Assisted and encouraged by his white conservative advisors, Reagan recruited officials from right-wing organizations in order to *weaken* federal civil rights enforcement and investigation agencies, including the important U.S. Commission on Civil Rights and the Equal Employment Opportunity Commission (EEOC). During the Reagan era, the existing civil rights laws and federal court desegregation (including affirmative action) decisions were often resisted, ignored, or weakly implemented by conservative officials in agencies that were supposed to enforce them. One moderate Republican Cabinet member, Terrel Bell, reported that at important meetings, he pressed for strong enforcement of civil rights laws, but *never* got support from other Cabinet members of the Reagan administration.[2] A rash of right-wing appointments to federal courts by the Republican administration further weakened the impact and enforcement of the civil rights laws and other antidiscrimination regulations.[3] Additionally, some federal agencies were pressed to surveil or reduce voter registration efforts and voter turnout campaigns for people of color. And toward the end of his administration, Reagan vetoed new U.S. civil rights legislation and legislation imposing economic sanctions on South Africa's white-run apartheid government. Not long thereafter, the next Republican President George H. W. Bush vetoed the important 1990 Civil Rights Act, falsely claiming it would impose "quotas" on employers and even though substantial majorities of both houses of Congress had voted for it.

Unmistakably, the Reagan administration and the follow-up George H. W. Bush administration mostly rejected prior federal commitments to end racial segregation and accelerate racial justice. The members of these two administrations typically operated out of a right-wing version of the still dominant white racial frame, and their administrative actions were thus often negative for the equality and justice interests of Americans of color. In fact, the Citizens Commission on Civil Rights concluded that President Reagan had generated "an across-the-board breakdown in the machinery constructed by six previous administrations to protect civil rights."[4] Clearly, elite and ordinary white concern about white-dominated institutions becoming too desegregated was central to backtracking on official commitments to racial desegregation and social justice. Moreover, since the Reagan era, this Republican backtracking on major racial change has moved many working-class and middle-class white voters to firm support of a more openly white supremacist Republican Party.

The Browning of U.S. Voters

Unquestionably, Americans of European descent are a decreasing percentage of the U.S. population. This demographic change is occurring in part because over the last five decades populations of color have generally had higher birth rates and in part because the end of highly racist U.S. immigration laws in the 1960s has allowed more immigrants of color. Over these decades the large-scale immigration of people of color from Latin America, Asia, Africa, and the Caribbean has changed not only the overall demographic makeup but also the character of the voting age population. A Center for American Progress report noted that

> Whites made up 69 percent of eligible voters in 2016—a figure expected to drop to 67 percent by 2020 and 59 percent by 2036. During this time period, the Hispanic population [of eligible voters] is expected to grow by 7 points—going from 12 percent in 2016 to 19 percent in 2036—while Asians and other racial groups grow...[from] 7 percent to 9 percent. The share of eligible voters who are Black will be mostly stable at around 13 percent between 2016 and 2036.[5]

As of 2020, voters of color were already more than 50 percent of eligible voters in Hawaii, New Mexico, California, and Texas, and by 2036 they are likely to be more than 40 percent of eligible voters in Nevada, Maryland, Georgia, Arizona, Alaska, Delaware, Florida, Illinois, Louisiana, Mississippi, New Jersey, New York, and Virginia. Some voting analyses indicate voters of color will be a national majority of voters by about 2052, and even earlier, by the early 2030s, a majority of younger voters.[6]

As of now, a significant majority of these voters of color opt for Democratic Party candidates at national, state, and local levels. Of course, the broad umbrella groups, such as Latina/o and Asian Americans, are politically diverse in terms of their numerous nationality subgroups. For example, in making sense of current political inclinations and voting, one needs to understand how Cuban Americans on the East Coast are more likely to vote Republican than are Mexican Americans across the Southwest. Also the backgrounds and experiences of Asian Americans vary greatly, and that too can affect their contemporary political actions. Nonetheless, significant majorities of these and other umbrella groups of color usually do vote for Democratic political candidates.

Thus, a mid-2020 Center for American Progress simulation of party majority changes by state—considering these racial-group voter effects and also generational voter effects—estimated that Michigan and Pennsylvania would likely become predictably Democratic in presidential elections by November 2020, which did in fact happen. They also estimated that by the late 2020s, Florida, Arizona, Ohio, Texas, Wisconsin, Georgia, and

North Carolina would be added to that Democratic Party column.[7] Substantial AP/Votecast data indicated that in the 2020 election the Democrat Joe Biden actually won seven states because a majority of his voters there were people of color—Wisconsin, Pennsylvania, Michigan, Virginia, Arizona, Nevada, and Georgia. He won the last three of these because of an increased number of these voters of color compared to previous elections. Overall he won 7,060,140 more votes nationally than did his Republican opponent Donald Trump.[8]

One major reason for this political trend favoring Democrats is the increasing Latina/o vote. In 2020, Biden won nearly two-thirds of that vote, although this varied by state. He got 69 percent of that vote in California and 62 percent in Texas, but only 54 percent in Florida. Substantial Latina/o majorities also voted for Democratic candidates down the ballot.[9] One reason for these voters' attraction to the Democratic Party is its generally more positive orientation to Latin American immigrants. For example, one policy report commissioned by the Justice Democrats organization examined survey data and found that 85 percent of Democratic primary voters supported a government path to citizenship for undocumented immigrants. The report also concluded that more progressive Democratic Party leadership on immigration and other liberal policy issues would not alienate the diverse and mostly progressive Democratic Party voters, but would likely increase the political clout of the Democratic Party.[10]

Underlying this voter pattern, now and in the likely future, is the significant growth in the Latina/o population, which as of 2021 was already a fifth of the country's total population. Social scientist Michael Rodriguez-Muniz has examined the views of leaders in the National Hispanic Leadership Agenda association, a nonpartisan organization working on government policy issues affecting their fast growing communities. He analyzes well beyond the heavy emphasis in most popular and social science analyses on how *whites* view these population and political changes. As he emphasizes,

> Political actors from minoritized groups are also bringing ethnoracial futures to bear on the present, in the process shaping contemporary politics and identities. It is important to take stock of how these projects and movements have also envisioned, mobilized, and pursued ethnoracial futures.[11]

He found that these Latina/o leaders generally frame their population "as a population of the future, one perpetually on the rise."[12]

One optimistic Latina civil rights leader made this point well:

> We are strong. Because progress is recognizing our potential at the voting booth. Eighty percent of Latinos who register vote.... The

mean age of the [new] Latino voter is eighteen years old. That is progress. Because when we come together as a community, when we're running young candidates, when we're setting ourselves high into the office of the president, when we are making sure that we are executives and mobilizing each other, uplifting each other like we did in Tornillo [Texas], we're unstoppable.[13]

Political Impacts of Geographical Dispersion

Another major factor affecting U.S. politics now and in the future is the geographical distribution and redistribution of Americans of color. This includes the recent and continuing migration of many Americans of color to areas where they once had relatively small populations, such as to states in the Southwest and Mountain West, which will probably continue the political liberalization there. In addition, the states of the old South are seeing more people move there from other regions than any other region. They have many of the country's fastest-growing cities and counties, and a third of the U.S. population. Much of that growth is in Black, Latina/o, and Asian American communities.

In recent decades, major Black migration *back* to the South, hundreds of thousands of people, has been significantly motivated by the economic growth there, especially in large cities like Atlanta, Houston, Dallas, and Miami. As a result, states like Florida and Texas have seen considerable growth in Black voters, and now have the second and third largest Black state populations (after New York) in the country. More than half of all Black Americans now live in the South, and that half is still growing. Cultural traditions, family ties, and much improved civil rights conditions compared to the harsh Jim Crow decades have played a role in making the new South and its changing economy more attractive. Indeed, without the sharply improved racial conditions, these southern areas would likely be in overall economic decline.[14] Actually, the five most residentially segregated U.S. metropolitan areas are now in the North, while the most residentially desegregated metropolitan areas are in the South and Southwest. Numerous southern and southwestern states are also seeing major growth in their Latina/o American and Asian American populations, with both internal and international migrants there mostly seeking better economic opportunities. Because of these shifts in migration patterns, most of the 3,100 U.S. counties have become less white in recent decades, thereby increasing the number with a minority white population.[15]

These in-migrations of people of color, together with frequent out-migrations of whites, are affecting the geographical distribution of Democratic and Republican voters, with their respective political impacts at local and state levels. In recent decades, we have seen that a growing dispersion of Democratic Party voters, often outward from older big city centers, is increasing Democratic power in many once Republican dominated areas. In the 2000s so far,

> All around the country, counties that experienced in-migration saw increases in Democratic vote share… and places experiencing out-migration saw increases in the Republican vote share. These in-migration counties that trended Democratic were mostly suburban, and the out-migration counties that moved toward the Republicans were both urban core and rural counties.[16]

Many examples of Democratic voter impacts can be seen in southern and southwestern states, including once bright-red Texas, Georgia, and Arizona. A white Democrat won an Alabama Senate seat in 2017, and Democrats had close or winning 2018–2019 political campaigns in Texas, Georgia, Florida, Kentucky, Louisiana, and Virginia. Numerous southern cities with growing populations of color have seen major Democratic victories, including elections of Black mayors in big cities like Houston, Dallas, and Atlanta.[17] As noted previously, the 2020 Democratic candidate Joe Biden won the major southern states of Virginia and Georgia substantially thanks to these voters of color. In addition, two liberal Democratic senators were elected in Georgia at that time. An optimistic aide to southern political activist Stacey Abrams has underscored the point that "In the South of the future, it will be voters of color supported by white voters, not the other way around."[18]

Indeed, another population dispersion tends to favor the Democratic Party—the development of new high tech industries in currently Republican-dominated states, including in the Midwest and Southwest. Such high tech development brings in many well-educated workers and their families, both white and nonwhite, with a majority often supporting the Democratic Party in state and national elections.[19] Considering these various population trends all together, where Republicans currently control the electoral redistricting constitutionally necessitated by the U.S. censuses indicating population change, and engage in gerrymandering or other suppression, the process of progressive political change from population growth or redistribution will be slowed, but eventually will have major political consequences usually favoring the Democratic Party.

In future decades, numerous historically white geographical areas and political organizations and institutions will experience much more racial diversification as people of color enter them and get greater political participation in them. As a result, it is likely that the Democratic Party will eventually become the dominant political party nationally and even in numerous now Republican-controlled states, although these changes may be significantly delayed by increased voter suppression in those Republican-controlled states.

Generational Diversity and Change: Voting Impacts

Another critical factor in current and future voting is the age composition of voters. Until relatively recently, most voters were Baby Boomers or members of the yet older Silent Generation, but in the 2020 election, the majority were in the younger Gen-X, Millennial, and Gen-Z generations. By about 2024, the Millennial and Gen-Z generations will be a larger percentage of eligible voters than the famous Baby Boom generation. A Brookings Institution report has underscored the diversity of these voters: "Younger, incoming generations of Americans are much more racially diverse than prior generations. As they come of voting age, they will slowly but surely alter the makeup of the electorate."[20] Most of this change will be from growth in Latina/o and Asian American voters.

One 2020 report by the Center for American Progress concluded that Millennial and Gen-Z voters are considerably more inclined to vote for Democratic candidates than earlier generations were when they were that young. Current data also suggests they will be more likely to *stay* Democrats as they age. The old adage "liberal when young, conservative when old" may not play out for these younger generations.[21] Additionally, a Democracy Fund Voter Study Group did surveys between 2011 and 2019 and found that the Millennial generation is "far more liberal than any generation before it, in part because it is more racially diverse, but also because millennial whites are just more liberal than their parents." Over those 2011–2019 years, the percentage of them inclined to vote Democratic did *not* decline.[22]

Other studies have found similar effects for the youngest segment of Gen-Z. The NBC 2020 presidential election exit polls indicated that two-thirds of voters aged 18–24 voted for Democratic candidate Joe Biden, and their turnout numbers apparently set a record. About half of these voters are nonwhite. One Gen-Z voter suggested why: "The issues that my age group and I most care about are issues that include immigration, reproductive rights, climate change, health care, unemployment among so many others."[23] They are very worried about their own future, their communities' future, and the country's and planet's future, seemingly more so than older generations. Clearly, a majority of them were not attracted to 2020 Republican candidate Donald Trump's views on the public policy issues they view as greatly affecting their personal and family futures. In November 2020, the total Gen-Z group's Democratic-Republican presidential split was by far the most Democratic of any generational group.

In spring 2021, the Harvard Youth poll found that 62 percent of those aged 18 to 29 (Gen-Z/younger Millennials) reported they had voted for Joe Biden in the previous November. Importantly too, this poll revealed a major racial split within this Gen-Z/younger Millennial group. A bare majority, 51 percent, of these younger whites said they voted for Biden, as compared with 85 percent of younger Blacks and 72 percent of younger Latina/os.[24] However, the voter exit polls during the actual November 2020 election showed a rather different racial split in this same young voter group. NBC News exit polls found that, as with older white generations, some 53 percent of the white Gen-Z and younger Millennial (18-to-29-year-old) voters said they had just marked ballots for Donald Trump, with only 44 percent saying they did that for Biden. As with the later Harvard survey a few months later, these exit polls did show that younger Black and Latina/o voters, 89 percent and 69 percent respectively, had just voted overwhelmingly for Joe Biden.[25]

Some polling analysts, such as Harvard's survey expert John Della Volpe, are optimistic about these younger white voters being significantly more progressive than their white elders and as likely staying more politically progressive as they become more politically powerful over coming decades. Yet his 2021 Harvard poll result for them (majority for Biden) is contradicted by the earlier exit polls of white voters done right after the 2020 election (majority for Trump). It may be that Harvard's months-later national survey of young white voters reflects social desirability effects—that is, some of those surveyed decided to claim they had voted for the election winner. Or perhaps they could just be misrepresenting how they voted in November 2020, given the violent insurrection of Trump supporters that occurred not long before the spring 2021 poll. Possibly too, some of these youth may not have actually voted, as this was a later general survey and not an immediate poll exit survey. Still, both the Harvard data and the NBC data on these younger white voters, when compared to exit poll data for older whites, do show that the former were significantly *less* likely to vote for the white nationalist Republican Donald Trump.

Younger White Generations: Superficial Liberalism?

Another piece of relatively good news for a future progressive multiracial America is that the younger generations of Americans, the Gen-Zers and Millennials, are the least conservative generations on an array of political, economic, and racial issues. They are the least likely to view right-wing cable and other news media on a regular basis. (Currently, only 20 percent of Fox News viewers are under 55 years old, and 92 percent are white.) Few participated in the January 2021 Capitol insurrection. As I noted previously, most people who did participate in that violent insurrection were middle-aged and older whites. Moreover, millions of younger Americans, white and especially nonwhite, have participated disproportionately in hundreds of Black Lives Matter (BLM) and similar protests against police malpractice and other systemic racism (see Chapter 6).[26]

We know from a major PEW Research Center survey that as a group the young Gen-Zers are similar to Millennials in being generally more politically progressive and supportive of government problem-solving than the older generations. They are also more likely to reject the notion that the U.S. is superior to all other nations. Like Millennials, two-thirds of Gen-Zers view Black Americans as suffering more discrimination than whites. And like Millennials, about six in ten approve of athletes kneeling in protest against racism, and they tend to look favorably on the country's growing racial and ethnic diversity. Also like Millennials, six in ten who are registered to vote favor the Democratic Party, while those identifying as Republican tend to be more moderate than Republican identifiers in other generations. In addition, another PEW survey found, like other surveys, that Gen-Z is the most racially diverse of completed U.S. generations, with just 52 percent being white, 25 percent Hispanic, 14 percent Black, 6 percent Asian, and the rest multiracial or some other racial group.[27] They are also likely to be the best educated U.S. generation by the time they finish their formal educations, and they are the most proficient of the generations in using social media.

In analyzing white racism, however, social psychologist Jennifer Richeson has pointed out the problem of optimistically assuming what she calls the generational fallacy, that *major* change in U.S. racism will necessarily take place as older racist whites are replaced by "enlightened younger people."[28] For one thing, there are certain category exceptions favoring older generations. For instance, one 2004–2005 survey of 35,580 faculty at 414 colleges and universities found that faculty support and advocacy for student racial diversity on campus was stronger among older faculty (presumably Baby Boomers and the Silent Generation) than younger faculty (presumably the Gen-Xers and the Millennials), possibly because some of these older faculty had been influenced by civil rights protest movements of the 1960s–1970s when they began their careers.[29]

Then there is the question of how strong younger whites' commitment to major racial change actually is? Research on the views of the youngest white generations indicates that, beyond their relatively liberal attitudes expressed in rather brief and often superficial surveys on racial issues, most are almost as conservative as their white parental generations in the critical area of supporting or pressing for major government action to bring real changes in historically white institutions, especially changes that would negatively affect their own white racial privileges, power, or wealth.

For example, several research studies indicate that most whites in all age groups do not support substantial material reparations for African Americans and other Americans of color for historical oppressions if that endangers their own individual or family's material circumstances in this still racially inegalitarian society. A survey of white Millennials in the Cooperative Congressional Election Study found they did have antiracist views on certain matters such as police brutality, yet they also have problematical views on other racial and class issues. That is, these white Millennials were

> no more likely than older whites to acknowledge that their racial identity is associated with certain advantages even though factual research shows that whites enjoy greater wealth, better health outcomes, and greater employment opportunities, and better treatment in the criminal justice system.[30]

Most of these younger whites also felt "that hard work is all it takes to be wealthy." They did not see, or did not want to see, the massive system of unequal racial privilege and power that whites in all current generations have in society.

In another major research study, sociologists Jennifer Mueller and DyAnna Washington analyzed an assignment given to young college students, asking them to study in detail the histories of wealth and privilege transmission over their own families' generations. They found that the important racial privilege insights gained by the white students in this class project did give them significant insights into how systemic racism worked and their role in that racism, but at that same time most showed little support of changing the racial status quo.[31] These young whites' apathy about significantly *changing* the systemic racism they observed in their intergenerational family histories sustains their own privileged material condition and, thus, the country's persisting racial inequality. Even a semester's worth of excellent education on systemic racism could not bring a perspectival shift toward making major racial changes for most of these younger white Americans.

Note too that much social science evidence suggests that younger Americans, and especially younger whites, still accent the phenotype ("racial look") of people in deciding their own and others' racial identities. As in the past, the process and reality of contemporary racialization still accents this personal phenotype in making specific racial identifications and in everyday interracial behavior linked to that identification. The younger white generations are not currently operating beyond this society's dominant white racial framing to any great degree.[32] We might also note that, though small in number, a very disproportionate percentage of the mass shooters in recent decades have been young white men, often with strong white supremacist views.[33]

Liberal White Democrats and Multiracial Coalitions

Generally speaking, the browning of American voters likely means a shift to the left in U.S. voting patterns. Even so, in most elections Democratic

Party candidates will need a multiracial voter coalition to win, one including numerous more liberal whites. This was demonstrably the case for the significant 2020 presidential electoral win by Joe Biden, one where exit polls showed a sizeable but still minority (42 percent) of white voters opting for him. Keeping this minority of white voters is critical for the Democratic Party as it tries to keep together a progressive multiracial voting coalition. That is, while Democrats will likely have continuing numerical advantages in the popular votes in future national elections, their victories in the undemocratic Electoral College "will likely require some combination of intensifying their support among voters of color and improving their margins among white, particularly white noncollege-educated, voters."[34]

Interestingly, an analysis by Drew Engelhardt of American National Election Studies surveys of whites found that their political "partisanship and racial attitudes are becoming increasingly aligned, and this is more a product of attitude change than shifting partisan attachments."[35] That is, many whites are changing their racial attitudes to fit their already-chosen political party, including in a significantly liberal direction for white Democrats in the most recent decade. Moreover, the fact that whites in the Democratic Party increasingly view African Americans positively has "profound implications for future political and policy contests."[36] Although the Democratic Party once had major internal divisions on racial matters, more recent white attitudinal changes "have reduced the degree to which racial concerns separate them from their co-partisans of color ... [and] may even serve to unite them, especially when juxtaposed with positions the Republican Party takes."[37]

Similarly, political scientist Cristina Beltrán cites data that demonstrate this liberalization of racial views among white Democrats, liberalization that has thereby increased the chasm within white communities between those inclined to overtly white supremacist views and those opposed to such blatantly racist views. In her view, declining numbers of whites now openly "embrace an ideology of whiteness and white democracy."[38] Optimistic about the less racist white minority in white communities, she suggests that

> Across the nation, white Americans have been engaging in what has been described as a "wave of self-examination" that has included reading books about racism and anti-racism, watching films and documentaries about African American history, researching their ancestry to learn about family connections to slavery, discussing anti-Black racism and white privilege with nonwhite friends and colleagues, and arguing with family members.[39]

Nonetheless, even with the more liberal white minority's interest in these contemporary racial justice issues, one has to keep in mind that most of

them are part of a substantial majority of white Americans who still frequently operate out of a strong white racial framing of society—especially
in regard to its central white virtuousness subframe (see Chapter 1). This is
obvious when they are asked explicitly about their views on such matters
as strong anti-discrimination enforcement programs or material reparations for racial oppression that might mean significant costs for them or
their families. That white majority does *not* support such powerful redres-
sive actions.[40]

Nonwhite Voter Impacts: Democratizing U.S. Politics

As the racial composition of the U.S. voting population changes, and
even with increased Republican attempts to limit that voting (see below),
its democratizing and other positive impacts are obvious and increasing.
For example, in the 2008 presidential election, American voters selected
the first ever president of color. In that election one-quarter of voters
were people of color, and a substantial majority gave their votes to Barack
Obama. As he ended his two-term presidency in 2016, President Obama
commented on the importance of his election in signaling the inevitabil-
ity of Americans of color gaining ever more political power: "A President
who looked like me was inevitable at some point in American history," he
emphasized. And then he added:

> It might have been somebody named Gonzales instead of Obama, but
> it was coming. And I probably showed up 20 years sooner than the de-
> mographics would have anticipated. And, in that sense, it was a little
> bit more surprising. The country had to do more adjusting and pro-
> cessing of it. It undoubtedly created more anxiety than it will twenty
> years from now, provoked more reactions in some portion of the pop-
> ulation than it will 20 years from now. And that's understandable.[41]

Moreover, when asked about the racist incidents and upheaval before
and after the 2016 presidential election of a racially reactionary Donald
Trump, Obama was quite optimistic: "You don't start worrying about
apocalypse. You say, O.K., where are the places where I can push to keep
it moving forward."[42] The significance of voters of color in that 2016 election can be seen in the fact that they constituted about 29 percent of all
voters, an increase from the previous election and again with most voting
for the Democratic Party candidate. That candidate, Hillary Clinton, was
also pathbreaking as the first female presidential candidate of a major U.S.
party, and she actually *won* a significant majority of voters nationally.[43]

As voting majorities change from majority white, we can expect
more politicians, including whites, to pay increased attention to the

socio-political concerns and needs of these voters of color. Recall from the Introduction that in her speeches during her 2016 presidential campaign and also in her Democratic convention speech, presidential candidate Hillary Clinton insisted this country needs to end racism: "Let's put ourselves in the shoes of young Black and Latino men and women who face the effects of systemic racism, and are made to feel like their lives are disposable."[44] In stark contrast, during that election year and ever since, a majority of Republican politicians have taken the opposite tack and instead appealed to conservative white voters with aggressive opposition to accurate teaching about the country's systemic racism in K–12 schools and in colleges and universities.

Nonwhite Voter Impacts: Local, State, Federal Policies

Already, too, increased racial diversity among voters has had major impacts on decisionmaking in an array of government settings, including in numerous local, state, or federal legislatures. Unsurprisingly, we are seeing progressive changes in these governments' policy priorities. For instance, voters and legislators of color have sought, often successfully, much better enforcement of civil rights laws and the creation or enforcement of laws supportive of immigrants of color.[45] As voting majorities change in a significantly less white and more multiracial direction in yet more areas, we will probably observe fewer white politicians opposing antidiscrimination laws, seeking to ban books and teaching about the U.S. racism targeting Americans of color, or pressing for laws restricting Latin American and Asian immigration.

As I showed previously, the nonwhite-white voter gap is overlaid with an age and generational gap, and this will become wider over time with the relatively faster growth of youth of color (e.g., Latina/o and Asian Americans). Demographer Bill Frey has summarized some of these age-related impacts: Nonwhite Americans are especially "interested in good schools, affordable housing, and greater employment opportunities, while the latter [whites] are concerned about preserving their retirement incomes and covering future medical costs."[46] At the local, state, and national government levels, we will probably see more political conflict between the disproportionately younger voters of color seeking greater legislative representation and more family support services (e.g., employment, education) and the disproportionately older white voters who continue to fight to keep certain government programs for these nonwhite Americans poorly funded but certain programs for themselves (e.g., Social Security, Medicare) well-funded. The latter will also seek to keep their local, state, and federal taxes down. In this way they attempt to preserve whites' economic and political interests and power. However, one might wonder whether workers of color will, in turn, challenge the economic and social reality of having to support many elderly whites (e.g., by paying into programs like Social Security whites now disproportionately benefit from) who have long maintained societal patterns of discrimination targeting people of color.

If the U.S. political system remains significantly democratic, voters of color will certainly strive for much greater input into political decisionmaking and for fairer representation in local, state, and federal government legislatures and agencies. Most voters of color have a different perspective on these political changes than most whites. They generally see such changes as very important and democratizing. Indeed, we already see the political results in our largest 100 cities, where the numbers of voters of color have been growing, often dramatically, in recent decades. In these large cities the white male percentage of city elective offices has been declining, to the point that in the year 2020 their percentage was substantially less than half, at just 36 percent in these cities. This indicates the growing numbers of candidates of color being elected in the majority of these cities—from Riverside, California, to Richmond, Virginia, over the past few decades.[47]

The prominent political analyst, Chauncey DeVega, has examined the browning of America from the viewpoints of Americans of color and accented the progressive policy changes that this demographic shift does and should bring to the U.S. He has noted that

> Black Americans and other people of color have only wanted full and equal rights with white Americans. For example, from the Civil War to the great experiment in democracy that was the Reconstruction, Black Americans worked very hard to expand opportunities for all people, including poor and working class whites. This dynamic continues into the present where public opinion polls show that Black and brown Americans consistently support policies which would expand the social safety net, civil rights and economic justice and opportunity for the average American—on both sides of the color line. Black and brown people are also on the frontlines of saving American democracy from the fascism and authoritarianism of Donald Trump and the Republican Party.[48]

Significantly, too, some government decisions by conservative white politicians who are fearful of these population and voting majority changes have already cost *them* and their own interests dearly in political and monetary terms. For example, after the 2020 Census, several Republican-controlled states in the Sunbelt did *not* get the extra congressional seats they expected because of intentional decisions by right-wing Republican officials there not to do effective Census-taking efforts in regard to correctly counting Americans of color, especially Latina/os in the states of Texas, Arizona, and Florida. As a result, these states each got one fewer member of Congress than expected. In contrast, states with effective Census outreach campaigns such as California, where population losses had been expected, did not lose as many congressional seats as expected. Republican-controlled states without aggressive Census campaigns—and thus getting lower than expected population counts—have also lost the important federal funding that usually accompanies increased Census population counts.[49]

A contrasting state-level impact of increases in residents of color can be seen in the much greater attention given to them by Democratic Party activists in other states. In California, for example, the substantial increase in voters of color there over recent decades helped to shift the state government from one periodically dominated by very conservative white Republicans to one now regularly dominated by moderate and progressive Democrats from various racial groups (see Chapter 6).

Are Republicans Losing Younger and Well-Educated Voters?

Since 1968, a majority of white voters have voted for Republican presidential candidates, candidates more politically conservative that those of the Democratic Party. Unsurprisingly, over these decades moderate Republican leaders have worried openly that in future this white voter majority will not be enough to win national elections. Indeed, several Republican Party reports have called on the Party to more aggressively seek out the growing number of voters of color. One important report concluded that "Unless the RNC gets serious about tackling this problem, we will lose future elections."[50]

In achieving such an elections goal, Republican leaders also face generational and educational problems. We saw earlier the strong tendency for majorities of younger voters, especially those in the Millennial and Gen-Z generations, to opt for Democratic Party candidates. In addition, a recent PEW Research Center survey found a generational issue within the Republican Party—that younger Republicans are more likely than their elders to be moderate politically and to view climate change and racism as serious societal problems needing to be addressed.[51] That is, their expressed views are not fully in sync with those of most current Republican legislators. Another issue is the impact of increasing education levels. A Center for American Progress report on future U.S. politics examined demographic and voter data and suggested that Republicans will likely have a difficult path to political victory as we move into the late 2020s and beyond. That is, future Republican political success will necessitate "mobilizing their strength among whites without college educations—a still-substantial but shrinking portion of the electorate—while attaining gains among at least some growing demographic groups."[52] In the 2020 election, there was a significant difference between white voters with college degrees (49 percent for Trump) and white voters without college degrees (64 percent for Trump).[53] Generally, as education increases white voters are more likely to be politically liberal. Current educational trends tend to disfavor the less liberal Republican Party.

Additionally, even with the anti-immigrant politics of Donald Trump and other leading Republican politicians, a PEW Research Center survey during Trump's presidential term found that 81 percent of Americans with graduate degrees, and 70 percent of college graduates, agreed with the vague statement that an "increasing number of people of many different races, ethnic groups and nationalities makes the U.S. a better place to live."[54] In contrast, among Americans with a high school degree or less, just 45 percent had such a positive view of this growing diversity. The majority of this latter group who were *positive* about this trend were likely respondents of color.

Generally, in the contemporary Republican Party, one finds a substantial majority that still believe hardcore misinformation about nonwhite immigration and replacement. One recent national poll asked respondents if they agree or disagree with this statement: "The Democratic Party is trying to replace the current electorate with voters from poorer countries around the world." Some 66 percent of Republican respondents agreed with this false conspiratorial idea, as compared with just 12 percent of Democrats. In terms of racial groups, whites had the largest percentage who agreed with it.[55] Interestingly too, this white nationalistic emphasis that voters of color are replacing white voters, a version of the "great replacement theory" discussed earlier, actually made less sense in explaining the Republican Party loss in the 2020 presidential election. In that election Donald Trump lost in part because he lost some *white* voters, especially in suburbia, that he had won before. He lost some college-educated white voters, and possibly others increasingly discontented with his extreme nativistic and nationalistic rhetoric. As political commentator Nate Cohn has pointed out, it is hard to view his 2020 loss as just a "great replacement" phenomenon because Trump "could have won in 2020 if only he had done as well among white voters as he did in 2016."[56]

Persisting Elite White Control: Undemocratic Political Institutions

White male dominance over the U.S. political system has been the societal reality for centuries. Over the first seven decades of the 20th century we saw that major political rights changes for people of color and for women of all backgrounds did occur, yet those changes had only modest impacts

on who actually rules at the top of U.S. society. Since 1790, all U.S. presidents but one have been elite white men. All speakers of the U.S. House
but one have been elite white men, as have all Senate majority leaders.
Today white men make up only about 29 percent of the adult population,
but hold 58 percent of the voting positions in the U.S. House and 67 percent of those in the Senate. House and Senate staffers are overwhelmingly
white, with most senior staffers being white men. White men are the
large majority of other important elected officials, including governors
and other statewide officials, major county officials, and sheriffs. Two major reasons for this white male dominance are that incumbent officials (i.e.,
usually white men) beat most challengers and that the Republican Party
puts up few candidates of color.[57]

Indeed, the U.S. has *never* been a real democracy. It has a substantially
undemocratic Constitution made only by white male slaveholders and other
elite white men, a document originally written with numerous provisions
protecting the slavery system. This U.S. Constitution still includes a Senate
elected by geography and not just voters, an undemocratic Electoral College
biased toward small-state Americans, and an unelected Supreme Court with
lifetime membership. Numerous members of the original Constitutional
Convention did not trust ordinary (then only white male) American voters
and made sure the Constitution had a white upper-class bias. The weaknesses have been clear in recent elections, including 2000 and 2016 when
the Republican Party lost the popular vote but still won the Electoral College and presidency. As one *New York Times* journalist noted, "Republicans
in the Senate haven't represented a majority of Americans since the 1990s,
yet they've controlled the chamber for roughly half of the past 20 years."[58]
Other counter-majoritarian problems include the Senate filibuster rule that
gives a minority of Senators (41 percent) the ability to block even legislation
popular among a substantial majority of the U.S. population. Much of our
current political framework clearly provides "a set of Americans who have
taken strongly to conservative ideology—rural [white] voters in sparsely
populated states in the middle of the country—more power than the rest of
the electorate."[59] These issues are made worse by the significant growth of
populations of color outside of these substantially rural states. Multiracial
democracy will, ultimately, require major changes in the structure of this
centuries-old essentially undemocratic political system.

In addition, today as in the past, major U.S. political and economic
institutions remain closely linked and integrated. The country's mostly
white economic elite substantially funds major politicians and their political campaigns, and thereby shapes many of their major policy decisions.
As the scholar Aaron Pacitti has noted, the economic elite's capture of
U.S. politics has long been routine, and that capture operates throughout
all major political institutions. Their business and other economic interests
continue to

dominate the staffing of key government agencies and create policies that directly benefit their firms and financial interests at the expense of everyone else. Government policy is created and used to increase the wealth of the elite, to the detriment of the average person and the U.S. economy as whole.[60]

Given their shaping and control of long-established political institutions, unsurprisingly, the elite white powerholders have great influence over the crafting and recrafting, circulation and recirculation, of this country's dominant framing of societal matters—including the dominant white racial frame, male sexist frame, and capitalist class frame. They ably adapt these and other major perspectival frames to new societal circumstances such as those of the currently changing racial demographics and shifting voting groups. The mostly white decisionmakers at the head of most powerful frame-manipulating institutions, including the major cable media and social media discussed in Chapter 3, often reframe important societal matters to maintain their political and economic control. Generally speaking, elite white men are the most influential elite group shaping and imposing class, racial, and gender statuses and identities on all Americans, historically and in the present. They have substantially controlled who gets identity-based capital such as W.E.B. du Bois's "public and psychological wage of whiteness" or the related public and psychological wages of advantaged class status and advantaged maleness in the gender system.

Of course, this dominant elite has factions that shift over time. Various factions of that white elite benefit from, even create, major societal crises to which they then provide their own political-economic solutions. Examples include the moderate/liberal faction that emphasizes and implements a moderate/liberal politics (e.g., in the 1930s New Deal) era or the far-right faction that emphasizes and implements very conservative politics in times of major national crisis and change (e.g., in the contemporary era since the 1980s). In such crisis periods, and generally, these elite white factions consciously mobilize powerful class, racial, and gender statuses and identities, and associated power and privilege, to facilitate their particular goals and politics of elite domination in U.S. society.

This country's ruling white elite is unlikely to allow major changes in their elite political control any time soon. Indeed, they cultivate an often militant white base that persists in fighting the elite's political battles. Collective white violence remains a constant political threat in near and distant future decades. The elite can sustain its power with nonviolent means or, if necessary, allow or encourage violent supporters to the forefront yet again, as in the January 6, 2021, U.S. insurrection at the national Capitol (see Chapter 6).

Recurring Political Legitimation Crises: The White Elite

The rapid browning of America has created, and will likely continue to create, recurring problems of political legitimacy for white-dominated federal, state, and local governments. Numerous social science analysts have argued that under capitalism the federal government (often termed the "state") regularly faces *legitimation crises* because it cannot protect well the political-economic needs of the small capitalist class and also the political-economic and other social needs of the rest of society, especially those of the majority that is working class and middle class. As the prominent European sociologist Jurgen Habermas has argued, the "exercise of the state's power within the social system" centrally involves "the shielding of the market mechanism from self-destructive side effects."[61] He has in mind pressures arising from periodically declining economic conditions for working and middle class workers in Western capitalistic societies.

However, like most European Marxist analysts, Habermas does not take into account that major questioning of the legitimacy of federal governments like that of the U.S. also comes from other oppressed segments of society, especially from those long oppressed by systemic racism or sexism. As U.S. social scientist Michael Dawson points out, the three societal systems of class, racial, and gender oppression have different societal logics that often come into conflict. For instance, if the substantial white proportion of society "believes that the state is undermining its traditional support for a white supremacist racial order, then the state will be perceived as increasingly illegitimate and can rapidly edge toward crisis."[62] That is, those societally classified as fully human and white, even if a class-oppressed white working or middle class, have been provided with much racial privilege (the public and psychological wage of whiteness) by elite whites who have historically controlled U.S. society. Indeed, ordinary whites have periodically demonstrated how angry they can get if their racial status and privilege are significantly threatened, as they sometimes are under government-supported racial desegregation programs or government-facilitated democratic political change. We saw an example of this at the January 2021 Capitol insurrection, a mostly white violent event that signaled a legitimation crisis for the contemporary U.S. political elite.

Certainly, the powerful white elite has profited greatly from maintaining a major societal division between ordinary whites and the oppressed racial groups "whose labor, property, and bodies could be subject to expropriation, exploitation, and violation without recourse to (particularly civic/political) resources available to those classified as fully human."[63] By racially dividing white and nonwhite Americans over the centuries, the white American elite has been able to implement a violent colonizing and oppression of people of color on several continents, including

Native Americans and African Americans in North America. Periodically, the legitimacy of this elite-run system of white-on-others oppression has been challenged, sometimes successfully, by Americans of color seeking humanistic liberation from the racialized exploitation of their labor and lands. Over the long course of U.S. history, we have seen many rebellions by Americans of color, including organized Native American resistance and Black slave rebellions and nonviolent civil rights movements.

Indeed, the partially successful 1960s civil rights efforts by African Americans and other Americans of color resulted in dramatic increases in federal voting protections and in accelerated registration of voters of color. Soon, however, these important democratizing changes in state and federal governments were met with reactionary political actions by the right-wing of the white elite and their supporters in the majority of ordinary whites. In their turn, they were questioning the legitimacy of the new more democratic governing. Their reaction included the 1960s development by Republican leaders of the "southern strategy" discussed previously, one designed to attract white voters using aggressive racist appeals.

This successful Republican political effort has substantially increased right-wing political power at the local, state, and federal government levels. Ironically, the ensuing Republican neoliberalist governing of recent decades has resulted in major cutbacks not only in taxes and regulations for rich elite Americans but also in social support programs benefitting ordinary Americans, including formerly privileged white workers and their families. Unsurprisingly, the latter whites have increasingly protested the decline in government support programs that once better assisted their family lives, although in their white racist framing of the cutbacks they have often blamed Americans of color. Of course, that major government program decline has also resulted in negative reactions from nonwhite Americans who, only relatively recently, have seen their family lives significantly improved by more egalitarian social programs.

Beginning in the 1970s, these white neoliberal government retrenchments and associated white racist governing have brought on decades of economic and other social problems for ordinary white and nonwhite Americans and thereby created *multiple* legitimation crises for a still mostly white-run U.S. government. As Dawson underscores,

> The deepness, pervasiveness, and perverseness of the current crisis in the United States indicates that the state cannot reconcile deep losses of legitimacy within multiple populations that have conflicting interests and ideologies. Blacks and Latinos ... are becoming increasingly disillusioned and angry due to the escalation of white supremacy within the United States. Conservative white men, because of their material and psychological reliance on hierarchies of race and gender, fear the loss of the privileges that they regard as their right.[64]

These significant socioeconomic and racial problems regularly create a difficult if not impossible political situation for the white-elite-run federal government—major legitimation crises from several oppositional social sectors at the same time. As these crises grow, they create more societal protest, violence, and social chaos. Certainly, there are opportunities for some capitalistic entrepreneurs to profit in such chaotic situations if they do not endanger the political-economic foundation of the society. However, in order for the capitalistic class as a whole to make substantial and continuing profits, top federal government officials are tasked with the critical job of keeping the societal peace—that is, keeping the corporate-tilted government legitimate, the stock market happy, and the dollar internationally stable. If spreading and repeated over time, large-scale social disorder such as the January 2021 Capitol insurrection is highly destructive for a profitable capitalist economy, as well as for the society generally.

Continuing Republican Suppression of Voters of Color

Suppression of Black voters by a white-run Democratic Party before the 1960s desegregation era, and by a white-run Republican Party since that desegregation era, have been *central* to U.S. political history. Since that desegregation era, in many geographical areas the Republican response to the browning of America has been to keep the population actually voting as white as possible, including by means of aggressively antidemocratic political strategies. Even the long-serving Chief Justice of the Supreme Court (1986–2005), William Rehnquist, openly admitted that he had worked to reduce the number of Black and Latina/o voters when he was a young white Republican operative in Arizona during those early desegregation decades. In addition, white Republican think-tank founders and their wealthy white funders have worked aggressively since the desegregating 1960s to reduce voters of color. A white co-founder of the now far-right Heritage Foundation once said "I don't want everybody to vote … our leverage in the elections quite candidly goes up as the voting populace goes down."[65]

Today, many Republican Party officials and voters are very concerned that the Party has *not* secured a popular vote majority in seven of the last eight U.S. presidential elections. Political analyst Kathleen Frydl has noted that "In an age when so much power is vested in the executive, the inability to run competitively for the White House will be a punishing blow to the Republican Party."[66] She further notes that the U.S. has always had one major political party that openly featured white power and privilege as a central societal goal, and in recent decades that has been the Republican Party. Unsurprisingly, because of this white orientation, Republican voters professing the overt racism of pro-insurrectionists, as well as their many sympathizers, will not simply fold their tents, renounce their views, and melt back into the landscape of American life.... [Whiteness] is not done wielding her ruinous force, promising to hobble the Republican Party in one way or another.[67]

Currently, a mostly white Republican Party can no longer win national elections without voter suppression efforts. Over the last decade or so it has become an openly antidemocratic U.S. party, one no longer committed to a constitutional right to vote. Thus, even without evidence of significant voting problems, Republican operatives and activists have pressed for needless voting changes over recent decades. They include "intimidating Republican poll watchers or challengers who may slow down voting lines and embarrass potential voters by asking them humiliating questions," "people in official-looking uniforms with badges and side arms who question voters about their citizenship or their registration," "warning signs... posted near the polls," and "radio ads... targeted to minority listeners containing dire threats of prison terms for people who are not properly registered—messages that seem designed to put minority voters on the defensive."[68] In addition, conservative white activists have mailed false voting information to Black and Latina/o voters. Another antidemocratic strategy involves "voter caging," wherein Republican operatives send letters to voters in areas they know have many Democratic voters, especially those of color, to find out if they will be returned unopened. For those voters whose letters are returned, their names are purged from voter rolls by local or state Republican officials or challenged at election time by Republican poll watchers claiming they are not legal voters. Moreover, before, during, and now after the 2020 presidential election period, some Republican officials have tried to make mail-in ballots difficult to get and return, to limit polling places in communities of color, and to interfere with or actually rig the counting of voters' ballots.[69] In the 1980s, such voter suppression strategies aimed at African American areas by the Republican National Committee were so problematical that a judge significantly restricted Republicans in their ability to do such challenges.[70] More recently, however, more conservative federal judges have been reluctant to get involved in these election law issues.

Another commonplace strategy targeting voters of color involves extreme partisan gerrymandering of electoral districts by Republican state legislators. They often use racial statistics in creating highly partisan voting district lines favoring Republican candidates. According to a law review article by Nicholas Stephanopoulos, federal court decisions on redistricting problems have shifted from the 1960s–1980s, when cases were mostly nonpartisan, to the 1990s-to-present era, when voting issues and cases have become hyperpartisan. He concludes that in the earlier period, "courts (properly) focused on nonpartisan line-drawing problems like rural overrepresentation and racial discrimination." Yet, in the more recent era, "courts have (regrettably) refrained from confronting directly the threat, partisan gerrymandering, that now looms above all others."[71] For instance, much partisan gerrymandering by white state legislators involves the assumption that African Americans will vote Democratic, so that racial population statistics can legally be used as a proxy for "Democratic voters" in drawing skewed electoral districts that cram most African Americans into one oddly shaped, gerrymandered district instead of plotting a more reasonable geographical distribution of them across two or more electoral districts. For the most part, judges have allowed such overtly racist framing to persist in much state legislative drawing of congressional and state electoral districts.[72]

Moreover, as of this writing, white right-wing politicians are increasing their anti-democratic efforts in many states to offset the demographic changes in voters of color with yet more laws designed to suppress their votes. More than 200 bills have been introduced, with two dozen passed so far. Right-wing Republican governors and legislators in states such as Georgia, Texas, Arizona, Iowa, and Montana have led this major attack on multiracial democracy. The laws include making mail-in ballots more difficult, reducing voting hours and places, ending same-day voter registration, setting limits on early voting, requiring more voter identification, and imposing more right-wing surveillance at voting sites. Indeed, there is yet more to this openly antidemocratic effort coming in the future. An analysis in *The Atlantic* magazine points out that

> Approved measures allow Republican-controlled state legislatures or election boards to sideline or override local election administrations in Democratic strongholds. This would allow state legislatures or their appointees to meddle in local decision making, purge voter rolls, and manipulate the number and location of polling places.[73]

A *New Yorker* magazine report also noted that many of the new voter laws and regulations enacted by right-wing state legislators are intended to undermine routine election administration. They do this "either by making it harder for officials to do their jobs or by removing them entirely... [this is] new terrain for the Republican Party."[74] Indeed, since the 2020 election, which Donald Trump lost badly to Joe Biden, Trump and other leading Republicans have falsely claimed that election was "stolen" from him by (imaginary) fraudulent voters. For a time, they pursued unsuccessful lawsuits and made other politicized attacks against the nonpartisan, Republican, and Democratic election officials involved in that fair election. In a long series of hearings, in which many Republican officials testified, the bipartisan congressional investigation into the January 6 Capitol insurrection found that Trump was told he lost the election by many of his close advisors, as well as some of his family members. Still, he ignored them and claimed, falsely, that the election was stolen from him. That congressional investigation also found that he had collected some 250 million dollars from supporters based on this false election claim. Later sessions of the congressional investigation revealed that a large group of Republican activists and officials, led or encouraged by Trump, had worked together in what the chair of the committee called a "coup" attempt to overthrow the legitimate election of Democratic Party candidate Joe Biden.[75]

Success in all these Republican voter suppression efforts will mean that the inevitable reality of more eligible voters of color does not necessarily translate into more votes by them in current and future elections. In his interviews on these voting matters, veteran journalist Ronald Brownstein found that many civil-rights advocates and leading democracy scholars view the state-level bills limiting voters' rights as the "greatest assault on Americans' right to vote since the Jim Crow era's blatant voting barriers." He quotes Derrick Johnson, president of the NAACP, as concluding that

> This is a huge moment. This harkens to pre-segregation times in the South, and it goes to the core question of how we define citizenship and whether or not all citizens actually will have access to fully engage and participate.[76]

Indeed, we might note the numerous other ways in which right-wing Republican operatives and officials have explicitly tried to limit the citizenship rights of Americans of color. Political analyst Harold Meyerson has noted that right-wing Republican legislatures and officials have

> required Latinos to present papers if the police ask for them; opposed the Dream Act, which would have conferred citizenship on young immigrants who served in our armed forces or went to college; and called for denying the constitutional right to citizenship to American-born children of undocumented immigrants.[77]

Other Antidemocratic Republican Politics

An increasingly right-wing U.S. Supreme Court has contributed substantially to reducing the deserved voting and other political clout of Americans of color. The important 2010 Court decision, *Citizens United* v. *Federal Elections Commission*, blocked federal and state legislative attempts to limit campaign expenditures for political electioneering by corporations, unions, and other groups.[78] As sociologist Glenn Bracey has underscored, this was a major reaction to the increasing political power of Americans of color. That is, the "combination of Black and Brown leadership, increased

Black and Brown voting activity, decreased white voting potential, and sufficient non-corporate funding pools for campaigns was a new threat to which whites were compelled to respond immediately."[79] As a result of this antidemocratic Supreme Court decision, often *huge* corporate electoral expenditures have disproportionately favored far-right and other right-wing candidates in local, state, and federal elections, many of them successfully elected. Consequently, the right-wing Republican Party and its largely white constituency have maintained substantial influence over U.S. government policies, even as whites are rapidly losing their demographic dominance. Unmistakably, too, since the 1970s, the Republican presidents' packing of the Supreme Court and other major federal courts disproportionately with right-wing judges has played a significant role in the suppression of voters of color, in election difficulties of candidates of color, and in other efforts to restrict multiracial democracy.[80]

The right-wing Republican political actions discussed in this chapter have measurably reduced the level of real democracy at local, state, and federal government levels. One research study developed a State Democracy Index with 61 indicators measuring aspects of democratic governing in U.S. states from 2000 to 2018. Using this Index, the study examined democratic expansion or backsliding "based in party competition, polarization, demographic change, and the group interests of national party coalitions."[81] It found little effect for these indicators except for Republican Party control of state governments. That one factor "dramatically reduces states' democratic performance during this period." In some states, democracy had actually "expanded in inclusive ways, expanding access to political participation, reducing the authoritarian use of police powers, and making electoral institutions more fair." However, in other states, principally Republican-controlled ones, "democracy narrowed dramatically, as state governments gerrymandered districts and created new barriers to participation and restrictions on the franchises."[82]

Conclusion

Throughout this chapter, much of the data and analysis suggests a key question for the democratic future of the U.S.: How long can a right-wing Republican Party remain in power with only a voter minority in major states, as is the current trend? It appears that the continuing voter suppression efforts of Republicans can only work in the short term, not in the long term, unless there is a nationwide fascist political revolution. University of Texas Policy analyst James Galbraith has summarized the long-term Republican dilemma if the U.S. retains its democratic voting institutions:

> In Texas, with 38 Electoral College votes—more than Pennsylvania and Michigan together—there has been an inexorable three-point swing

toward the Democrats every four years: Obama got 40% in 2012, Clinton got 43% in 2016, and Biden got 46% in 2020. Republican legislatures, especially in southern and southwestern states, have done the math and are terrified. That is why they have worked to reverse the great ballot-access experiments of 2020. The GOP's unspoken watchword is: Get American voters back into long lines (without drinking water)! The point is to discourage as many as possible from voting at all.[83]

An optimist about the U.S. future, Galbraith then suggests that even if Congress does not act to rein in these Republican voter suppression efforts, their current antidemocratic tactics will only *slow* the ongoing U.S. electorate change favoring the Democratic Party. That is, current voter suppression efforts "can't save the Republicans. Voting is a habit, and habits are hard to break."[84]

Notes

1 Steven Neal, "D-e-a-v-e-r Spells Insensitivity," *Chicago Tribune*, May 9, 1985, Zone C, p. 19.
2 Terrel Bell, *The Thirteenth Man* (New York: Free Press, 1988), p. 103.
3 In this section I draw on Bob Herbert, "Righting Reagan's Wrongs?" *New York Times*, November 13, 2007, http://www.nytimes.com/2007/11/13/opinion/13herbert.html?_r=2 (accessed March 10, 2011); Kathanne W. Greene, *Affirmative Action and Principles of Justice* (Westport, CT: Greenwood Press, 1989), pp. 5ff; and Joe Davidson, "Reagan: A Contrary View," MSNBC.com, June 7, 2004, http://www.msnbc.msn.com/id/5158315/ns/us_news-life/ (accessed March 10, 2011). See also Barbara J. Flagg, "'Was Blind but Now I See': White Race Consciousness and the Requirement of Discriminatory Intent," *Michigan Law Review* 91 (1993): 953; Wendy Moore, *Reproducing Racism* (Lanham, MD: Rowman & Littlefield, 2008).
4 Quoted in Joe Davidson, "Reagan: A Contrary View," msnbc.com, June 7, 2004, http://www.msnbc.msn.com/id/5158315/ns/us_news-life/ (accessed March 10, 2011).
5 Rob Griffin, Ruy Teixeira, and William H. Frey, "America's Electoral Future: The Coming Generational Transformation," *American Progress*, October 19, 2020, https://www.americanprogress.org/issues/politics-and-elections/reports/2020/10/19/491870/americas-electoral-future-3/ (accessed November 22, 2021).
6 Ibid.; and "Exit Polls," *CNN*, November 23, 2016, https://www.cnn.com/election/2016/results/exit-polls (accessed February 18, 2018). See also Adia Harvey-Wingfield and Joe R. Feagin, *Yes We Can: White Racial Framing and the Obama Presidency*, 2nd ed. (New York: Routledge, 2013), Chapter 10.
7 Griffin, Teixeira, and Frey, "America's Electoral Future."
8 Nate Cohn, "Why Rising Diversity Might Not Help Democrats as Much as They Hope," *New York Times*, May 4, 2021, https://www.nytimes.com/2021/05/04/us/census-news-republicans-democrats.html (accessed November 28, 2021).
9 Harold Meyerson, "The State of the Parties," Prospect.Org, November 25, 2020, https://prospect.org/politics/the-state-of-the-parties/ (accessed

January 7, 2021); and Jens Manuel Krogstad, "Most Cuban American Voters Identify as Republican in 2020," PEW Research Center, October 2, 2020, https://www.Pewresearch.org/fact-tank/2020/10/02/most-cuban-american-voters-identify-as-republican-in-2020/ (accessed August 5, 2021).

10 Sean McElwee, *The Future of the Party: A Progressive Vision for a Populist Democratic Party* (Data for Progress, April 2018).

11 Michael Rodriguez-Muniz, *Figures of the Future* (Princeton, NJ: Princeton University Press, 2021), p. 4.

12 Ibid., p. 3.

13 Quoted in Ibid., p. 195.

14 Greg Toppo and Paul Overberg, "After Nearly 100 years, Great Migration Begins Reversal," *USA Today*, February 2, 2015, https://www.usatoday.com/story/news/nation/2015/02/02/census-great-migration-reversal/21818127/ (accessed January 7, 2021).

15 William Frey, *Diversity Explosion* (Washington, DC: Brookings Institution, 2015), Kindle loc. 198, 305, 327.

16 Jonathan Rodden email to Thomas B. Edsall, cited in Edsall, "There's an Exodus From the 'Star Cities,' and I Have Good News and Bad News," *New York Times*, May 12, 2021, https://www.nytimes.com/2021/05/12/opinion/New-York-San-Francisco-after-covid.html (accessed May 12, 2021).

17 Karim Farishta and Jackson Miller, "Reclaiming the Southern Strategy: How Democrats Win Back the South in the 2020s," *Harvard Graduate Capstone*, April 2020, https://harvardgradcapstone.wixsite.com/reclaimingthesouth (accessed July 3, 2022).

18 Quoted in Ibid.

19 Data cited in Edsall, "There's an Exodus from the 'Star Cities,' and I Have Good News and Bad News."

20 Griffin, Teixeira, and Frey, "America's Electoral Future."

21 Ibid.

22 Sean McElwee and Colin McAuliffe, "Progressives Control the Future," *Data for Progress*, June 14, 2020, https://www.dataforprogress.org/blog/6/14/-progressives-control-the-future (accessed March 28, 2021).

23 Abigail Johnson Hess, "The 2020 Election Shows Gen Z's Voting Power for Years to Come," CNBC.com, November 18, 2020, https://www.cnbc.com/2020/11/18/the-2020-election-shows-gen-zs-voting-power-for-years-to-come.html (accessed March 28, 2021).

24 Data provided by John Della Volpe, Harvard IOP, January 22, 2022.

25 Hess, "The 2020 Election Shows Gen Z's Voting Power for Years to Come."

26 Amy Harmon and Sabrina Tavernise, "One Big Difference about George Floyd Protests: Many White Faces," *New York Times*, June 12, 2020, https://www.nytimes.com/2020/06/12/us/george-floyd-white-protesters.html (accessed February 7, 2022).

27 Kim Parker and Ruth Igielnik, "On the Cusp of Adulthood and Facing an Uncertain Future: What We Know about Gen Z So Far," *Pew Research Center*, May 14, 2020, https://www.Pewresearch.org/social-trends/2020/05/14/on-the-cusp-of-adulthood-and-facing-an-uncertain-future-what-we-know-about-gen-z-so-far-2/ (accessed July 29, 2021).

28 Jennifer Richeson, "Americans are Determined to Believe in Black Progress," *The Atlantic*, August 2020, https://www.theatlantic.com/magazine/archive/2020/09/the-mythology-of-racial-progress/614173/ (accessed July 1, 2022). Interestingly, a review of 20 studies of U.S. workplaces involving thousands of employees found that the workplace preferences and values of

millennial employees differed little from those of earlier generations. D. P. Costanza, J. M. Badger, and R. L. Fraser, *et al.*, "Generational Differences in Work-Related Attitudes: A Meta-analysis," *Journal of Business and Psychology* 27 (2012): 375–394. DOI: 10.1007/s10869-012-9259-4

29 Julie J. Park and Nida Denson, "Attitudes and Advocacy: Understanding Faculty Views on Racial/Ethnic Diversity," *Journal of Higher Education* 80 (July–August 2009): 415–438.

30 Candis Watts Smith and Christopher DeSante, "The Racial Views of White Americans—Including Millennials—Depend on the Questions Asked," *Scholars Strategy Network*, January 12, 2018, https://scholars.org/contribution/racial-views-white-americans-including-millennials-depend-questions-asked (accessed August 17, 2020). See also Christopher D. DeSante and Candis Watts Smith, *Racial: Stasis: The Millennial Generation and the Stagnation of Racial Attitudes in American Politics* (Chicago, IL: University of Chicago Press, 2020).

31 Jennifer C. Mueller and DyAnna K. Washington, "Anticipating White Futures: The Ends-Based Orientation of White Thinking," *Symbolic Interaction* (June 2021): 18–20. ISSN: 0195-6086 print/1533-8665 online.

32 I am indebted here to discussions with sociologist Jennifer Mueller. See also Joe R. Feagin, *The White Racial Frame*, 3rd ed. (New York: Routledge, 2020).

33 "Why Are Almost All Mass Shooters Men?" *The Violence Project*, https://www.theviolenceproject.org/media/why-are-almost-all-mass-shooters-men/ (accessed July 1, 2022).

34 Griffin, Teixeira, and Frey, "America's Electoral Future."

35 Drew Engelhardt, "White People's Racial Attitudes Are Changing to Match Partisanship," *Data for Progress*, March 21, 2019, https://www.dataforprogress.org/blog/2019/3/20/racial-resentment-is-the-defining-feature-of-american-politics (accessed May 6, 2021).

36 Ibid.

37 Ibid.

38 Cristina Beltrán, *Cruelty as Citizenship* (Minneapolis: University of Minnesota Press, 2020), p. 120.

39 Ibid., pp. 120–121.

40 See Mueller and Washington, "Anticipating White Futures," and Feagin, *The White Racial Frame*, passim.

41 This is from an interview with David Remnick. John Gruber, "David Remnick: 'Obama Reckons with a Trump Presidency,'" *DaringFireball*, November 27, 2016, https://daringfireball.net/linked/2016/11/27/remnick-obama-trump (accessed August 4, 2021).

42 Ibid.

43 "Exit Polls," *CNN*, November 23, 2016, https://www.cnn.com/election/2016/results/exit-polls (accessed February 18, 2018). See also Harvey-Wingfield and Feagin, *Yes We Can: White Racial Framing and the Obama Presidency*.

44 *Los Angeles Times* Staff, "Transcript: Hillary Clinton's DNC Speech, Annotated," *Los Angeles Times*, July 28, 2016, http://www.latimes.com/politics/la-na-pol-hillary-clinton-convention-speech-transcript-20160728-snap-htmlstory.html (accessed February 19, 2018).

45 See Harvey-Wingfield and Feagin, *Yes We Can*, Chapter 10.

46 Frey, *Diversity Explosion*, p. 356.

47 Women Donor's Network, "Confronting the Demographics of Power: America's Cities 2020," August 2020, https://wholeads.us/wp-content/uploads/2020/08/CONFRONTING-POWER-CITIES-Report.pdf (accessed April 22, 2022).

48 Chauncey DeVega, "What Fuels 'White Anxiety'? The Baffling Hypocrisies behind White Paranoia Politics," June 26, 2018, https://www.salon.com/

2018/06/26/what-fuels-white-anxiety-the-baffling-hypocrisies-behind-white-paranoia-politics/ (accessed November 28, 2021).

49 Dudley L. Poston and Rogelio Sáenz, "A Wasted Chance for a Third House Seat," *The Eagle*, May 2, 2021, https://theeagle.com/opinion/columnists/a-wasted-chance-for-a-third-house-seat/article_f03b4cda-organization01-11eb-8af7-3b69fd474251.html (accessed May 6, 2021).

50 Quoted in Yoni Appelbaum, "How America Ends: A Tectonic Demographic Shift is Underway. Can the Country Hold Together?" *The Atlantic*, December 2019, https://www.theatlantic.com/magazine/archive/2019/12/how-america-ends/600757/(accessed December 8, 2021).

51 "Ezra Klein Interviews Kristen Soltis Anderson," https://www.nytimes.com/2021/03/26/podcasts/ezra-klein-podcast-kristen-soltis-anderson-transcript.html (accessed August 8, 2021).

52 Griffin, Teixeira, and Frey, "America's Electoral Future."

53 "Women More Likely than Men to have Earned a Bachelor's Degree by Age 31," *TED Economics Daily*, December 6, 2018, https://www.bls.gov/opub/ted/2018/women-more-likely-than-men-to-have-earned-a-bachelors-degree-by-age-31.htm (accessed July 1, 2022); and Jennifer Lawless and Paul Freedman, "What the Exit Polls Are Telling Us," UVA Today, November 6, 2020, https://news.virginia.edu/content/what-exit-polls-are-telling-us (accessed May 9, 2021).

54 Hannah Fingerhut, "Most Americans Express Positive Views of Country's Growing Racial and Ethnic Diversity," June 14, 2018, *Pew Research Center*, https://www.Pewresearch.org/fact-tank/2018/06/14/most-americans-express-positive-views-of-countrys-growing-racial-and-ethnic-diversity/ (accessed July 5, 2020). See also Bruce Drake and Jacob Poushter, "In Views of Diversity, Many Europeans Are Less Positive Than Americans," *Pew Research Center*, July 12, 2016 (accessed July 1, 2022).

55 "The Democratic Party Is Trying to Replace the Current Electorate with Voters from Poorer Countries around the World," *UMass Poll*, December 14–21, 2021, https://polsci.umass.edu/sites/default/files/Replacement_Dems.pdf (accessed April 27, 2022).

56 Nate Cohn, "Why Rising Diversity Might Not Help Democrats as Much as They Hope," *New York Times*, May 4, 2021, https://www.nytimes.com/2021/05/04/us/census-news-republicans-democrats.html (accessed July 30, 2021).

57 Women Donors' Network, "System Failure: What the 2020 Primary Elections Revealed about Our Democracy," May, 2021, https://wholeads.us/wp-content/uploads/2021/05/reflectivedemocracy-systemfailure-may2021.pdf (accessed April 22, 2022); and Capitol Hill Staffers, "Congress by the Numbers," Legistorm.Com, https://www.legistorm.com/congress_by_numbers/index/by/house/mode/race/term_id/64.html?type_id%5B%5D=gender&gender_id%5B%5D=Major; https://iop.harvard.edu/get-involved/study-groups-0/spring-2019-aisha-moodie-mills (accessed May 4, 2022).

58 Osita Nwanevu, "Trump Isn't the Only One to Blame for the Capitol Riot," *New York Times*, January 4, 2022, https://www.nytimes.com/2022/01/04/opinion/capitol-riot.html (accessed January 4, 2022).

59 Ibid.

60 Aaron Pacitti, "The Elite Capture of Politics," HuffPost, https://www.huffpost.com/entry/the-elite-capture-of-poli_b_13710494 (accessed November 8, 2021).

61 Quoted in Michael C. Dawson, "Hidden in Plain Sight: A Note on Legitimation Crises and the Racial Order," *Critical Historical Studies* 3 (Spring 2016): 145. DOI: 10.1086/685540

62 Ibid., p. 149.
63 Ibid.
64 Ibid., p. 155.
65 Quoted in Clare Malone, "The Republican Choice: How a Party Spent Decades Making Itself White," 538.com, June 24, 2020, https://fivethirtyeight.com/features/the-republican-choice/ (accessed August 19, 2021).
66 Kathleen J. Frydl, "The Future of American Politics: A Party Built on Whiteness Is Collapsing; Two-party Dominance May Go with It," *American Prospect*, January 21, 2021, https://prospect.org/politics/future-of-american-politics/ (accessed February 15, 2021).
67 Ibid.
68 Chandler Davidson, Tanya Dunlap, Gale Kenny, and Benjamin Wise, *Republican Ballot Security Programs: Vote Protection or Minority Vote Suppression—or Both?* Report to Center for Voting Rights and Protection, September 2004. See also Roy L. Brooks, Gilbert Paul Carrasco, and Michael Selmi, *The Law of Discrimination: Cases and Perspectives* (New Providence, NJ: LexisNexis, 2012). For more detail on these racialized political issues, see Joe R. Feagin, *White Party, White Government: Race, Class, and U.S. Politics* (New York: Routledge, 2012), passim.
69 Matt DeRienzo, "New and Age-Old Voter Suppression Tactics at the Heart of the 2020 Power Struggle, Center for Public Integrity, October 28, 2020, https://publicintegrity.org/politics/elections/ballotboxbarriers/analysis-voter-suppression-never-went-away-tactics-changed/ (accessed July 29, 2021).
70 Chandler Davidson, Tanya Dunlap, Gale Kenny, and Benjamin Wise, "Vote Caging as a Republican Ballot Security Technique," *William Mitchell Law Review* 34 (2008): 533–562; Josh Gerstein, "RNC on Verge of Escaping Aging Court Decree on 'Ballot Security,'" *Politico*, November 29, 2017, https://www.politico.com/story/2017/11/29/republicans-ballot-security-267717 (accessed December 21, 2017).
71 Nicholas Stephanopoulos, "The Dance of Partisanship and Districting," *Harvard Law & Policy Review.* 13 (2019): 507.
72 Ibid., pp. 507–537.
73 Steven Levitsky and Daniel Ziblatt, "The Biggest Threat to Democracy Is the GOP Stealing the Next Election," *The Atlantic*, July 2021, https://www.theatlantic.com/ideas/archive/2021/07/democracy-could-die-2024/619390/ (accessed January 7, 2022).
74 Sue Halpern, "Threats against Election Officials Are a Threat to Democracy," *New Yorker*, June 29, 2021, https://www.newyorker.com/news/news-desk/threats-against-election-officials-are-a-threat-to-democracy (accessed July 15, 2021).
75 Ryan Bort, "Trump Scammed Supporters Out of $250 Million for Non-existent Fraud Fund," *RollingStone*, https://www.rollingstone.com/politics/politics-news/trump-fundraising-scam-jan-6-hearing-1367359/ (accessed July 1, 2022).
76 Ronald Brownstein, "Democrats' Only Chance to Stop the GOP Assault on Voting Rights," *The Atlantic*, March 3, 2021, https://www.theatlantic.com/politics/archive/2021/03/democrats-need-hr-1-and-new-vra-protect-voting-rights/618171/ (accessed March 25, 2021).
77 Harold Meyerson, "GOP's Anti-Immigrant Stance Could Turn Texas into a Blue State," *Washington Post*, March 3, 2011, https://www.washingtonpost.com/opinions/gops-anti-immigrant-stance-could-turn-texas-into-a-blue-state/2011/03/01/ABBivaL_story.html (accessed July 4, 2022).

78 *Citizens United v. Federal Election Commission*, 558 U.S. 08-205 (2010).
79 Glenn Bracey, "A White Supremacist Century: Supreme Court as White Oligarchical Power," http://www.racismreview.com/blog/2010/01/24/a-white-supremacist-century-supreme-court-as-white-oligarchical-power/ (accessed April 12, 2011).
80 See Cord Jefferson, "Voting Rights Act at 45: What's to Celebrate?" *The Root*, August 6, 2010, http://www.theroot.com/views/voting-rights-act-45-whats-celebrate?page=0,1 (accessed August 3, 2011; and Feagin, *White Party, White Government*, Chapter 10.
81 Jacob M. Grumbach, "Laboratories of Democratic Backsliding," Unpublished research paper, University of Washington, March 28, 2021, pp. 23–24.
82 Ibid.
83 James K. Galbraith, "America's Democratic Future," *Project Syndicate*, https://www.project-syndicate.org/commentary/america-electoral-map-turning-democratic-by-james-k-galbraith-2022-01, January 7, 2022 (accessed January 13, 2022).
84 Ibid.

Chapter 6

America at a Historical Crossroads

The pathbreaking African American legal scholar Derrick Bell was an early founder of the now much attacked and misrepresented "critical race theory." In a seminal 1992 law journal article, he questioned the liberal idea of thorough racial integration in the U.S. as naïve, underscoring the (now demonstrable) reality that most whites would *not* accept major racial transformation in the next few generations. In his famous "racial realism" perspective, the best those committed to racial justice can do is continue the courageous struggle against white racism so that *existing* gains are not dismantled. He underscores his point about this courageous struggle by recounting his walk with a fearless 1960s civil rights activist in the Black community of Harmony, Mississippi:

> Some Harmony residents, in the face of increasing white hostility, were organizing to ensure implementation of a court order mandating desegregation of their schools the next September. Walking with Mrs. Biona MacDonald, one of the organizers, up a dusty, unpaved road toward her modest home, I asked where she found the courage to continue working for civil rights in the face of intimidation that included her son losing his job in town, the local bank trying to foreclose on her mortgage, and shots fired through her living room window. "Derrick," she said slowly, seriously, "I am an old woman. I lives to harass white folks."[1]

In the 2020 national election Stacey Abrams, the progressive African American founder of the New Georgia Project, demonstrated this courage by leading Democratic Party activists in pathbreaking grass-roots mobilization of Georgia voters. They engaged in extensive legwork to get out a more diverse array of eligible voters, especially voters of color. Abrams summarizes that effort:

> Early investments in infrequent voters? Check. Consistent, authentic progressive messaging? Check. Outreach in multiple languages?

DOI: 10.4324/9781003359883-7

Check. Centering the issues of communities of color and margin-
alized groups typically exiled to the fringes of statewide elections?
Check. The results of these efforts on the Democratic side of the ballot
had been incredible: We had tripled the turnout rates of Latino and
Asian American Pacific Islander (AAPI) voters.[2]

Because of these savvy strategies, to the surprise of many political pundits,
Democrat Joe Biden won Georgia's presidential electors, and two progressive Democratic senatorial candidates won. Assessing this progressive shift
in Georgia, many media analysts have emphasized a shift in moderate white
suburban voters there, but far more important were increases in the numbers and turnout of voters of color and their effective political organization.[3]

In this concluding chapter, I examine in detail what the political, economic, and social future of the U.S. might look like, especially in the
2025–2050 era. Some societal changes are certain. We know from data
cited previously that the future population will certainly be ever more
racially and ethnically diverse, with European-descended whites increasingly a statistical minority. We know that now dominant white generations, including famous Baby Boomers, will give way in population
dominance to younger and more racially diverse Millennial, Gen-Z, and
Gen-Alpha generations. However, just what the other major societal consequences of this huge demographic shift will be, and how and when they
will occur, remain a speculative or murky matter as of today.

In the rest of this chapter, I first examine briefly the suggestions of
social analysts that the U.S. may become a racialized society more like
certain Latin American countries or South Africa. Then, since the U.S.
has a strong federal system with powerful state governments and a powerful central government, I look closely at the impact of the browning of
America on the political-economic realities of our two largest states, California and Texas, states often suggested as future developmental models for
other states and the U.S. as a whole. I conclude this section of the chapter
with a discussion of certain analysts' suggestions that the U.S. political-
economic structure may go the way of that in the late 19th-century post-
Reconstruction era—that is, of a "cold" civil war between the states and a
much more "divided states of America" structure for the U.S. as a whole.

After that discussion, I will revisit critical political-economic issues
raised in previous chapters, especially the character of the growing progressive organization and struggles of ordinary and elite Americans for an
authentic multiracial democracy.

Latin Americanization of U.S. Society?

Considering other contemporary countries' societal development models, several possibilities suggest themselves in regard to the future racial

hierarchy and power structure of the U.S. Taking a broad view, some analysts suggest that this country's future might involve a Latin Americanization or South Africanization restructuring. Let us briefly consider both possibilities.

Some scholars and popular analysts have forecasted that, as the U.S. population becomes much less white in future decades, the country will become more like a common Latin American three-tiered racial system with powerful whites in the top group, relatively powerless darker-skinned people at the bottom, and a middle group of more white-acceptable people of color with some power and privilege. An array of renovated political, economic, and other social institutions will reflect this shifting racial framework.[4]

Yet, this Latin Americanization argument often ignores certain relevant racial and racial-power differences across the many Latin American countries. There are at least two different racial hierarchy systems in Latin America. There is the reality of a central white-to-Black hierarchy in Brazil (and various Caribbean countries), while other Latin American countries mainly have a central white-to-mestizo hierarchy. In addition, another major problem with a tri-level Latin Americanization argument is that the "middle tier" of mixed-race and other people of color is usually much closer in socioeconomic condition to the bottom tier than to the top white tier. That is, they are not really in the middle.[5] The scholar Christina Sue has noted that because of this variation a viable Latin Americanization theory "would avoid a number of conceptual problems if, instead of positing a theory of the 'Latin Americanization' of the US, it predicted the 'Brazilianization' or 'Puerto Ricanization' of the US." She adds the important consideration that the U.S. "may be moving towards mirroring the Latin American situation in terms of outcomes but … the underlying mechanisms that led to these outcomes are quite distinct in these two regions … the process is just as important as the outcome."[6]

One key feature of U.S. society, and of primarily white-to-Black hierarchical societies like Brazil, is that once a person or family is firmly categorized in racial terms, it is difficult to move out of that socially imposed racial identity. In the U.S., as in Brazil, there is also a common assumption that those in lower ranked racial groups will benefit economically from a "trickle down" effect, with in-between "model minorities" getting somewhat more benefits. Those in the bottom tier typically get very little. Historically, Brazil's racialization process and hierarchy have categorized and called out mixed-race groups and placed them in a middle socio-racial status between Brazilians mostly of African ancestry at the societal bottom and those with substantial European ancestry at the societal top. The middle mixed-racial groups are socially more acceptable to whites than the more visibly African Afro-Brazilians. White Brazilians still mostly rule at the society's pinnacle, both in the capitalistic economy and its national political system. About half of the Brazilian population, the darker-skinned Afro-Brazilians, remains relatively powerless in major societal institutions.[7]

Possibly then, a fully developed tripartite Brazilian pattern might be the U.S. future by the 2050s. That is, white-positioned, white-named, and white-favored intermediate nonwhite groups such as lighter-skinned (and middle-class) groups among Asian Americans and Latina/o Americans will then provide a societal buffer between a population minority of white-constructed "whites" at the top rank and a larger population of white-constructed "Blacks" in the bottom rank. Over the past few decades, especially among some scholars and media analysts, the idea of such tripartite racial intermediation has increased in importance because the U.S. population is rapidly becoming composed of fewer European-descended whites.[8]

South Africanization of U.S. Society?

Or perhaps South Africanization is more likely for the U.S. future? For most of its history, the U.S. societal system has been very hierarchical, with a minority white elite at the top, a huge supporting white acolyte group in the middle, and a mostly subordinated nonwhite category below. That large-scale nonwhite subordination only began to change significantly in a democratic direction in the 1960s–1970s as a result of the civil rights movements, and the demographic dominance of whites has been declining since that era as well. As European-descended whites become a national population minority in the near future, this situation might regress to be more like that of the old South African *apartheid*, wherein a small white group (about 16 percent of population then) had great political, economic, and social power over a substantial nonwhite population majority (with a small mixed-race middle group). This racially oppressive, highly undemocratic apartheid lasted a long time, officially from 1948 to 1991 and unofficially much longer.[9]

Indeed, the current Black president of the NAACP Legal Defense and Educational Fund has offered a pessimistic take on the socio-political impact of the browning of America, underscoring that

> I think we have to rely less on the idea that demography is destiny, because it is not. There is such a thing as minority rule. It's very ugly. Many of us know it from South Africa. It's brutal. We shouldn't assume that just because there are numbers that there's power.[10]

Other civil rights leaders and groups have expressed a similarly cautious view noting the possible antidemocratic impacts of ongoing racial demographic change.

Indeed, detailed data in previous chapters suggest that a significant, racially fearful segment of the white population is currently moving in a direction of supporting something like the old South African apartheid wherein an ever smaller white minority runs the country autocratically with repressive police and other organized violence. During that apartheid era, much overt white racial violence, like that of the Jim Crow segregation era in the U.S. South, was essential to maintaining white political-economic dominance and extreme racial inequality.

Thus, one future U.S. possibility is that whites will react to the country becoming minority white by creating yet more racial segregation like that of South African apartheid or the Jim Crow South. As I showed in Chapter 2, for decades now, a great many whites have already chosen mostly segregated residential communities and schools. Many have been moving to whiter counties and states, such as those away from more progressive and racially diverse coastal areas. Significant numbers, still relatively small but growing, are joining or otherwise supporting armed white militias and violent insurrections, as was demonstrated in the January 2021 U.S. Capitol attack.

Or, perhaps, the *current* racial reality of post-apartheid South Africa might anticipate that of a future U.S. With the 1990s downfall of South African apartheid, Black South Africans have gained much political control, yet only modest improvements in socioeconomic conditions and status in the South African economy.[11] A substantially co-opted Black political elite runs much of the country's government, but a white corporate elite, local and international, still controls most of the economy. The minority white population also controls most of the land and other valuable assets like good housing, and decent-paying skilled jobs are still mostly in white hands. The racial wealth gap remains huge. Nearly 80 percent of the working population is Black, yet Black South Africans are less than 15 percent of top managers and hold only 3 percent of corporate stock, decades after the official end of apartheid.[12] One scholarly analyst has noted that whites are still

> able to use their oligarchic power—and grand corruption—to maintain the status quo....White oligopoly power is so effective in marginalising Blacks because it has one or two friends in the ANC government. The [Black political] governing party does not enforce its own transformation or land distribution laws. Instead, it may use state power to protect white oligarchs.[13]

This current South African structure might presage a U.S. future—say, after the end of an era of white right-wing Republican political dominance for the next few years—with African Americans and other Americans of color eventually gaining much greater political power, especially in political representation at the national level and in certain major states. Nonetheless, if the country does become like contemporary South Africa, these state and national political systems dominated by officials of color will still be rather undemocratic in actual operation. They too will face a mostly white economic elite firmly in control of the capitalistic U.S. economy, as well as behind the scenes in funding conservative white and sell-out politicians of color in political institutions who continue to coordinate with white-run corporations. In this possible scenario, there is no way for Americans of color to get major control over the U.S. capitalistic system where much real societal power lies.

A Minority White State Model: The California Case

Recognizing the browning of America, the social analysts who discuss and debate the possible Latin Americanization or South Africanization of the U.S. tend to focus on national impacts, especially on the national racial hierarchy and associated political-economic power. Interestingly, yet other analysts assessing the browning of America have examined this demographic change as it shapes particular states' racial hierarchies and political-economies. They detail state changes not only in racial demography and racial hierarchy but also in specific government taxing, regulation, and public welfare actions affecting elite and ordinary state residents now and in the future. Several analysts have debated whether the current more democratically-run state of California or the much less democratically-run state of Texas might be the better political, economic, and public welfare model for other states, or for the U.S. nationally. Both states have relatively recently become minority white in their total population composition.

First, let us consider California. In the mid-1990s, the prominent journalist Dale Maharidge wrote a book titled *The Coming White Minority* in which he anticipated and focused on the coming white minority reality of California. Already at that time, many whites there, leaders and ordinary citizens, were upset and dreading "the unknown and not-so-distant tomorrow.... They fear losing not only their jobs but also their culture."[14] A few years later in 1999, California did become the first state in the continental U.S. to have a (non-Hispanic) white minority population.

California is also a conspicuous political-economic case showing how much liberal social welfare progress can be made even after long eras of conservative political administrations—change substantially generated or facilitated by racial demographic change there. My first academic job out of graduate school, in the late 1960s, was at the University of California (Riverside), when the state was substantially governed by a very conservative, mostly white Republican Party headed by then Governor Ronald Reagan (1967–1975). At that time, the state was so conservative that university faculty were required to sign a McCarthy-type loyalty oath. In the decades after the conservative Reagan administration, the state of California has had alternating Democratic and Republican government administrations, some of the latter (e.g., Governor Pete Wilson in 1990s) pressing hard for very conservative anti-immigrant and very pro-corporate deregulation policies.

Over these same decades, and sometimes before, California has incubated and sustained not only these right-wing Republican politicians and political movements, but also the less well-known and left-leaning political activists and movements that have helped to create the contemporary, more liberal Democratic Party in the state and nationally. From the 1940s to the present, generations of liberal California leaders and activists have generated and maintained a political perspective and movement extending the social democratic ideals of the 1930s New Deal. In contrast to the 1930s, moreover, contemporary progressive leaders and activists have become ever more racially diverse, and their organizations include an array of Black, Latina/o, and Asian American civil rights organizations, labor unions, and LGBTQ rights organizations fighting for enforced civil rights, greater political democracy, and more social democratic programs.[15]

The sharp difference in California politics between the very conservative Republican state administrations of the Reagan 1960s and Wilson 1990s and the progressive Democratic state administrations of the 2010s–2020s is remarkable. California became a politically progressive state in part because decades of racial demographic change brought many more progressive voters, organizers, and candidates of color into political organizations and state politics, at various government levels, and especially in larger cities (see below). This progressive political direction, from which a substantial majority of the state's citizens have benefited, is one where increased numbers of voters of color have added their political efforts to those of earlier progressive coalitions and helped elect a much more racially diverse and progressive state legislature.

Sociologist Manuel Pastor has documented how progressive California government policies have begun to seriously address socioeconomic inequality by imposing reasonable taxes on the wealthy, significantly increasing the minimum wage, and better funding public schools. This progressive state government has supported programs for greater socioeconomic mobility for its increasing Latin American and Asian immigrant and immigrant-descended populations and has vigorously moved on major climate change issues, including setting up stricter programs to reduce greenhouse gas emissions. These progressive legislative efforts were made possible by major political reforms that significantly increased truly democratic policymaking.[16]

Still, California does have continuing environmental and cost-of-living problems, including major increases in wildfires, coastal gentrification, and high housing costs. However, the significant change in the state's population to a nonwhite political majority and the increased political clout of its voters and politicians of color have made for significant improvements in its democratic decisionmaking and action on these critical and continuing public welfare issues as well. Additionally, the economic shift in California from older industries such as manufacturing to new high-tech companies has increased the number of relatively liberal corporate executives more sympathetic to significant government action on such matters as climate change. Reviewing California history and its ever more nonwhite population, Manuel Pastor concludes optimistically that, in spite of periodic right-wing political shifts there historically, the state's healthy economy, good public schools and colleges, and generally effective local and state governments are linked to an old social contract recognizing the "need to welcome new arrivals and invest in future generations."[17]

Given this contemporary reality, numerous social analysts have suggested that diverse California's social democratic decisionmaking can or should be a political–economic model for other states or for the U.S. as a whole. If an expansion of progressive voters proceeds similarly in other majority-minority states in the future, we could see those states, and eventually the country as a whole, move in the direction of California's expanded social democratic programs. National opinion polls already show that these programs reflect the desires of a majority of Americans for better political, economic, and social lives.

A Minority White State Model: The Texas Case

Meanwhile, there are numerous dissenters to this idea of progressive California as a governing model for other political jurisdictions. Conservative analysts like Joel Kotkin and Wendell Cox, as well as leaders of right-wing organizations like the American Legislative Exchange Council (ALEC) and the Texas Public Policy Foundation, have argued that California's increased business regulation, higher taxes on the wealthy, and expanded social democratic programs are key reasons that state has lost some population in recent years.[18] In their view, progressive California policies offer undesirable models for current or future political efforts by other state governments or the U.S. as a whole.

Numerous conservative analysts, most of them white, cite Texas—also now a majority-minority state—as their preferred counter model to California governing and policy development, given Texas's much weaker corporate regulation, cheaper oil and gas, weakly zoned urban sprawl, lack of a state income tax, and right-wing politics at the state level. (A frequent subtext here is that white-run Texas limits the political power of residents of color). In addition, many conservative analysts accent the outmigration of residents from California to Texas to prove their case. Generally speaking, however, their view of these Texas virtues is the one emphasized by its *well-off* citizens, especially affluent whites.

Certainly, for several decades now, Texas has mostly had a state government dominated at the top by well-off white Republicans. Yet their pro-corporate bias, often extreme right-wing legislative policies, and periodic governing incompetence have cost the state's less affluent and increasingly diverse population greatly. Their political conservatism includes seriously underfunding educational and other important community-welfare programs—and even unnecessary illness and deaths, such as during the collapse of the under-regulated Texas energy grid in an early 2021 weather crisis.[19]

The social analyst Kenneth Miller's interesting book, *Texas vs. California*, compares the two states' political-economic conditions. He likes this particular two-state comparison and asserts that the "national dialectic between right and left, red and blue, Texas and California, contributes to America's remarkable vitality."[20] He too is less optimistic about contemporary California being a model for other states or a future U.S., yet is also critical of certain parts of a full-fledged Texas model. Recognizing the growing racial diversity of the state, he foregrounds the conservative Texas model of development over several decades, describing in mostly positive terms the conservative program of less government, lower taxes, weaker business regulation, cheaper labor, development of oil and gas, and relatively conservative social policies.[21]

Miller also discusses the decline and rise of California, from being what he calls a "failed state" in the 2007–2009 Great Recession to making a major economic comeback soon thereafter. He attributes this comeback substantially to the rapid growth of new high-tech enterprises, which eventuated in California becoming a "leader in information technology, biotech, green energy, telecommunications, entertainment."[22] However, in his view, one major California problem is that high-tech expansions have reinforced a two-tiered California economy with its well-off, well-educated, and well-paid workers on the one hand, and a larger class of workers with less education and lower pay on the other. In Miller's view, many workers in California's economic middle, and many middle-class jobs, have moved out of the state to "more business-friendly states or shuttered altogether," especially to states like Texas.[23]

We can pause here to note that the frequently cited migration from California to Texas is generally misunderstood and misrepresented. For example, under a conservative *Republican* California administration that was business-friendly, during 2005–2008, an average of about 75,000 Californians moved to Texas each year (less than two tenths of one percent of the California population). However, during six years soon thereafter (2011–2017), with a more liberal Democratic California governor and legislature, that migration figure *dropped* to about 65,000 a year. Contrary to white conservative analysts' commonplace assertions, the significantly greater legislative liberalism in that later period did *not* increase the migration out of California.[24]

Then, in 2018–2020, that outmigration did significantly increase. Clearly, over recent years, the number of Californians moving to Texas has oscillated up and down. Strikingly, too, over recent years (2005–2019) some 35,000–40,000 *Texans moved to California* each year. That is, the net migration figure for Texas for these years is actually a modest 20,000–30,000 people. Scholars like Miller, and those more aggressively defending the Texas model, usually do *not* note or analyze this Texas-to-California migration reality. Moreover, a recent Rice University report indicates that most California migration to Texas does *not* reflect the Texas job opportunities, corporate deregulation, or lower taxes alleged by conservative analysts but mainly the differential cost of housing, which until recently has grown faster in California. The driving force behind much of this migration "is not a pull into Texas but a push out of California: home prices."[25] However, even that pull housing factor is now lessening in importance because the cost of homes has recently increased faster than average family income in Texas than it has in California. Many economically thriving U.S. states have such housing problems today.

Miller does recognize some of the reasons why most Californians, and many migrants from outside the state, prefer to come, live, and stay *there*. Most states are not like California in terms of attractive high-tech job opportunities, environmental conditions like pleasant climate, and geographical beauty that bring or keep most people there. In his view, the way to slow contemporary interstate movements of middle- and upper-class people out of California, which he too exaggerates, is a federal government effort to bring some of the significant California improvements in family living conditions there to all the states, which would require increased taxes on well-off Americans *everywhere*.[26] Presumably, this would include impoverished Texas. Consider, for example, that Californians have not had to deal with the very negative impacts of the poor legislative funding of Texas government in regard to educational, health, and other community welfare programs. In numerous ways, California is a better place for moderate- and middle-income families to live because it has effectively and fairly taxed its richer residents. Indeed, Texas community welfare problems are much worse than analysts like Miller describe, as Texas is currently at or close to the *bottom* of all 50 states in per-child school spending, women's health insurance ranking, child hunger, and numerous other measures of public health and welfare.[27]

In his conclusion, Miller expects California will probably stay politically progressive and Democratic for the foreseeable future. His forecast for Texas is less certain. He recognizes that Texas, like California, is already a majority-minority state in its population and voters, but underscores the current right-wing Republican control of state politics. In his view, the likely future scenario for Texas is a "move into a period of two-party competition in which Democrats occasionally win elections, but Republicans remain largely in charge. This expectation is reinforced by the fact that Texas has become the essential cornerstone of the national Republican Party."[28]

Missing in this incomplete political picture is the continuing dominance of extreme white nativism and political authoritarianism in the Texas Republican Party, one dedicated to numerous antidemocratic political goals (e.g., banning honest teaching about Texas and U.S. racism in public schools) and to little compromise with the Texas Democratic Party and its racially diverse state legislators. Indeed, downplayed or omitted in many analyses of Texas state politics is the role of these powerful white reactionaries who still control much of the majority-minority state, directly as top politicians or indirectly as politicians' rich white corporate funders. Mainstream analysts like Miller view the contemporary reality of a politically polarized U.S. in "both-siderism" terms that incorrectly assume we now live "in a free, pluralistic, democratic society, [where] disputes over politics and policy are natural."[29] States like Texas have long been controlled in its major political-economic institutions very disproportionately by elite conservative white men. That control has substantially created, and still maintains, the Texas model of relatively weak democracy and weak community-welfare programs. Unsurprisingly, that condition makes it a political-economic model for many right-wing Americans.

Nonetheless, Texas is changing in population rapidly, and in its politics more slowly. While it is well known that California is a majority-minority state, most Americans do not seem aware that Texas too is already a majority-minority state in terms of its population and of its eligible voters—changes largely because of decades of in-migration by people of color (mainly not recent migration) and of a white population aging and reproducing much less. One current estimate puts the Texas eligible voter population at 18.9 million, with about *51 percent* of that now being nonwhite.[30] In the future some three quarters of growth in this eligible voter population will continue to be nonwhite. Soon a majority of eligible voters will likely be active Democratic-leaning voters whose turnout will then reshape the results of local, state, and national elections. If Texas still has democratic voting institutions—which are currently under attack from right-wing Republican legislators—it will eventually be a state where a majority of the state's voters regularly vote for statewide Democratic candidates. That likely will bring an end to a competitive Republican Party in Texas and nationally.

Note too that the country's largest and most prosperous metropolitan areas include Houston, Dallas, Austin, San Antonio, and El Paso, all of which demonstrate fast-growing racial diversity in both population and voters. The majority of voters in these metropolitan areas went for Democratic presidential candidates in 2016 and 2020. Like other big cities, these cities are increasingly linked into the diverse social, political, and economic institutions of the national and global spheres. Speaking from Houston, the country's fourth largest metropolis, former liberal Mayor Annise Parker has emphasized what she learned about her city's racially and ethnically diverse dynamism: "Every language of business spoken anywhere in the world is spoken in Houston by native speakers with global connections."[31]

In an important book on Houston, termed the "prophetic city," sociologist Stephen Klineberg is optimistic about the progressive future of a white-minority Texas and country. He underscores the progressive attitudinal shifts in that city's ever more racially diverse population. Once a predominantly white and Jim Crow segregated city just a few decades back, the city itself now has a minority white population. Drawing on decades of Houston opinion surveys, Klineberg notes:

> Across the traditional divides, respondents in the more recent surveys have been expressing significantly more support than in earlier years for policies to reduce the inequalities and address the needs of the poor; they have been calling for more spending on public education and for more stringent controls on development to reduce the region's vulnerability to future flooding and enhance its quality-of-life attributes.[32]

That is, even once politically far-right and demographically majority white Houston now is far more racially diverse in population and is becoming much more progressive and social democratic in its population's attitudes and politics.

Indeed, given its dramatic majority-minority reality now, and even more so in the near future, the actual Texas future may see its political-economic development being much more like California than the reverse.

A Divided States of America?

The veteran CNN political analyst, Ronald Brownstein, has summarized well the already sharp, and increasing, political realities of a divided states of America:

> States where the GOP controls both the governorship and state legislature are moving in unprecedented numbers to restrict abortion, limit access to voting, ban books, retrench transgender rights and constrain teachers' ability to discuss race, gender and sexual orientation at public K-12 schools and increasingly at public colleges and

universities. Many of the same states are simultaneously rescinding restrictions on gun ownership, stiffening penalties for people engaged in unruly public protests and, in a new twist, empowering private citizens to bring lawsuits to enforce many of these initiatives.... The striking implication of the GOP's ongoing revolution from below is that the coming decade may see the nation's 50 states diverge between those two paths more than they have at any point since the Supreme Court and Congress began nationalizing more civil rights and liberties over half a century ago.[33]

An opinion survey right after the January 2021 Capitol insurrection found that *45 percent* of the Republican voters supported that anti-democratic coup attempt; in great contrast, *96 percent* of Democratic respondents clearly indicated they were opposed to it. This political divide decreased some in later polls, but remains wide as of this writing.[34] Recent national surveys also show major party differences in acceptance of extreme white nationalistic and nativistic framing, with that framing being well-received by a great many white Republicans. Given this huge partisan divide, analyst Bernard Harcourt has suggested that the continuing growth of white nationalist and other antidemocratic framing in the Republican Party might reach a national tipping point that could "involve a consensual separation, with citizens throughout the country sorting themselves into two or more sovereign states. The borders could be along red and blue divisions, or urban and rural lines."[35] This separation might, he and numerous other analysts suggest, result in a severely split country with ongoing cold or hot "civil wars" between red and blue states or regions. Already, national polls have found a significant number of Americans, young and old, feel there is a good chance of a "second civil war" in the near future.[36]

Still, considering U.S. geographical realities, actual physical separation into two contiguous sovereign state complexes seems impossible because of the dispersion of more politically liberal states on both coasts and in the middle of the country (e.g., Illinois, Minnesota). Such an unlikely geographical scenario would require massive population migrations—conservatives to conservative areas, liberals to liberal areas—across most state lines. Strikingly, major interstate migrations are currently going in directions that *counter* conservative white political dominance in some states. To take a major example, there is the relatively recent and ongoing migration of Democratic-leaning African Americans from northern states to southern states that their ancestors once fled because of Jim Crow segregation. Additionally, Democratic-leaning Mexican Americans and other Latina/os are moving from the entry border states of their ancestors to numerous other U.S. states, including those once predominantly white. Then, too, there are numerous new middle-class immigrants of color from African, Caribbean, Asian, and Latin American countries who are mostly

Democratic-leaning. So far, these important internal and external non-white migrations are gradually contributing to political liberalization of the traditionally conservative socio-political climates of states like Texas, Arizona, Georgia, and Florida. Certainly, these internal and external migrations present long-term challenges for a geographical "two sovereign states" scenario.

A more likely divided-states scenario, especially in the short term, is similar to what happened in the U.S. after the 1860s Civil War—which was a war not only over the slavery system but also geographically between southern states and border/northern states. For a time after that bloody war, a remarkable Reconstruction era showed what a multiracial democratic society in the South could be like, with African Americans freed from slavery, officially given U.S. citizenship, and often free to be politically active and provide better control over their families' social and economic lives. In fact, the Reconstruction era brought significant multiracial democracy to many southern areas. Bold federal congressional action was essential to this revolution—especially passage of the 13th, 14th, and 15th Constitutional amendments and 1866 Civil Rights Act, the disenfranchising of top Confederate leaders, and federal enforcement of new federal civil rights laws. This Reconstruction era has accurately been called the "second American revolution," and these constitutional amendments greatly expanded all Americans' constitutional rights.

All too soon, however, most northern white government officials, and associated white corporate officials, tired of this southern civil rights enforcement effort. Together with re-enfranchised former Confederate officials, they generated a *white counter-revolution* to the Black liberation and multiracial democracy. While some northern liberal members of Congress continued to press for African American rights, most of the northern corporate-dominated elite, backed by a conservative white Supreme Court, agreed to let the white southern political and economic elite retake totalitarian control of their states and resume extreme racial oppression, this time in the form of near-slavery segregation ("Jim Crow") of their African American population. White southerners came to call this renewed white supremacist control the "Redemption" era—that is, white totalitarian redemption from burgeoning multiracial democracy.

Today, the very divided U.S. political reality has similarities to that of this "Redemption" era. In the 1950s–1970s, soon after major civil rights movements and laws began to dismantle this country's racial segregation, a substantial majority of the white population supported political and other societal efforts to reduce, stall, or end that significant racial progress. As in the 19th century, an organized white counter-revolution (another white "Redemption") began during the early stage of racial desegregation, and it has reappeared, albeit in fluctuating organization and strength, since that multiracial democratic civil rights revolution. Conspicuous examples of continuing racial desegregation in recent years, such as election of first African American president Barack Obama, have brought yet more aggressive white racialized pushback. We saw that pushback in the openly white nationalist organizing for Donald Trump's successful election in 2016, in his similar 2020 attempt at re-election, and in his encouraging of the January 2021 Capitol insurrection, the first violent political coup attempt since the Civil War.

Continuing into the present day, the counter-revolutionary efforts against expanded multiracial democracy of a great many whites, including a majority of Republicans, show that the U.S. is again in an extraordinarily difficult political era—an era where multiracial democratic institutions are again under direct and serious threat. Legal scholar Julie Novkov argues that, given the currently intense racial and political polarization of the Republican and Democratic Parties, the

> compromise that ended Reconstruction may begin to look like a plausible way out: leaving states to develop and implement policies based on the world views of those who control their dominant parties, with all that that could mean for those living there.[37]

That is, another possible divided-states' scenario for the U.S. is a sort of contemporary white-racist "redemption" federalism. On the one hand, there is the likely reality of western and northern states like California and New York becoming more nonwhite in population and voters and staying Democratic in political terms. On the other hand, major states in southern and southwestern areas like Texas and Florida also become more nonwhite in population and voters but stay white conservative Republican-dominated at the state government level by means of voter suppression and other antidemocratic efforts by Republican officials in those states. This latter reality would be backed by antidemocratic Republican officials at the federal government level such as the right-wing justices currently in full control of the Supreme Court (see Chapter 5 on voter suppression).

In this regard, we need to remind ourselves that the U.S. was long ago constitutionally founded by elite white men as a so-called federalist country wherein government power is shared between the federal government and the state governments—with states being of greatly varying population size but having the same clout in an undemocratic U.S. Senate. Many elite white founders openly said they feared the country's "masses," and they then had in mind ordinary white men. Their expectation, largely confirmed since their time, was that elite white men would very disproportionately control the U.S. state and federal governments forever. According to political scientist William Riker, "it is impossible to interpret federalism as other than a device for minority tyranny" and "If one approves of the goals and values of the privileged minority, one should approve of federalism."[38] Contemporary white right-wing Republican control of numerous states has led to their governments already accelerating "states rights" resistance to federal government programs, laws, and decisionmaking considered "too liberal," including progressive policies supported by a majority of their own state residents.

Today, this reinvigorated states-rights rhetoric is true even for states like Texas where whites are already in a significant *minority* among state residents and a larger percentage but still a *minority* (about 49 percent) of eligible voters. The mostly white right-wing Republican government currently there is zealously trying to suppress democratic voting by, and fair political representation of, its citizens of color. This white-minority political tyranny may eventually be true of numerous other states. Importantly too, the current right-wing U.S. Supreme Court majority has been lenient in allowing white Republican-controlled state governments to act against the interests of their Democratic Party voters, including voters of color.[39] Moreover, the scholar Julie Novkov notes that this significant white right-wing control at the state level also facilitates national Republican congressional dominance "gained from more than 30 Republican-controlled states' changes to districting and election laws."[40] Eventually, this white right-wing control may further sabotage democratic majority rule not just within those states, but also in the U.S. Senate and other national political institutions.

Measuring Democratic Decline

Central to these demographically changing, shifting political-economic models of a future U.S. is the question of multiracial democracy. That is, will an increasingly majority-minority America be able to sustain its now partially democratic political institutions and expand them to create an authentic multiracial democracy, one where citizens of all racial backgrounds have truly equal political rights?

There seem to be two major paths involving large-scale citizen action on U.S. democracy. One path involves much civil conflict involving whites organized in counter-revolutionary actions, nonviolent and violent, against a liberalizing multiracial-democratic society—a counter-revolution moving in an undemocratic fascist-type direction that attempts to maintain or expand currently disproportionate white political and economic power even as whites become a smaller population minority. In contrast, there is the vigorous pro-democracy path that began in earnest with the large-scale 1950s–1960s civil rights movements and consequent racial desegregation and has recently involved large-scale collective organization by diverse millions of Americans pressing for expanded and meaningful multiracial democracy (see below). In my view, this latter organizational path is the only one with any hope of turning back continuing white nationalist attempts to overthrow U.S. democratic institutions.

The U.S. already seems to be moving well along this first dangerous path. A recent report on the global status of democracy by the International Institute for Democracy and Electoral Assistance rated, for the *first* time, the U.S. as a "backsliding" democracy. The reason cited was the visible deterioration in U.S. democratic norms. Since 2019, there have been

> declines in civil liberties and checks on government ... [which] indicate that there are serious problems with the fundamentals of democracy.... A historic turning point came in 2020–21 when former president Donald Trump questioned the legitimacy of the 2020 election results in the United States.[41]

Additionally, the Center for Systemic Peace assessed U.S. democratic conditions in the Donald Trump era and scored the country, on a scale from 1 to 10, as just a 5—that is, as only a partial and deteriorating democracy. This score was well down from the top democracy score (10) it had received in the past. More recently, that previous high score was mostly regained with Joe Biden's 2020 election and 2021 inauguration. Assessing such disturbing findings, political scientist Barbara F. Walter has described this Trump era U.S. political condition as an "anocracy," as partly democratic and partly authoritarian:

> We are no longer the world's oldest continuous democracy. That honor is now held by Switzerland, followed by New Zealand, and then Canada. We are no longer a peer to nations like Canada, Costa Rica, and Japan, which are all rated a +10 on the Polity index.[42]

Contemporary Movement to Racialized Fascism

In Chapter 5, I discussed the periodic legitimation crises faced by ruling elites in countries like the U.S. As the U.S. undergoes a demographic and political transition from majority white to minority white, that ruling white elite and the political, economic, and other societal institutions they have created and now maintain will face ever more pressures from a racially divided population—on the one hand from nonwhite Americans demanding more political power and social equality, and on the other from white Americans demanding the continuation of the disproportionate power and social privilege they have had for centuries.

One such legitimation crisis was dramatized in the January 6, 2021, Capitol insurrection and its continuing politically polarized aftermath, to the present day. As we learned months after the 2020 presidential election from media and congressional investigations, there was extensive backstage organization and covert cooperation among white Republican leaders and operatives in a serious attempt to overthrow a legitimate U.S.

election result. They included the then President Donald Trump and his mostly white right-wing presidential advisors, many Republican legislators and other Republican officials, wealthy backers, and leaders and activists in major far-right organizations. Much of Trump's governing as president and his attempted and violent political coup were motivated by antidemocratic goals, indeed centrally by the racist-right ideologies of white nationalism and nativism documented throughout this book.[43]

Donald Trump's and other Republican leaders' white nationalist governing, attempted coup, and continuing antidemocratic efforts represent a new incarnation of the U.S.'s distinctive tradition of *racialized fascism*. In a 1995 address at Howard University, the ever insightful African American novelist and essayist Toni Morrison anticipated the contemporary Republican racist-fascist goals. In this era, she argued,

> Racism may wear a new dress, buy a new pair of boots, but neither it nor its succubus twin fascism is new or can make anything new. It can only reproduce the environment that supports its own health: fear, denial and an atmosphere in which its victims have lost the will to fight.... Fascism talks ideology, but it is really just marketing—marketing for power. It is recognizable by its need to purge, by the strategies it uses to purge and by its terror of truly democratic agendas. It is recognizable by its determination to convert all public services to private entrepreneurship; all nonprofit organizations to profit-making ones—so that the narrow but protective chasm between governance and business disappears.[44]

Morrison is referencing the very long history of this country's racialized fascist institutions and movements, especially as they have negatively affected Americans of color.

Over the last century, the U.S. has seen dozens of white fascist organizations emerge with thousands of members, and millions of white sympathizers. In the 1930s era, these included the paramilitary Black Legion, the Ku Klux Klan, the Silver Legion of America, the German American Bund, and the popular movement of radio commentator Father Charles Coughlin, among others.[45] In this era, President Franklin Roosevelt and his New Deal liberalism were often the target of these influential organizations. Disturbed at growing fascist views and efforts among the country's white corporate elite and ordinary white citizens, Roosevelt commented thus on U.S. fascism:

> The first truth is that the liberty of a democracy is not safe if the people tolerate the growth of private power to a point where it becomes stronger than their democratic State itself. That, in its essence, is fascism—ownership of government by an individual, by a group or by any other controlling private power.[46]

After World War II, the U.S. corporate-connected fascist movement declined in power somewhat, but its ideas, organizations, and tactics have reappeared in an oscillating fashion ever since.

Most scholars of fascism today agree that dictatorial corporate or individual dominance of a nation state has been a common feature of fascism since the early 20th century. In 2004, the prominent social scientist Robert Paxton, who specializes in the study of fascism, described yet other major features. Fascism is

> marked by obsessive preoccupation with community decline, humiliation or victimhood and by compensatory cults of unity, energy and purity, in which a mass-based party of committed nationalist militants, working in uneasy but effective collaboration with traditional elites, abandons democratic liberties and pursues with redemptive violence and without ethical or legal restraints goals of internal cleansing and external expansion.[47]

Recently, Paxton has described the Donald Trump political era as *clearly fascist* in these ways.

In addition, commenting specifically on the Trump political era, the fascism scholar Ruth Ben-Ghiat emphasizes that Trumpites have used

> fascist tactics, from holding rallies to refresh the leader-follower bond to creating a "tribe" (MAGA hats, rituals like chanting "lock them up," etc.) to unleashing a volume of propaganda without precedent by an American president. Yet the political cultures that form him and his close supporters... reflect a broader authoritarian history.... In the 21st century, fascist takeovers have been replaced by rulers who come to power through elections and then, over time, extinguish freedom.[48]

In the 2016 and 2020 presidential elections, Donald Trump demonstrated well these characteristics of a fascist political leader. Numerous other Republican leaders have used these often racialized fascist tactics, including celebrating a white individual as a cult-type leader, setting up ritualized rallies, and spreading much false political propaganda at state and federal levels. Moreover, some of Trump's Republican advisors and allies have had close ties to white supremacist and other authoritarian groups, while others have worked with or spoken positively about fascist dictators overseas.

Unsurprisingly, given this U.S. racist-fascist history, numerous societal analysts fear that another political coup attempt by Donald Trump or another far-right Republican candidate will come during the 2024 or 2028 national elections. Indeed, political actions that might facilitate an overt fascist coup, including racist gerrymandering and other representational suppression strategies targeting progressive voters, are now expanding in Republican-controlled states. Moreover, the majority of white voters have shown little concern about the possibility of U.S. elections being manipulated by their conservative state officials, who have already put into place significant voter suppression strategies.[49] Substantial research by election researcher Jennifer Cohn has demonstrated with empirical evidence that during the 2016 and 2020 elections, it is likely there were some illegally manipulated local vote tallies by Republican operatives or by Russian hackers' internet intrusions.[50]

Such treasonous antidemocratic efforts will likely increase in the U.S. political future. Reviewing future scenarios, historian Alfred McCoy has pessimistically suggested that

> in 2024, as the continuing erosion of America's global power creates a crisis of confidence among ordinary Americans, expect … a militant demagogue with thundering racialist rhetoric, backed by a revanchist Republican Party ready, with absolute moral certainty, to bar voters from the polls, toss ballots out and litigate any loss until hell freezes over. And if all that fails, the muscle will be ready for another violent march on Washington.[51]

Unsurprisingly, billionaire-funded far-right groups like the ALEC policy organization have already argued for a new U.S. Constitutional Convention, implemented under the current U.S. Constitution's Article V that allows the states to originate such a meeting. The goal would be would to give further power over the federal government and its budgets to mostly white-run corporate America.[52]

A Growing White Nationalist "Army"?

Recall from Chapter 2 that several white terrorists who perpetrated mass shootings in the U.S. and elsewhere have portrayed themselves as heroes, expressed much anger over white population decline, and emphasized their white supremacist vision of a coming "race war." In addition, across the U.S. the number of white supremacist and neo-Nazi paramilitary groups with similar views has grown significantly in recent decades. Given ongoing white population decline, we will likely see more whites joining or otherwise supporting such racist-fascist groups. The scholar Matthew Feldman has pointed out that "Democratic regression and political polarization are not unique to the U.S. Having more guns than people is. So are militias, usually formed of lower- and middle-class white Americans harboring anti-government sentiments."[53] Similarly, historian Charles King has underscored national surveys showing that Americans are "more armed, more forgiving of extrajudicial killing, and more comfortable with state-sanctioned confinement and execution than the citizens of any other free country."[54]

As the January 2021 Capitol insurrection and other riotous protests against state and local governments have demonstrated, many whites in white supremacist and related far-right political organizations will use collective violence to impose their extremist racial and political framing. As Andrew Whitehead sums up the national situation, white Christian nationalists

> see the nation as their own both historically and theologically and so any Presidential election that does not produce the desired result must be illegitimate. True patriots, in this understanding, have the right— the duty, even—to take it back, by force if necessary.... Just as the January 6th insurrection and recent voting laws are not aberrations but a reflection of similar events in our nation's history, they too may be a bellwether of events to come if we do not acknowledge and confront Christian nationalism.[55]

It is noteworthy too that, as of now, only a modest number of the thousands of January 2021 Capitol insurrectionists have been significantly punished for their actions. Disturbingly too, 13 percent of those so far arrested are actually serving in the military or are military veterans, twice their percentage in the general population.[56] Moreover, recent national surveys have shown that about 17 percent of Republicans support the use of violence to put Donald Trump or a similar fascist Republican back into the U.S. presidency.[57]

Social scientist Anthony Weems has suggested that this contemporary white commitment to political violence often seems like the building and activation of a "white army."[58] We certainly see much evidence of many whites arming themselves and creating the aforementioned white militias and other army-like organizations. In the future, if the U.S. does establish fully undemocratic minority white rule at the federal government level like that of the old South African apartheid, that white ruling elite might well make use of fearful armed whites and related white nationalist organizations as a paramilitary "white army" to achieve, maintain, and protect its reactionary sociopolitical goals.

This bodes ill for the survival of the democracy in, or even the country of, the U.S. Assertive pro-democracy organization and action against the growing power of white nationalist and other fascist movements in the U.S. will necessarily involve much sacrifice. One major issue regarding future U.S. antiracist and pro-democracy protests is what the response of these progressive protesters, white and nonwhite, will be if their large and peaceful demonstrations are met with much repressive policing or even military repression that results in many democratic protestor injuries and deaths. This has already happened in a few cities which had protests against police brutality and malpractice. If this accelerated policing violence happens, will millions of white and nonwhite protestors continue to flood the streets protesting for racial changes? Will they too arm themselves? Or will most Americans, including most who are progressive, just be political bystanders. Significantly, one analysis of citizen resistance to aggressive German Nazi actions in European countries in the violent 1930s–1940s era found that "most of the population in Germany and France was passive; it was natural to look the other way as human rights abuses occurred, and care for oneself and one's family."[59]

The Yale historian of political authoritarianism, Timothy Snyder, has recently suggested the following scenario of total U.S. political-economic chaos and collapse if a far-right political candidate is imposed on U.S. society illegally by Republican legislators in state and federal governments and/or by violent insurrectionary activity:

> Tens of millions of people protest. Paramilitaries on both sides emerge. Violence leads to fake and real stories of deaths, and to revenge. Police and armed forces will know neither whom they should obey nor whom they should arrest. With traditional authority broken, those wearing uniforms and bearing arms will become partisans, take sides, and start shooting one another. Governors will look for exit strategies for their states. Americans will rush to parts of the disintegrating country they find safer, in a process that looks increasingly like ethnic cleansing. The stock market and then the economy will crash. The dollar will cease to be the world currency.[60]

Recently too, an outside observer and leading Canadian political scientist, Thomas Homer-Dixon, put it this way, with a future Trump-type presidential figure in mind:

> In 2014, the suggestion that Donald Trump would become president would also have struck nearly everyone as absurd. But today we live in a world where the absurd regularly becomes real and the horrible commonplace. By 2025, American democracy could collapse, causing extreme domestic political instability, including widespread civil violence. By 2030, if not sooner, the country could be governed by a rightwing dictatorship.[61]

Important Barriers to Expanded U.S. Fascism

Still, there are several reasons for some optimism in regard to actual barriers to such increased U.S. fascism and associated violence. First, consider the political difficulties facing an increasingly fascistic Republican Party in 2024 and later presidential elections. In interviews with leading political analysts, *New York Times* journalist Thomas Edsall found several who argued former president Donald Trump cannot be reelected in future elections unless he can get more non-college-educated ("working class") white voters to turn out for him than he did in 2020—that is, at the same high rate of 2016. These analysts cite national surveys showing that Trump voters have included a large percentage of weak or reluctant supporters.[62] Moreover, many conservative Republican voters seem convinced that because of Trump's obsessive "stop the steal" rhetoric about the 2020 election, their votes did not matter, and will not matter in the future. This could mean that even with Republican voter suppression efforts, some future election battleground states will see Trump or a similar Trump-type Republican candidate losing previous voters who will not turn out. Others may even vote for Democrats, especially those disturbed at the violent 2021 Capitol insurrection. As Edsall concludes, looking toward future elections Trump "embodies the party's predicament: Candidates running for the House and Senate need him to turn out the party's populist base, but his presence at the top of the ticket could put Congress and the White House out of reach."[63]

Currently, new far-right political voices are appearing on the political scene. As of this writing, Trump's political power seems to be waning. His lack of serious involvement in many legislative efforts for Congress and his lesser media presence and smaller rally crowds since 2020 suggest to numerous contemporary political observers that he may be losing significant numbers of Republican voters to rising right-wingers like Florida's authoritarian governor Ron DeSantis. Conservative *Washington Post* columnist Henry Olsen has argued:

> Those who say that the GOP is Trump's fiefdom are wrong. The barons are restless, and many of the peasants want a new king. Don't be surprised if these factors depose Trump from his metaphorical throne before the next presidential cycle begins.[64]

Additionally, other media reports have indicated that some of Trump's more famous supporters are in a struggle with each other over both Republican funders and followers—and that Trump was upset at his new rival DeSantis.[65] Still, as of early 2023 Trump's complete removal from the Republican leadership throne in the near future seems unlikely, but if he is demoted from that throne other less charismatic right-wing Republicans are waiting to quickly replace him. This should not be surprising because, as I have shown previously, organized fascist-type politics has a very long history in the U.S., a movement much larger than just one political figure.

One possible strategy for a declining white Republican Party has long been to broaden its voter base by recruiting more voters of color. As we saw in Chapter 5, some political analysts argue that more open-minded white conservatives might build new majority conservative coalitions by recruiting certain Asian or Latina/o voters and treating them as "honorary whites." At present, however, few Republican leaders seem interested in this broader political strategy, even though there was a small shift to Donald Trump from 2016 to 2020 among voters of color. Nonetheless, substantial majorities of these nonwhite groups are still voting for Democratic candidates, and a racially broader Republican coalition seems unlikely in the near future.

Another important voter group likely affecting Republican and Democratic political success in the future is college-educated white voters, and especially college-educated white women voters. In 2020, a majority (54 percent) of college-educated whites actually voted for Democrat Joe Biden, including 58 percent of college-educated white women. These percentages were a significant increase over Hillary Clinton's presidential results in 2016. Yet, Biden only got 44 percent of all white voters, although this too was more than Clinton's 41 percent in 2016.[66]

Americans Organizing for Democracy: A Long History

The most important barrier to this expanding U.S. fascism is, or can be, the successful organization of the majority of Americans—those still firmly committed to U.S. democracy--to protest regularly in an array of anti-fascist demonstrations and to vote in overwhelming numbers for political candidates with strong commitments to present and future multiracial democracy. Both of these efforts are already conceptualized, planned, and being implemented by a number of progressive democratic activists and organizations, new and old. In this last section of the book, after a brief historical review, I will detail some of these democracy-saving efforts.

Centuries of African American Efforts for Democracy

Anti-fascist resistance has a long history in the U.S. For centuries, Americans of color have demonstrated the reality and importance of efforts to expand and buttress American democracy in the face of actual and threatened racialized fascism. By way of illustration, let us briefly review the history of African American efforts in building coalitions for expanded democracy. Of all American groups, African Americans have the longest continuing history in fighting collectively for full freedom and social justice for all Americans.

Consider, for example, that in the Civil War hundreds of thousands of African American soldiers, sailors, and support troops—many of them formerly enslaved—fought in the U.S. (Union) military for democracy. Their courageous efforts helped mightily to give the U.S. its first multiracial democratic institutions. The democratic impact of that war can be seen in the postwar passage of the U.S. Constitution's 14th amendment with its provisions for due process and equal protection of the laws, thereby expanding democratic institutions for Americans of all racial backgrounds. In *How Blacks Built America*, I have emphasized with much data that the

> large-scale, recurring resistance and counter-framing of Black pamphleteers, abolitionists, Civil War soldiers, and civil rights activists have been critical factors in the significant progress this country has made in implementing, if still only partially, its much-heralded ideals of freedom, justice, and democracy.[67]

Indeed, a pathbreaking feature of the famous 1950s–1970s civil rights movements was their Black leaders' repeated insistence on these broad progressive ideals. These were large-scale, racially integrated movements committed to multiracial democracy. The great civil rights activist, Ella Baker, emphasized the radical democratic goals of these civil rights movements:

> In order for … oppressed people to become part of a society that is meaningful, the system under which we now exist has to be radically changed. This means we have to learn to think in radical terms. I use the word radical in its original meaning—getting down to and understanding the root cause.[68]

Later on, activist-scholar Cornel West accented that this antiracist counter-framing is

> fundamentally committed to the priority of poor and working people, thus pitting it against the neoliberal regime, capitalist system, and imperial policies of the U.S. government. The Black prophetic tradition has never been confined to the interests and situations of Black people. It is rooted in principles and visions that embrace these interests and confront the situations, but its *message is for the country and world*.[69]

Moreover, at various times in the 1960s and 1970s, numerous African American civil rights organizations—the Student Nonviolent Coordinating Committee, Southern Christian Leadership Conference, NAACP, National Urban League, and Black Panther Party—joined in marches or otherwise supported the mostly Latino and Filipino United Farm Workers (UFW) union's strikes for economic and social justice. To the present day, African Americans have participated in many such multiracial protest efforts across the country.[70] They have also been leaders in conceptualizing the importance of continuing social justice protests for the country and across the globe. For instance, the African American scholar Robin D. G. Kelley has recently emphasized that the path to racial liberation, social justice, and democracy is not fixed but constantly changing and globalized:

> What we are witnessing now, across the country and around the world, is a struggle to interrupt historical processes leading to catastrophe.... [The] forces we face are not as strong as we think. They are held together by guns, tanks, and fictions. They can be disassembled, though that is easier said than done. In the meantime, we need to be prepared to fight for our collective lives.[71]

Contemporary Diverse Movements: Black Lives Matter Protests

Recently, the African American population has again demonstrated these continuing collective commitments to social justice and authentic democracy. Together with millions of other people of color and progressive whites, a great many African Americans have participated in large-scale multiracial protests against the killings of Black and Brown men, women, and children, especially since the murder of Florida teenager Trayvon Martin in 2012. Soon thereafter in summer 2013, intense discussions of Black Lives Matter (#BLM), with that term and hashtag, became common in the ever expanding online media. That year, three African American women created the Black Lives Matter Network, which helped to integrate numerous local protest organizations into a national multiracial network working against policing racism and other systemic racism. Two years later, the Movement for Black Lives was created as an even larger multiracial coalition of more than 50 local activist groups, including the BLM groups.[72] This loosely integrated network of organizations has been influential in providing information about police and other racist malpractice in various media and in getting millions of Americans of diverse racial and ethnic backgrounds to participate in local antiracist protests.

Most dramatically so far, during summer 2020, there was a major increase in nonviolent protests against police brutality and other systemic racism, much of which was triggered by yet more police killings of Black Americans. During that summer police brutalization of George Floyd, a Black man murdered in Minneapolis in May 2020, was a major motivation for these large-scale protests. One *New York Times* analysis of opinion polls estimated total participation in these 2020 antiracist protests to be at least 15 million people, and perhaps as many as 26 million. In addition to millions of Black demonstrators, there were millions of whites and other people of color. Such numbers indicate this was probably the *largest* collective protest in U.S. history. About 6–10 percent of all the survey respondents polled nationally indicated they had participated in these multiracial demonstrations, which took place in at least 1,360 U.S. counties, about three quarters of those being predominantly white. Many survey participants said media coverage of police violence against people of color or against other protesters had influenced their decision to participate, and half said they were participating in such antiracist protest for the first time.[73]

One media report in summer 2020 suggested that these large-scale demonstrations had already generated some significant policing changes nationwide:

> In Minneapolis, the multiracial City Council pledged to dismantle its police department. In New York, lawmakers repealed a law that kept police disciplinary records secret. Cities and states across the country passed new laws banning chokeholds. Mississippi lawmakers voted to retire their state flag, which prominently includes a Confederate battle emblem.[74]

However, while some of these reforms are today still in place, the Minneapolis council pledge only ended up in a small cut to the city's policing budget. Numerous pledges nationwide have had a similarly modest or backtracking result.

One of the African American developers of authentic critical race theory, law professor Kimberlé Crenshaw, has summarized what the diverse George Floyd marches meant for the country as a whole, especially for continuing antiracist action:

> Every state in the union had a march. The majority of people out there were not of color. Language was being shared widely for the first time: "systemic racism," "institutionalized patterns of marginality," "racial power." People were saying these words in a way that they hadn't—ever!…. With no real literacy beyond that, with no capacity to actually say: Okay, so tell us what that means, what needs to be done. Tell us what the policies are that allow us to unravel the institutionalized forms of inequality that you are now talking about. And if you don't have the ability to do it, you've picked a fight with a giant, and you don't have ammunition…. This was produced by a singular moment, and that moment is increasingly looking like it may be singular if we're not prepared in this moment to actually say: "This really is what structural racism is."[75]

Learning terms like "systemic racism" is important, but far more important is teaching more Americans, and especially white Americans, what that concept *really means* in everyday practice. The recent white racist-right attack on "critical race theory" noted in previous chapters is actually an attack on teaching honest histories of these systemically racist experiences of Americans of color. In this process of knowledge suppression these racist-right activists help to keep most whites (and many others) of all ages illiterate about much of this country's actual racist history. Unquestionably, that racist-right effort is an overt white attack on Black Americans and other Americans of color and their critical perspectives on the systemically racist experiences that have long endured.

Multiracial Political Coalitions: The Role of Diverse Gen-Zers

In recent decades, majorities of voters of color in most age groups—including African Americans, Native Americans, Asian Americans, and Latina/o Americans—have generally stayed with the more progressive Democratic Party in state and national elections. Typically, they do so because of right-wing Republican Party attacks on, or neglect of, their social justice and socioeconomic goals for their families and communities. One result of the future browning of America may be that Americans of color will build yet more effective political coalitions across their groups and with progressive whites in a Democratic Party coalition. In this way, they can secure the goal of breaking down persisting discriminatory barriers and racialized institutions and move the U.S. toward a much more democratic society, one with greater social justice and equality. The most likely white participants in this collective effort are the youngest white generations.

Recall from Chapter 5 that the young Gen-Z generation, now about 70 million strong, is more socially and politically progressive than any of the older Silent, Baby Boomer, Gen-X, and Millennial generations. In the 2020 national election, these younger Americans turned out in relatively high numbers and as a group voted overwhelmingly for Democratic Party candidates, including Joe Biden for president. As a group, numerous opinion polls show, they are very racially diverse and are worried about—and committed to social and political action on—climate change, gun control, economic inequality, and racial inequality. A few nonrandom online polls have found that most, especially those who are nonwhite, have very progressive racial views and action commitments. A nonrandom 2020 Yubo poll of thousands of U.S. Gen-Zers, most of whom (64 percent) identified as nonwhite, found that 88 percent felt Black Americans suffered discrimination, almost 90 percent supported the BLM movement, and 83 percent felt the police often used too much force. In terms of activism, a majority of this group said they had participated in a protest for Black equality (77 percent) and were willing to get arrested during a peaceful protest for racial equality (62 percent). In addition, most (86 percent) thought peaceful protest was essential for significant societal change. Unsurprisingly, this survey also found that these respondents had often used social media to express support for BLM and for equality for Black Americans.[76]

Significantly, too, very few Gen-Zers and younger millennials participated in the violent January 2021 Capitol insurrection. In contrast, millions of them, white and nonwhite, have participated in hundreds of BLM and similar protests against policing and other systemic racism. Some rough estimates indicate that at least three quarters of those in the BLM protests were Gen-Zers and younger Millennials, with at least half of those being white.[77] These hundreds of large demonstrations suggest that a significant, mostly younger, segment of the white population has aligned more with the antiracist views and sentiments of Americans of color about racist policing than with the views of the mostly older white whites who buttress the contemporary Republican Party. Large-scale protest participation by younger whites suggests they are at least more open than other older whites to racial justice changes in U.S. society.[78]

However, as I noted in Chapter 5, for many in the younger white generations their relatively progressive understandings of U.S. racism and of racial change are often relatively superficial, and they too are in great need of much more critical education about this country's long history of both systemic racism and antiracism. Indeed, several studies discussed earlier suggest most are not committed to large-scale racial change if that change significantly affects their own socioeconomic situations and their current or future racial privileges in U.S. society.

Contemporary Resistance to Multiracial Organization: Moderate Whites

Beyond the younger white Gen-Z and Millennial generations, one can inquire about the role of the racially moderate whites of older generations in the current and future cause of racial and other social justice. For instance, the BLM protests in summer 2020 did see many white participants of various ages marching with people of color, although younger participants were the substantial majority.[79] The presence of many thousands of older whites, many of them doubtless political "moderates," gives one some hope of somehow reaching more of them in future social and political efforts for multiracial democracy causes. Still, as of now, such innovative recruitment efforts mostly remain to be done (see below).

Actually, the number of racially diverse protests against racist policing, other policing malpractice, and systemic racism generally, which had once spread greatly, soon declined significantly just a few months after summer 2020. One *New York Times* analysis found that in general the white majority's attitudes had become more *opposed* to such demonstrations: "Whereas support for Black Lives Matter remains relatively high among racial and ethnic minorities, support among white Americans has proved both fickle and volatile."[80] While many whites became more supportive of BLM policing protests after George Floyd's murder, over the next year that support declined to less than before that police murder.

One important reason for this white attitudinal decline seems to have been the white right-wing media's and most Republican politicians' reinvigorated politicization of, and attacks on, the policing reform proposals and other racism reform issues coming out of these pathbreaking demonstrations.[81] In more recent years the mainstream news media have not provided the necessary scale of counter programming to the often false and misleading conservative media presentations on policing and other systemic racism issues.

Additionally, there is a centuries-old history of very negative white responses to multiracial organizing and organizations that needs to be considered. Most members of the white elite have long feared organized democratic rebellions by multiracial coalitions, especially those with significant white participation. To forestall white participation in such democracy protest movements, that elite has regularly provided and extended the seductive "public and psychological wage of whiteness" to ordinary whites discussed in previous chapters. The white elite's creation of a large-scale colonial, and later U.S., slavery system in which only Black and Native Americans were enslaved was coupled with energetically accenting racial solidarity across white social classes.[82] Moreover, after the Civil War, there was a very substantial increase in ordinary Black and white workers joining partially integrated alliances and mutual-aid organizations seeking major progressive political and economic goals. These included militant farmers' organizations working for better farm trade conditions for both poor white and poor Black farming communities. These partially integrated organizations were frightening to elite whites in the South and North.[83] Historian James Horton has noted:

> All through the late 19th century, there is this constant message hammered at poor white people: "You may be poor, you may have miserable lives right now, but the thing that is most important, the thing we want you to focus on, is the fact that you are white."[84]

Note too that somewhat similar elite messages worked well during the civil rights movement era, when a majority of whites in national polls were opposed to the civil rights movement and had negative views of leaders such as Dr. Martin Luther King, Jr. For example, in a 1963 national Gallup survey 60 percent of white respondents said they had a negative view of the 1963 March on Washington, led by Dr. King and other African American activists.[85] Using various socio-political resources, the white elite has long created the equivalent of contemporary conservative

Fox-type media to con and pressure ordinary whites away from progressive democratic political coalitions with Americans of color.

Today, attempts at large-scale multiracial democratic organizing also run into the problem of the majority of ordinary whites being isolated in relatively segregated housing areas and being concerned with protecting their white racial status and privilege instead of seeking social class alliances with people of color. The elite white dominance strategy continues to be successful to the present. Many white participants in the aforementioned white supremacist groups and other far-right political groups, as well as in the political campaigns of white nationalist candidates like Donald Trump, have been working-class and middle-class whites who suffer significant wage suppression and other class oppression at the hands of the white capitalist elite. If they could break significantly with the centuries-old "wage of whiteness" tradition and organize with Americans of color for democratic change, most ordinary white individuals and their families would likely see their socioeconomic lives dramatically improved. Such multiracial farmers and urban workers coalitions were successful for a time in the late 19th century, until aggressive white elite counter-action—much of it race-baiting and accenting white supremacist organization—brought them to an end.[86]

Today, such large multiracial coalitions would again have the power to implement the important social democratic programs (e.g., national health care, better wages and benefits) sought by union activists, civil rights leaders, and other progressive activists. White workers and their families badly needing these social democratic programs have been constantly conned by white elites to think and work against their material interests, now for several centuries. Current maintenance of the high level of class inequality in U.S. society requires that ordinary whites' social discontent—feelings of resentment and of being socioeconomically oppressed—be directed, not at the actions of the elite capitalist villains, but at mostly imaginary threats from people of color.

Contemporary Grassroots Organizing for Democracy

Lessons from California's Grassroots Organization

Undoubtedly, the *democratic* political and economic future of several hundred million U.S. residents lies in the actions of progressive movements like those that brought effective multiracial social democracy to states like California (see above). Greatly expanded progressive movements and organizations seem essential if there is any chance to save the U.S. from moving permanently to a white nationalistic and fascist federal government—or a country with many such fascistic state governments.

How can the successful progressive efforts in states like California be multiplied on a larger scale nationally?

Comparing California's oscillating political history to the troubled U.S. today, sociologist Manuel Pastor argues that the U.S. today is quite like California in its very troubled 1990s—then "wracked by racial tension, anxious about its economic future, and willing to follow leaders with simplistic solutions."[87] The California progressive vision and successes appeared over the course of the early 2000s thanks to a large array of liberal activist groups, whose strength won elections and pressured the executive and legislative branches of state government to make dramatic changes in a multiracial and social democratic direction. For some years now, grassroots movements for such progressive goals as better wages, paid family leave, unionization, immigrant rights, and environmental restrictions have been successful there.

Pastor summarizes four lessons for democratic organizers in other states and the country as a whole that emerge from these California grassroots efforts:

> The first is how organizations decided to both scale up their own work and *connect with others through statewide networks*; organized labor, environmental justice groups, faith-based networks, and multiracial grassroots advocates proved willing to work effectively with one another and to build an ecosystem for change. The second is the role of a hardheaded analysis of power, a strategy that helped to ease the usual leftist schism between those who *emphasize protests and those who stress policy proposals and electoral politics* by lifting up the fact that both are important. The third is... [that] progressives recognized that while increasing urbanization might give them an edge, they also needed to *stretch into the inland and suburban parts of California....* The fourth is... [that] organizers didn't just passively count on demographic shifts but rather developed an "integrated voter engagement" program—one that *combined ongoing community organizing with concentrated efforts to get out the vote.*[88]

Successful multiracial leadership development, movement-building, and cooperative integration of numerous grass-roots organizations and movements were major keys to their ultimate political success in elections and legislatures. Pastor sees that success as an organizing model for the U.S. today. If California politicians can be influenced by well-organized progressive movements, it should be the case that other progressives across the country can also "double down on understanding power, taking geography seriously, developing long-lasting alliances, constructing an alternative values-based vision, and working to get the people out when the vote really counts."[89] Pastor ends his analysis by listing other lessons from California's move to being very progressive, both politically and socioeconomically. These include accenting a broad *social compact* shared across most racial groups and social classes; understanding the importance of generation gaps; emphasizing the role of intersectionally linked, grassroots movements; fighting restrictive voting laws; recognizing rural *and* urban diversity; including the more liberal faction of the capitalist class; and boldly asserting progressive economic and other social goals.[90]

As I noted earlier, national political reactions to the progressive California movements and political impacts have varied dramatically. During Donald Trump's term in office, his arch-conservative administration fought repeatedly with California officials over a range of progressive policies, including environmental protection, homelessness, and climate change. He often disparaged the liberal state government, especially after they passed a bill requiring presidential candidates to make tax returns public.[91]

In contrast, during the 2020 political campaigns, Michael Bloomberg, a former New York City Republican mayor and billionaire entrepreneur, was a Democratic presidential candidate. He had much praise for California's progressive policies and programs. An Associated Press report summarized his positive take on California's policies on gun control, climate change, and criminal justice: "I think that California can serve as a great example for the rest of this country." In spite of their housing and other problems he underscored, California "is something the rest of the country looks up to. California has been a leader in an awful lot of things."[92]

Moreover, in his first years in office, President Joe Biden, supported by talented Californian Vice President Kamala Harris, tried to implement some progressive policies similar to those already operational in California, including a higher minimum wage and a required family leave program. One California magazine summarized this increasingly progressive state and federal government reality:

> History will remember 2021 as the year when a windfall of government spending sought to address years of inequality, poverty and a growing population left behind. Trillions of dollars were spent by the federal government, but California's state government, facing the nation's highest poverty rate, also saw an unprecedented budget surplus that the state's supermajority Democrats used to expand health and education programs as well as climate change efforts and assistance for the poor.[93]

Today, a large majority of Americans back an array of federal government support programs—indeed, an expanded social welfare state—that improve living conditions for individuals and families. In a recent Center for American Progress Strategies online poll of 2,000 representative registered voters, a substantial majority of Democrats and Republicans supported federal action to insure that local communities had clean water, good public education, good food access, and adequate housing, all of these being considered "basic human rights." A substantial majority also supported large-scale infrastructure investments, guaranteed employee sick days, paid family and medical leave, and food and housing assistance for those in need.[94] Democratic Party commitments to expansion of such progressive federal programs to meet basic human needs will likely grow with the browning of that Party, perhaps also increasing the movement of political independents and former Republicans into it.

Innovative Progressive Strategies: The Race-Class Narrative Project

Other recent progressive efforts have also developed innovative political strategies to bring more social democratic reforms to the U.S. For example, since 2017 a multiracial group of race scholars, racial justice activists, and polling specialists have developed what they term the Race-Class Narrative Project to build progressive political strategies and coalitions. They have conducted state and national interviews and focus groups to establish the best strategies to build political coalitions that include both progressive voters of color and progressive white voters. In a goals statement, they note that economic justice *and* racial justice are "core progressive priorities, but too often campaigns discuss them as if they were separate," adding that "our opponents promote racial fears to turn out white voters, pitting working people against each other and against good government." Drawing on substantial interviewing and polling data, they have discovered effective ways to build multiracial voter solidarity. This includes foregrounding candid discussions with white voters about how society's dominant white racist framing is a "divide-and-conquer tactic that creates distrust, undermines belief in government, and causes economic pain for everyone, of every color."[95]

In one major poll, some 59 percent of white respondents were found to be "persuadables" who hold two contradictory racial orientations in their heads—"one that views talking about race as necessary and desires racial fairness and progressive values; and another that hears conversations about race as problematic and orients them toward racial resentment and conservative fears."[96] Given this contradictory white reality, the successful progressive political strategy must include frank discussions of racism issues, but at same time one countering the white racial resentment fostered by white right-wing politicians: "Pointing out this strategic racism and tying it to the class war that wealthy [white] reactionaries are winning helps connect the experiences of targeted people of color and the experiences of economically anxious white people."[97] In their insightful perspective building, a successful progressive coalition requires recurring and forthright discussions of how white right-wing politicians and their wealthy white backers have used this divide-and-conquer political strategy to intentionally separate anxious white voters from voters of color. After truly candid discussions with white voters about this underlying racial-class reality, then a full discussion of how these two groups can join together in political action on both racial justice and economic prosperity is necessary, action that will greatly benefit both groups of politically progressive Americans.[98]

These progressive political activists have concluded that this race–class narrative works well in developing political strategies across an array of different groups. Large unions like the Service Employees International Union (SEIU) and the American Federation of Labor and Congress of Industrial Organizations (AFL-CIO), rural organizing groups like People's Action, and the North-Carolina-based Poor People's Campaign have endorsed this race–class fusion approach.[99] A survey of Latina/os voters by Project Junto found that a political approach accenting a race–class narrative also works best in attracting them to a multiracial political coalition. Thorough analysis of the survey found that elite white

> attacks on Latinos often use proxies like immigration status, national origin, and language, which many Latinos see as distinct from their racial group issues. Expressly naming race works best among Hispanics when presented as one important source of societal division among important others, for instance when associated with nationality and ethnicity.[100]

These perceptive race–class analysts suggest that using a political language of calling out divisive white elite political strategies and phrasing their own efforts as joining together with "other groups," instead of just "racial groups," works to keep a broad progressive strategy for Latina/os in the forefront. "Unlike the colorblind liberal strategy, the race–class approach directly challenges racism. Unlike the call out racism message, it frames powerful elites, rather than whites in general, as the problem."[101]

In a recent *New York Times* commentary, Democratic Party strategists Tory Gavito and Adam Jentleson have emphasized that this joint race–class approach is practical for actually organizing voters. Instead of letting Republicans force discussions of the racial issue into their own terms, the Democrats

> must confront it and explain that powerful elites and special interests use race as a tool of division to distract hard-working people of all races while they get robbed blind. Then pivot back to shared interests....The strategy we suggest here is a middle way: It is more

powerful than a racial-justice-only frame but also more powerful than a strategy that ignores race altogether.... By confronting race as a tool of division, and then pivoting to shared interests, Democrats can offer an optimistic, inspiring and even patriotic vision.[102]

Nonetheless, although this somewhat white-appeasing approach might bring in some moderate white voters to a multiracial coalition, it does explicitly reject the critical antiracist perspectives of many voters of color who insist systemic racism involves whites of all classes and must be forth-rightly challenged. These voters of color do seem to hold the ethical and social justice high ground, but the U.S.'s systemic white racism probably does necessitate something like the race-class approach to actually build enduring and successful multiracial voter coalitions.

Moreover, the majority of whites, especially those who are not college-educated, remain very resistant to any type of political approach that brings racial matters to the center of attention.[103] Numerous white Demo-cratic Party leaders have long called on the Party to work harder and spend more funds to bring into it more ordinary white voters, especially white working-class voters considered to be "swing" voters. Today, that task is challenging, if not impossible, because a substantial majority of white voters have bought strongly into a white-racist framing of U.S. society, including a very negative view of the browning of America. As I have emphasized here and in previous chapters, that white majority has been conned by the white elite with promises of continuing white racial status and racial privilege over the centuries to the present. Unsurprisingly, thus, the traditional Democratic Party approach to these ordinary white voters is to just accent "kitchen table" economic issues, while neglecting their strong white racist framing. Significantly, Heather McGhee, an African American lawyer working with the Race-Class Narrative Project, has written about extensive discussions with the ordinary whites across the country who face serious economic crises. She too reports that most do *not* understand how their own difficult socioeconomic conditions—including loss of public goods like good schools and parks, and loss of good-paying jobs and affordable health care—stem from greedy profit-centered efforts of the wealthy white corporate executives, the ones who con ordinary whites with racialized right-wing rhetoric into letting their government-dismantling and privatization efforts proceed and succeed.[104]

Still, McGhee remains optimistic. In numerous places across the country, she reports discovering a major "solidarity dividend" that comes when whites and people of color do manage to collaborate for economic and racial justice goals ultimately benefitting both groups. In those cases, the race-class narrative did work in getting some white voters to understand how they are being exploited by that white elite. Assessing the white fear of the demographic and political rise of Americans of color, McGhee further argues that whites' fear of being replaced, and insistent zero-replacement goals, must be aggressively countered and removed from their dominant framing of society: "Until we destroy the idea, opponents of progress can always unearth it and use it to any action that benefits us all."[105]

Another relevant issue here is the fact that many white left-wing critiques of contemporary capitalism call out its inegalitarian class hierarchy and class oppression well, but are weak on recognizing the role of systemic racism in founding, shaping, and perpetuating contemporary capitalism. They relegate race-based conceptualizations of capitalistic oppression and related anti-oppression organizing to what they problematize as distracting "identity politics."[106] Such white critics do not seem to understand that systemic racism is *foundational* to the rise and reality of Western capitalism, especially in countries like the U.S.

That is, slavery capitalism's organized features—royal colonizing and enslaving companies, profitmaking plantations, slave shipping companies, banking and other professional slavery support organizations—were the first large-scale capitalistic enterprises in Europe and North America. For centuries, the U.S. ruling class—mostly elite white men—has regularly made political-economic decisions motivated and shaped by their white racist framing of society, as well as their capitalistic framing of society. Significant aspects of that long-dominant white racist frame predate the capitalist-class framing of the white decisionmakers at the helm of major economic institutions. Indeed, many white left critiques of "identity politics" do not even mention, much less analyze and foreground, the racial (and gender) identity, positioning, and actions of the elite *white male* capitalists who are constantly engaged in early and later racialized decisionmaking. Racially oppressed Americans are by no means the only ones with relevant societal "identities" shaping their decisionmaking. The failure by some key white analysts and activists in U.S. left organizations to understand and emphasize the constantly intertwined reality of racial and class oppression helps to explain why some progressive movements have difficulties in organizing collectively for major societal change. Thus, a race-class approach to progressive organizing can make sense in a society where race and class realities are always intimately and integrally intertwined.

Racially Smart Progressive Campaigns: Focusing on the Nonwhite Base

The African American political activist Steve Phillips argues for yet another Democratic Party campaign approach that firmly emphasizes the Party's growing nonwhite and progressive white base. In his view, the mostly white Democratic Party leadership has historically insisted too much on heavily funding political strategies aimed at certain white "swing voters," especially the aforementioned working-class whites. This Democratic leadership folly is demonstrated in Democratic losses to Republican politicians in numerous state and national elections, including to George W. Bush in the early 2000s and to Donald Trump in 2016. In his view, Democratic leaders should instead focus more on, and heavily fund, registering and turning out the growing number of mostly progressive non-white voters and the minority of progressive whites, termed the "New American Majority." That means a strategy centering voters of color and progressive whites, *not* the failed strategy of focusing mainly on the white working class and other supposed white swing voters. He perceptively underscores this political reality:

> The absolute top priority for the progressive movement and progressive politics must be expanding the participation of and securing the lasting loyalty of this majority. That means moving large amounts of money to voter registration, door-to-door organizing, and culturally compelling communications.[107]

Phillips further insists that the progressive government policies most desired by this new political majority in many areas should be boldly promoted by Democratic leaders and political candidates. As he summarizes, "The way to win—the only way Democrats have won at the national level in the past sixteen years—is to inspire, invest in, organize, and galvanize the New American Majority—especially people of color who didn't vote in 2016" and the more progressive whites who sometimes vote for neither major party and choose libertarian or Green Party candidates.[108] Central to this vigorous multiracial-base strategy is also to bring into the Democratic leadership many more nonwhite and progressive white leaders whose lived experience—i.e., authentic cultural competence—is different from that of most whites in the current Democratic Party leadership and among its major political consultants. Successful campaigning

> means strengthening organizations and nurturing leaders who come from and can speak to the communities who make up the New American Majority. It means turning the growing analytics engine of the progressive movement to the critical questions of how to engage America's communities of color and their progressive White allies.[109]

Further, Phillips insists that mobilizing these Democratic voters by direct personal contacts is essential, instead of relying heavily on television ads as often has been traditional. Wiser Democratic leaders would also utilize culturally competent consultants who know better how to communicate with both nonwhite and more liberal white voters, including helping the latter to better understand and resist white nationalism:

Most White consultants are clueless about how to effectively talk about racial issues, and as a result they allowed Trump's race-baiting campaign to become normalized and an acceptable option for just enough Whites to allow him to capture the presidency.[110]

Related to this suggestion is Phillips' call for all Democratic Party leaders to more openly discuss the centrality and dangers of systemic white racism, to confront it head-on as a now critical feature of U.S. politics. In this important way, his approach emphasizes much more centrally the perspectives of voters of color than does the race-class approach.

Much progressive organizing has successfully utilized innovative grass-roots strategies that accent mobilization of millions of neglected voters of color. This has now been very successful in numerous political campaigns. As I noted in the opening to this chapter, in the 2020 election a pathbreaking mobilization of Georgia voters of color was led by progressive Democratic activists like Stacey Abrams. Extensive grass-roots efforts focused on legwork to contact and get out a diverse array of eligible voters, especially voters of color.[111] As a result, there was a dramatic upsurge in the numbers and turnout of Democratic voters, and Joe Biden won traditionally conservative Georgia's important presidential electors. Extensive mobilization of voters of color was demonstrably the key.[112]

Additionally, a recent Harvard political report argues that old South states like Georgia are set for yet more political changes favoring the Democratic Party. The report's authors contend that the South

> is entering what could be described as a Third Reconstruction.... some of the most innovative social justice campaigns in the country ... are conceived and led by local organizers in the South. A region of immense promise and potential that, with the right investments, could drive a period of profound change for the entire country.[113]

For example, the Georgia organizer Stacey Abrams has emphasized the major voting reforms that are now necessary at the state and national level: "The key to creating permanent voting rights lies in major federal change. When the right to vote is left to the states, implementation is fragmented, racist, and plain suppressive."[114] Recent political discussions in many Democratic Party settings, including in the major states of North Carolina and Pennsylvania, have accented the importance of the Abrams approach that emphasizes aggressive voter registration and much more voter education as necessary to grass-roots mobilization for successful expansion of multiracial democracy.[115]

Note too that only a minority of whites are racially and politically progressive, yet they are still essential to building and sustaining this "New American Majority." Political scientists Richard Fording and Sanford

Schram have argued from much election data that they are essential to the critical process of driving a "wedge between white moderates and white racial extremists."[116] They note this will be difficult because white Republican moderates, especially corporate executives, have benefitted from joining with these white nationalist extremists and thus winning national and local elections, thereby securing very favorable government action related to their business profitmaking. The only viable progressive alternative, Fording and Schram argue, is to vigorously mobilize racially liberal white and nonwhite voters to defeat this reactionary Republican coalition at the ballot box: "A defeated Republican Party is the best thing that could happened in the struggle to beat back rising white nationalism in U.S. politics."[117]

In addition, a critical shift in the racial framing of many white progressives is necessary. They too, for the most part, operate out of a version of the dominant white racial frame, one that still prizes much white history, social norms, and general virtuousness. The pioneering African American philosopher George Yancy has strongly suggested that a major step in dealing with white moderates and progressives is to press them to do the hard work of deframing that dominant white racial frame by actually listening to, and carefully hearing, African Americans and other Americans of color in their views on personal racism experiences and on how to counter white racism with personal and collective antiracist strategies. In this process, progressive and other whites must acknowledge that being white is often a serious handicap in understanding how to be a truly human being in a dehumanizing racist society. In contrast, Americans of color learn about that white inhumanity and racial danger quickly in growing up, as a matter of everyday lived experience battling white dehumanization of their lived reality. Yancy advises that these whites practice "active silence" in the place between their situational reflection and their interactive engagement, when they must choose how to proceed in interactions with people of color. The hard part is that progressive whites, indeed like all whites, must learn to hold back on reacting just according to their well-learned white racist norms and framing—a very difficult thing to do on a regular basis—and instead react in terms of what they hear and learn from the more humanized norms and values signaled by racially experienced people of color. Yancy also presses whites to *openly challenge* the white discriminatory actions, individual and collective, that constantly uphold the massive racial inequalities central to U.S. society today.[118]

Mobilizing Corporate Groups for Multiracial Democracy

Numerous political experts in the mainstream media and in academia have called on corporate America to more seriously defend U.S. democratic institutions in the face of growing white nationalism and political fascism.

Political scientist Richard Hasen has suggested that neither U.S. laws nor the Democratic Party can by themselves preserve the current level of U.S. democracy, but that "all sectors of society need to be mobilized in support of free and fair elections.... business groups, civic and professional organizations, labor unions and religious organizations all can help protect fair elections and the rule of law."[119]

The 2016 and 2020 elections involved New York entrepreneur Donald Trump and his voter base's white nationalist views and other far-right framing. As we have seen in this and other chapters, numerous other rich white businesspeople, including some top corporate leaders, have colluded in and helped to fund this white nationalist political resurgence. This political reality has made it more difficult for top corporate executives with more moderate political views to speak out on needed societal reforms without alienating the white far-right part of their investor base, corporate employees, and customers. Nonetheless, after white nationalist violence such as the 2017 Charlottesville riots or the January 2021 Capitol insurrection, numerous major corporate CEOs and certain important business associations have briefly spoken out against such racialized social and political violence. Sometimes, they have openly criticized ex-President Donald Trump's racist framing of such matters as Latin American immigration and racialized police shootings. However, as I noted in a previous chapter, many of them did backtrack a few months later from their critical statements and, more importantly, from their promises to end their corporate contributions to white racist-right political candidates.

Significantly, at a meeting of 45 CEOs from Fortune 100 companies that Harvard professor Jeffrey Sonnenfeld set up after the November 2020 election, the discussion centered on Donald Trump's and his followers' unfounded allegations of that presidential election being "stolen." At that meeting, a progressive Yale scholar of authoritarianism, Timothy Snyder, made a presentation to these top executives on political authoritarianism and the Trump presidential coup attempt just days before. In discussions about appropriate corporate responses to the political coup attempt, the CEO group agreed on the need for a stable law-respecting society if a capitalistic market economy is to function well. They jointly crafted a statement for the mainstream media upholding the 2020 election result, a statement followed by similar ones from other major business groups. There were more such top CEO meetings like the Harvard one for some weeks after the 2020 election, most again concerned with countering the far-right efforts to delegitimate the national election. Indeed, in some joint meetings after the January 2021 Capitol attack, top executives unanimously favored the impeachment of Trump, and many signed onto a major newspaper ad opposing the Georgia legislature's new voter suppression laws. Significantly, too, during the chaotic 2017–2021 Trump administration, numerous CEOs had already rejected requests to serve on his important business committees, and many openly rejected his extremist policies on immigration, transgender issues, or climate change.[120]

Additionally, leading corporate organizations which are part of the traditional donor class bankrolling Republican politicians have occasionally issued statements critiquing the white nationalist political trend, especially the January 2021 Capitol insurrection. An example of this corporate reaction can be seen in a statement on the anniversary of that event by the Business Roundtable's CEO Joshua Bolten:

> The lawless and violent attack on the U.S. Capitol one year ago today was an assault on American democracy, which Business Roundtable condemned at the time. Today, we reiterate our strong condemnation of the perpetrators and the falsehood of an illegitimate 2020 presidential election. January 6 is a day for recommitting ourselves to the principles of our democracy and for honoring the heroes who saved lives and fought to protect the Capitol on that tragic day.[121]

As the progressive critic of U.S. capitalism, Noam Chomsky, has put it, Trump's

> entire legislative program was designed to pour money into the pockets of the super-rich, benefit corporations, and eliminate regulations that protect people but interfere with profits. As long as he was doing that, they were willing to tolerate him. But January 6 was too much. And almost instantly, the major centers of economic power—the Chamber of Commerce, the Business Roundtable, major corporate executives—moved very quickly and told Trump straight out, this is enough: get lost.

Chomsky then speculates on what they might do in the future: "Are they going to listen to the donor class and restore a more genteel version of Trumpism? Or are they going to be swept away by the forces that remain in Trump's pocket?"[122]

To this point, major corporations' political donations to extremist right-wing members of Congress tell a mixed story. Though at first critical of Republican members of Congress and other Republican leaders for not supporting the congressional certification of legitimate 2020 election returns, some major CEOs and corporations soon began to make political donations even to the seditious Republican representatives voting not to certify Joe Biden as president. In March 2021, the U.S. Chamber of Commerce issued a statement that, on a case by case basis, they too would continue to provide funding for these seditious members of Congress.[123]

In an early 2022 analysis, journalist Judd Legum found that 79 major corporations were keeping their previous pledge *not* to donate to these

Republican election objectors, while 26 others had backtracked on some but not all such funding. Significantly, 58 had backed off their pledge entirely.[124] Moreover, in his examination of Federal Election Commission filings for 2019 and 2021 by thousands of Political Action Committees (PACs), Legum found that corporate PAC monetary funding of the Republican members of Congress who voted against certifying Joe Biden as president had dropped overall by two thirds. Legum summarizes thus:

> So while the media narrative is that corporate PAC contributions to Republican objectors have returned to normal, the reality is that they've dropped by 60 percent....Most Republicans have not been able to replace their lost corporate cash with small-dollar donations from the Republican base.[125]

Whether these top CEOs, their corporations, and corporate PACs will persist in this funding withdrawal from extremist Republican politicians in future national elections remains to be seen. Hopefully, there is a growing recognition in this powerful economic elite that likely future political chaos and violence will destroy the U.S.'s capitalistic economy. Large-scale insurrection attempts or large-scale violent clashes between substantial U.S. political factions will of course create major and lasting crises in the U.S. stock market and for much routine profitmaking of these major corporations, not to mention the international reactions to such political and economic chaos. The U.S. economy and underlying socio-political stability would be destroyed. Such chaotic, economy-destroying impacts are not imaginary, but very likely given that the majority of Americans still support significant democracy for the country and will not tolerate a full-fledged fascist American revolution.

Nonetheless, beyond just not funding far-right members of Congress, and sometimes making modest environmental, social, and governance (ESG) commitments for their firms, most CEOs and their corporations have *not* made the much needed political and funding commitments to progressive attempts to expand public educational programs, health programs, and other social programs necessary to building up the public U.S. infrastructure—and thereby a much less inegalitarian country. Recall that Stephen Klineberg's book on economically successful Houston shows an urban population that is far more diverse than a few decades back and now moving attitudinally to much greater support of a social welfare state. However, he further argues:

> It remains to be seen whether the [conservative white] business and civic leaders of Houston can build on these attitude changes and undertake the critical investments that will be needed to position the

region for sustained prosperity in this new era of economic, demographic, and technological transformation. These are the challenges facing all of America. The jury is out, not only for Houston, but for the rest of the country as well.[126]

Mobilizing an Array of Progressive Groups

As social scientist Richard Hasen has underscored, the consumers and customers of these major business organizations "need to continue to pressure business groups to hold the line" on commitments to democratic institutions.[127] Beyond these customer actions, it seems clear that, from now well into the future, large-scale civic organizing and protests by progressive Americans of all backgrounds will be necessary if multiracial democracy is to fully develop and characterize this highly troubled society. Today there are many such efforts to extend and institutionalize full democracy. One is that of the journalist organization Report for America (RFA), created in 2017. The RFA is a national service program that works to put thousands of racially diverse journalists in local newspapers in the U.S. and overseas, many of the latter in serious financial trouble, to cover important local topics. Funded by an array of individual and foundation donors, their "mission is to strengthen our communities and our democracy through local journalism that is truthful, fearless, fair and smart." In one recent year (2020), they provided support for almost 300 journalists "in 14 countries, 48 states, Washington D.C. and Puerto Rico, producing more than 11,000 stories."[128] They accent their being strongly committed to racially diversify these journalists so as to get better news coverage in many currently under-covered communities.

Several media-oriented progressive groups have mobilized to deal with the high level of political misinformation that the rise of major social media firms has greatly facilitated. As I demonstrated in Chapter 3, numerous right-wing online news and social media platforms are helping to destroy what is left of U.S. democracy. During the 2020 election, both Russian troll farms and domestic white extremists had a widespread internet presence on Facebook, Twitter, and other social media platforms and constantly published white nationalist and nativistic messages, videos, and photos designed to attract white Americans who could be influenced by their efforts. As one critical media analysis concludes, during the 2020 election era, right-wing extremists,

> including elected officials actively promoted destabilizing misinformation through their social media channels, leading to threats of violence against elections workers and culminating in the events of January 6. Indeed, the January 6 insurrection was extensively planned by domestic actors on social media platforms.[129]

In spite of these well-documented antidemocratic actions and resulting white violence, major social media organizations have so far taken only *modest* action to stop white extremist actions now or the future.

One effective group working to increase this corporate action is the Lawyers' Committee for Civil Rights Under Law, which was created in the 1963 civil rights era to get private lawyers involved with legal efforts to end racial discrimination. As they put it,

> The principal mission of the Lawyers' Committee for Civil Rights Under Law is to secure, through the rule of law, equal justice for all, particularly in the areas of criminal justice, fair housing and community development, economic justice, educational opportunities, and voting rights.[130]

This Lawyers' Committee's Digital Justice project has worked to deal with such discrimination in a range of mainstream and social media. In March 2019, after long months of pressure from this group, Facebook (Meta) executives decided to ban white nationalist and separatist postings as hate speech. Kristen Clarke, the Lawyers' Committee president, viewed this as a modest first step:

> While we are pleased that Facebook is taking long overdue action, we know well that communities are still reeling from the rise in hate and racially motivated violence, and that extensive remedial action must be taken to ensure that hate is eliminated root and branch across the platform.

This organization has continued with a legal fight against "predatory commercial data practices, discriminatory algorithms, invasions of privacy, disinformation, and online hate [that] disproportionately target and harm communities of color, especially Black Americans, immigrants, women of color, and LGBTQ people of color."[131]

Additionally, Karen Kornbluh, Director of the Digital Innovation and Democracy Initiative of the (U.S.) German Marshall Fund, has pressed for state and federal government action to improve racial and other disinformation and misinformation problems in contemporary social media. She has argued that the Federal Trade Commission and state attorneys general already have consumer protection laws against deceptive trade practices they could use "to investigate platforms' potential material failures to honor commitments in their own terms of service or unfair actions in failing to guard against significant harms to consumers."[132] Clearly, progressive organizations, especially those focused on the digital world, can put even more pressure on online social media corporations to be much more restrictive on domestic and foreign white nationalist and other antidemocratic messaging.

Still, one continuing problem here is that major social media companies are controlled by white corporate founders and top executives committed to profits first and only to our weak regulatory status quo, so significant digital racism will likely persist until major structural change desegregating and democratizing this internet social media decisionmaking takes place.

Note too that, for more than two centuries, the U.S. has seen the development of major civil rights organizations by Americans of color that work at local, state, and national levels for substantial changes in U.S. patterns of racial discrimination. This includes those working to racially diversify the mainstream media. Examples are the National Association of Black Journalists, the National Association of Hispanic Journalists, the Native American Journalists Association, and the Asian American Journalists Association.[133] All have worked hard to democratize employment and reporting in U.S. mainstream media. In addition, there are numerous other civil rights organizations that have worked for racial change and equity in many other U.S. institutions. Among these are national Latina/o organizations like the Mexican American Legal Defense and Education Fund and the LatinoJustice PRLDEF; Native American organizations like the American Indian Movement; and Asian American organizations like the Japanese American Citizens League, Asian Pacific American Advocates, and the Asian American Legal Defense and Education Fund. These antiracist civil rights groups are often joined in collective protest efforts by an array of other human rights groups, including women's rights and LGBTQ rights organizations.

Unsurprisingly, coalitions of these groups have developed to accelerate and support greater social justice and equality in U.S. society. One of the largest is the Leadership Conference on Civil and Human Rights:

> The Leadership Conference's founders came together in 1950 out of the belief that the fight for civil rights could not be won by one group alone, but needed to be waged in coalition. Our members—which have grown from 30 civil and human rights organizations at our founding to more than 200 today—differ in size, scope, and structure. But what transcends our differences and unites The Leadership Conference coalition is our enduring common purpose: full equality for all.[134]

In early 2022, the national Leadership Conference published an analytical report on the progress of civil and human rights by the Joe Biden presidential administration, one calling out both advances and much needed legislative and executive branch actions yet to be done:

> The sheer breadth of this document is a testament to the commitment of the Biden-Harris administration and the 117th Congress to advance

civil and human rights in their first year. Yet we remain disappointed by a lack of urgency on reforming the criminal-legal system, dismantling inhumane immigration policies and practices, and ensuring that civil rights are front and center in the nation's technology and AI policies. We hope the administration will prioritize these issues in 2022 and beyond.[135]

Yet other social justice organizations are working at the local and regional levels for racial change. To take a major example, in 2004 two antiracist activists, Herb Perkins and Margery Otto, established a midwestern antiracist organization, Antiracism Study-Dialogue Circles (ASDIC), to stimulate awareness of racism, antiracist discussions, and change efforts in their local communities. Responding to the realities of white racist resistance to the browning of America, ASDIC activists have used well-crafted dialogue and study workshops to educate and empower people of diverse backgrounds to speak out on community patterns of racism and to help them protest for a more just and democratic society, locally and nationally. They have developed a racial equity curriculum for specific community groups and generated extensive networking among social justice change agents across the Midwest. The ASDIC founders and activists emphasize racially diverse dialogue groups where there is what psychologist Gordon Allport called equal-status contacts, a high frequency of such contacts, and meaningful (non-casual) contacts with intensity and substantial duration—all conditions that are necessary for changing a person's white racist framing of society.[136] The ASDIC approach is to get local groups of people from different racial and ethnic backgrounds into dialogue groups over weeks of antiracist dialogue meetings. The participants are encouraged

> to talk about race and racism as a legacy—an un-asked-for but nevertheless received legacy, as a system of ideas about the place they and others are to occupy, the social arrangements they are to take as normative, the worldview, beliefs, values, assumptions and interpretations they are to take as conventional and unproblematic. Would such an approach free participants from wallowing in unproductive guilt and shame? Free them to break their silence and come to more thoughtfully reflect on ways they might be implicated in current social arrangements, and begin to question how those arrangements might be privileging them? Could such an approach free them to look at the horrific history of U.S. racism rather than turning from it, denying its enduring consequences on them and others?[137]

This candid ASDIC approach has been very effective, and ASDIC activists have facilitated more than 100 workshops and dialogue circles with more than 2,200 community participants in antiracist activism—teachers, students, government staff, and members of religious organizations. Their antiracist curriculum has been used in college courses, in communities with major incidents like racialized police killings, and in Sunday church forums on social justice.[138]

The white participants in ASDIC groups are quietly pressured to do what Robert Jones, a scholar of religion and race, has suggested is necessary—have a *frank* confrontation with the history of white racist framing of society and its continuing implementation of white supremacy within U.S. institutions and culture:

> Even rearranging the words—from "white supremacy" to "supremacy of whites"—gets us closer to a clearer meaning: the continued prevalence of the idea that white people are superior to, or more valuable than, black and other nonwhite people... this subtle transposition gets us to what's really at stake: that white people's superior nature thus entitles them to hold positions of power over black and other nonwhite people.[139]

To counter the contemporary resurgence of white nationalist propaganda in much of the media, such as Fox News and right-wing talk radio (see Chapter 3), and to celebrate the positive impacts of a multiracial democratic America, one very important progressive strategy would be to dramatically expand these antiracist dialogue groups to *all* local and regional areas of the U.S. and to interconnect them in an effective national association collectively working against the systemic white racism still operative across the country.

Conclusion

Clearly, there is no time to waste in this national antiracist and social justice effort, for white nationalists and nativists are becoming yet more organized and widespread in their aggressive, even violent actions against a majority-minority America. In recent years, Republican-controlled legislatures in many states have moved backward on human rights matters. They are passing laws that cut back on voting and other civil rights, LGBTQ rights, and women's rights. Republican officials are passing laws and issuing executive orders that ban books and teaching on equality and social justice topics in schools, colleges, and libraries. As I discussed previously, these laws need to be assertively challenged as flagrant violations of the Constitution's First Amendment, which stipulates that "Congress shall make no law ... abridging the freedom of speech."

African American psychologist Jennifer Richeson has underscored the need for extensive organized action to redress this antidemocratic backtracking:

This is the time to strike, the time to take audacious steps to address systemic racial inequality—bold, sweeping reparative action. The action must be concrete and material, rather than solely symbolic, and must address current gaps in every significant domain of social well-being: jobs, politics, education, the environment, health, housing, and of course criminal justice.[140]

Prominent white journalist Ronald Brownstein has argued that U.S. history so far has demonstrated that "while the voices resistant to change may win delaying battles in politics, they cannot indefinitely hold back the future." He cites as evidence the fact that Donald Trump

twice demonstrated that he could mobilize a powerful coalition around a message of resistance to the way America is changing demographically, culturally and even economically. But he could not amass a national majority [of voters] for that backward-looking vision of restoration ... in either of his campaigns, and that math will only grow more difficult in the years ahead.[141]

As the younger and more diverse generations come to dominate the eligible voter population, a more liberal popular culture will likely have its impact. As I noted in the opening to this book, the brilliant young African American poet Amanda Gorman wrote and delivered a social justice poem at President Joe Biden's inauguration, and there she proclaimed that we are still striving to forge "a country committed to all cultures, colors, characters and conditions."[142]

That striving must include an expansion of legally imbedded and enforced human rights that are essential to any modern democracy, especially one composed of racially diverse and different Americans. Famous American leaders have suggested the need for an aggressive move to more U.S. democracy for generations now. For example, in his 1944 State of the Union address, the democratically inclined creator of the modern U.S. social welfare state, Franklin Roosevelt, assertively pressed for a major "Economic Bill of Rights."[143] In his presentation, this expanded Bill of Rights should encompass broad economic and social rights for all Americans regardless of their racial, class, or religious group. Without full respect for the diversity of individuals, communities, and cultures, there could be no authentic democracy. Yet one more sign that the U.S. today is *not* the full-fledged democracy celebrated on holidays such as July 4 is the fact that the U.S. Constitution has not yet been amended to include progressive President Roosevelt's important economic bill of rights. Moreover, while numerous reforms and executive orders during the Roosevelt era and since have further democratized the U.S., they have not done away with antidemocratic institutions such as the electoral college and its power to put candidates into major political offices like the presidency without a majority of the popular vote or the power of a minority of U.S. senators to filibuster and block major presidential appointments and critically needed democratizing legislation.[144]

Changing these undemocratic institutions will require a further democratization of the U.S. Constitution and its implementation. This will likely require a new and truly democratic constitutional convention at which all U.S. population groups are fairly represented and at which the central goal is creating a truly multiracial democracy. For centuries now, those who have struggled most against persisting oppression have underscored the great importance of continuing this difficult struggle for social justice and democracy. In an 1857 speech in New York state a few years before the Civil War, the great Frederick Douglass accurately described the dimensions of the bloody struggle for slavery's abolition and for real U.S. democracy. Formerly enslaved and then a leading antislavery abolitionist, Douglass knew from much experience what he was talking about:

> The whole history of the progress of human liberty shows that all concessions yet made to her august claims, have been born of earnest struggle…. If there is no struggle there is no progress. Those who profess to favor freedom and yet depreciate agitation, are men who want crops without plowing up the ground, they want rain without thunder and lightning. They want the ocean without the awful roar of its many waters…. Power concedes nothing without a demand. It never did and it never will. Find out just what any people will quietly submit to and you have found out the exact measure of injustice and wrong which will be imposed upon them, and these will continue till they are resisted with either words or blows, or with both. The limits of tyrants are prescribed by the endurance of those whom they oppress.[145]

Notes

1 Derrick Bell, "Racial Realism," *Connecticut Law Review* 24 (Winter 1992): 379. Italics added.
2 Stacey Abrams, *Our Time Is Now* (New York: Henry Holt and Co., 2020), pp. 136–137.
3 Ronald Brownstein, "The Price Republicans Paid in Georgia," *The Atlantic*, January 6, 2021, https://www.theatlantic.com/politics/archive/2021/01/-georgia-senate-results-trump-hurt-republicans/617568/ (accessed February 22, 2021).
4 For example, Eduardo Bonilla-Silva and David R. Dietrich, "The Latin Americanization of Racial Stratification in the U.S.," in *Racism in the 21st Century*, ed. Ronald E. Hall (New York: Springer, 2008), pp 151–170.
5 I am indebted here to discussions with sociologist Eddie Telles.
6 Christina Sue, "An Assessment of the Latin Americanization Thesis," *Ethnic and Racial Studies* 32 (2009): 1064.

7   See Lia Vainer Schucman and Willamys Da Costa Melo, "White Supremacy, Brazil Style," *NACLA Report on the Americas* 54 (2022): 197–202.
8   I am indebted here to discussions with sociologists Randolph Hohle and Eileen O'Brien.
9   See Pierre Van den Berghe, *South Africa, a Study in Conflict* (New York: Praeger, 1980).
10 Quoted in Michael Rodríguez-Muñiz, *Figures of the Future: Latino Civil Rights and the Politics of Demographic Change* (Princeton, NJ: Princeton University Press, 2021), p. 195.
11 Mohammad Amir Anwar, "White People in South Africa still Hold the Lion's Share of All Forms of Capital," *TheConversation*, April 24, 2017, https:// theconversation.com/white-people-in-south-africa-still-hold-the-lions-share-of-all-forms-of-capital-75510 (accessed January 2, 2022).
12 Thanti Mthanti, "Systemic Racism behind South Africa's Failure to Transform Its Economy," *TheConversation*, January 31, 2017, https://theconversation. com/systemic-racism-behind-south-africas-failure-to-transform-its-economy-71499 (accessed January 3, 2022).
13 Ibid.
14 Dale Maharidge, *The Coming White Minority: California's Eruptions and America's Future* (New York: Random House, 1996), p. 11.
15 Jonathan Bell, *California Crucible: The Forging of Modern American Liberalism* (Philadelphia: University of Pennsylvania Press, 2012).
16 Manuel Pastor, *State of Resistance: What California's Dizzying Descent and Remarkable Resurgence Mean for America's Future* (New York: The New Press, 2018), pp. 3–10.
17 Ibid., pp. 20–21.
18 Joel Kotkin and Wendell Cox, "California Fleeing," *City Journal*, July 13, 2021, https://www.city-journal.org/california-demographic-decline?wallit_nosession=1 (accessed August 13, 2021).
19 Mandi Cai, Erin Douglas, and Mitchell Ferman, "How Texas' Power Grid Failed in 2021—And Who's Responsible for Preventing a Repeat," *Texas Tribune*, February 15, 2022, https://www.texastribune.org/2022/02/15/ texas-power-grid-winter-storm-2021/ (accessed July 4, 2022); and Ty Ross, "Lights Out: Energy Prices Soar As Texas Power Grid Fails Again," May 15, 2022, https://occupydemocrats.com/2022/05/15/lights-out-energy-prices-soar-as-texas-power-grid-fails-again/ (accessed July 4, 2022).
20 Kenneth P. Miller, *Texas vs. California: A History of Their Struggle for the Future of America* (New York: Oxford University Press, 2020), pp. 258–259.
21 Ibid., p. 4.
22 Ibid., p. 252.
23 Ibid., p. 253.
24 See William Fulton, "It Seems like All of California Is Moving to Texas. Is That True? *Urban Edge* (Rice University), March 3, 2021, https://kinder.rice. edu/urbanedge/2021/03/03/californians-moving-to-texas-covid-migration (accessed January 20, 2022).
25 Ibid.
26 Miller, *Texas vs. California*, pp. 256–257.
27 Louis Jacobson, "Fact Check: Does Texas Rank Last or Near Last in Children's and Women's Health?" *Austin American-Statesman*, September 19, 2021, https://www.statesman.com/story/news/politics/2021/09/19/texas-ranks-last-near-last-some-childrens-health-metrics/8378932002/ (accessed January 20, 2022).

28 Miller, *Texas vs. California*, pp. 255–256.

29 Ibid., p. 258.

30 "18.9 Million Votes: See the Demographics of Texas' Voting Population," *Stacker Newswire*, November 3, 2021, https://stacker.com/texas/189-million-votes-see-demographics-texas-voting-population (accessed January 17, 2022).

31 Quoted in Stephen L. Klineberg, *Prophetic City: Houston on the Cusp of a Changing America* (New York: Simon & Schuster, 2020), p. 150.

32 Ibid., pp. 285–286.

33 Ronald Brownstein, "Red States are Remaking the Civil Liberties Landscape," CNN, https://www.cnn.com/2022/02/22/politics/republicans-civil-liberties-abortion-voting-race/index.html (accessed December 31, 2022).

34 James Walker, "45 Percent of Republican Voters Support Storming of Capitol Building," *Newsweek*, January 7, 2021, https://www.newsweek.com/45-percent-republican-voters-support-storming-capitol-1559662 (accessed July 1, 2022).

35 Bernard E. Harcourt, "The Fight ahead," *Boston Review*, January 2021, https://bostonreview.net/race-politics/bernard-e-harcourt-fight-ahead (accessed March 12, 2021).

36 See surveys cited in Jamelle Bouie, "Why We Are Not Facing the Prospect of a Second Civil War," *New York Times*, February 15, 2022, https://www.nytimes.com/2022/02/15/opinion/why-we-are-not-facing-the-prospect-of-a-second-civil-war.html?referringSource=articleShare (accessed February 15, 2022).

37 Julie Novkov, "Some Say the U.S. is Headed toward Civil War. History Suggests Something Else," *Washington Post*, January 4, 2022, https://www.washingtonpost.com/politics/2022/01/04/jan-6-civil-war-democracy/ (accessed May 1, 2022).

38 William H. Riker, *Federalism: Origin, Operation, Significance* (New York: Little Brown, 1964), as quoted in John Stoehr, "Federalism is the Source of Fascism, American-Style," *The Editorial Board*, https://www.editorialboard.com/federalism-is-the-source-of-fascism-american-style/ (accessed January 31, 2022).

39 John Dinan, "The Institutionalization of State Resistance to Federal Directives in the 21st Century," *The Forum*, September 21, 2020, DOI: 10.1515/for-2020-1001 (accessed January 6, 2022); and Novkov, "Some Say the U.S. is Headed toward Civil War. History Suggests Something Else."

40 Novkov, "Some Say the U.S. is Headed toward Civil War. History Suggests Something Else."

41 Agence France-Presse, "US Added to List of 'Backsliding' Democracies for First Time," *The Guardian*, November 1, 2021, https://www.theguardian.com/us-news/2021/nov/22/us-list-backsliding-democracies-civil-liberties-international (accessed November 22, 2021).

42 Quoted in Dana Milbank, "'We are Closer to Civil War Than Any of Us Would Like to Believe,' New Study Says," *Washington Post*, December 17, 2021, https://www.washingtonpost.com/opinions/2021/12/17/how-civil-wars-start-barbara-walter-research/ (accessed December 18, 2021).

43 Sean Collins, "Trump Once Flirted with White Nationalism. Now It's a Centerpiece of His White House," vox.com, July 21, 2020, https://www.vox.com/21313021/trump-white-nationalism-supremacy-miller-bannon-immigration (accessed February 18, 2022).

44 Toni Morrison, "Racism and Fascism," *Journal of Negro Education* 64 (1995): 384–385. When interviewed recently, several experts thought the terminology

for what the current Republican majority seeks should include terms like *fascist, authoritarian, right-wing populist,* and *ultranationalist,* and its top leaders termed as *demagogues, plutocrats,* and *oligarchs.* Dylan Matthews, "Is Trump a Fascist?" Vox.com, October 23, 2020, https://www.vox.com/policy-and-politics/21521958/what-is-fascism-signs-donald-trump (accessed December 16, 2021).

45 See Stanley G. Payne, *History of Fascism 1914–45* (Madison: University of Wisconsin Press, 1996); and Jason Stanley, *How Fascism Works: The Politics of Us and Them* (New York: Random House, 2018).

46 Quoted in "Anti-Monopoly," *Time,* May 9, 1938, https://web.archive.org/web/20080505122815/http://www.time.com/time/magazine/article/0,9171,759590,00.html (accessed June 1, 2022).

47 Robert O. Paxton, "I've Hesitated to Call Donald Trump a Fascist. Until Now," *Newsweek,* https://archive.org/details/anatomyoffascism00paxt_0 (accessed January 27, 2022). See also Robert O. Paxton, *The Anatomy of Fascism* (New York: Knopf, 2004).

48 Cited in Dylan Matthews, "Is Trump a Fascist?" Vox.com, October 23, 2020, https://www.vox.com/policy-and-politics/21521958/what-is-fascism-signs-donald-trump (accessed December 16, 2021).

49 See Jennifer Cohn, "Public Officials Provided False Assurances about the Legitimacy of Trump's Poll-Defying Win in 2016," https://jennycohn1.medium.com/why-have-so-many-people-spread-misinformation-about-voting-systems-and-internet-connectivity-247bd9877419 (accessed December 17, 2021).

50 Ibid.

51 Alfred McCoy, "Recurring Nightmares: How the American Coup Attempt Summoned Memories of Another," *Salon,* https://www.salon.com/2021/11/07/recurring-nightmares-how-the-american-coup-attempt-summoned-memories-of-another-_partner/ (accessed December 5, 2021).

52 Jim Freeman, *Rich Thanks to Racism* (Ithaca, NY: Cornell University Press, 2021), p. 25.

53 Cited in Dylan Matthews, "Is Trump a Fascist?" *Vox.com,* Oct 23, 2020, https://www.vox.com/policy-and-politics/21521958/what-is-fascism-signs-donald-trump (accessed December 16, 2021).

54 Charles King, "The Fulbright Paradox: Race and the Road to a New American Internationalism," *Foreign Affairs,* July/August 2021, https://www.foreignaffairs.com/articles/united-states/2021-06-18/fulbright-paradox (accessed June 20, 2021).

55 Andrew Whitehead, "The Growing Antidemocratic Threat of Christian Nationalism in the U.S.," *Time.com,* May 27, 2021, https://time.com/6052051/antidemocratic-threat-christian-nationalism/ (accessed May 5, 2022).

56 Talia Lavin, "The U.S. Military Has a White Supremacy Problem," *New Republic,* https://newrepublic.com/article/162400/us-military-white-supremacy-problem (accessed February 21, 2022).

57 Dana Milbank, "'We are Closer to Civil War Than Any of Us Would Like to Believe,' New Study Says," *Washington Post,* https://www.washingtonpost.com/opinions/2021/12/17/how-civil-wars-start-barbara-walter-research/ (accessed December 18, 2021).

58 Email discussion (2022) with Anthony Weems. Used by permission.

59 Jonathan Wilson-Hartgrove, "Who Poisoned Talk Radio?" *Sojourners,* May 2020, https://sojo.net/magazine/may-2020/who-poisoned-talk radio (accessed January 12, 2021).

60 Timothy Snyder, "A Dream of Power, an Awakening to Destruction," https://snyder.substack.com/p/a-dream-of-power-an-awakening-to (accessed January 6, 2022).

61 Richard Luscombe, "US Could Be under Rightwing Dictator by 2030, Canadian Professor Warns," *The Guardian*, https://www.theguardian.com/us-news/2022/jan/03/us-rightwing-dictatorship-2030-trump-canada (accessed February 24, 2022).

62 Thomas Edsall, "Why Trump Is Still Their Guy," *New York Times*, April 21, 2021, https://www.nytimes.com/2021/04/21/opinion/trump-republicans.html?campaign_id=39&emc=edit_ty_20210421&instance_id=29494&nl=opinion-today&regi_id=54115655&segment_id=56003&te=1&user_id=6a44bcdea3628e8ce52c97f8996a95fe (accessed January 10, 2022). See also Michael Scherer and Josh Dawsey, "A Weakened Trump? As Some Voters Edge Away, He Battles Parts of the Republican Party He Once Ran," *Washington Post*, February 13, 2021, https://www.adn.com/nation-world/2022/02/13/a-weakened-trump-as-some-voters-edge-away-he-battles-parts-of-the-republican-party-he-once-ran/ (accessed February 24, 2022).

63 Edsall, "Why Trump Is Still Their Guy."

64 Henry Olsen, "Why Donald Trump May Lose Influence in the Republican Party," *Washington Post*, June 9, 2021, https://www.washingtonpost.com/opinions/2021/06/09/why-donald-trump-may-lose-influence-republican-party/ (accessed July 5, 2021).

65 Drew Harwell, "Since Jan. 6, the Pro-Trump Internet Has Descended into Infighting Over Money and Followers," *Washington Post*, January 3, 2022, https://www.washingtonpost.com/technology/2022/01/03/trump-qanon-online-money-war-jan6/ (accessed January 3, 2022).

66 Andrew Prokop, "New Report Complicates Simplistic Narratives about Race and the 2020 Election," catalist.com, May 10, 2021, https://catalist.us/2021/05/a-new-report-complicates-simplistic-narratives-about-race-and-the-2020-election/ (accessed February 24, 2022).

67 Joe R. Feagin, *How Blacks Built America* (New York: Routledge, 2016), p. 95.

68 Quoted in Charles E. Cobb Jr., *This Nonviolent Stuff'll Get You Killed: How Guns Made the Civil Rights Movement Possible* (New York: Basic Books, 2014), p. 246.

69 Cornel West and Christa Buschendorf, *Black Prophetic Fire* (Boston, MA: Beacon Press, 2014), Kindle loc. 2497–2505. Italics added.

70 Lauren Araiza, *To March for Others: The Black Freedom Struggle and the United Farm Workers* (Philadelphia: University of Pennsylvania Press, 2014).

71 Robin D. G. Kelley, "Foreword," in *Black Marxism: The Making of the Black Radical Tradition*, ed. Cedric J. Robinson, 3rd ed. (Chapel Hill: University of North Carolina Press, 2021), p. xxviii.

72 Kevin Zeese, "Dismantling White Supremacy in World," *CounterCurrents*, October 10, 2017, https://countercurrents.org/2017/10/dismantling-white-supremacy/ (accessed March 7, 2022).

73 Larry Buchanan, Quoctrung Bui, and Jugal K. Patel, "Black Lives Matter May Be the Largest Movement in U.S. History," *New York Times,* July 3, 2020, https://www.nytimes.com/interactive/2020/07/03/us/george-floyd-protests-crowd-size.html (accessed April 8, 2021).

74 Ibid.

75 Quoted in K. K. Ottesen, "An Architect of Critical Race Theory: 'We Cannot Allow All of the Lessons from the Civil Rights Movement Forward to Be Packed up and Put Away for Storage'" *Washington Post*, January 19, 2022, https://www.washingtonpost.com/lifestyle/magazine/an-architect-of-critical-race-

theory-we-cannot-allow-all-of-the-lessons-from-the-civil-rights-movement-forward-to-be-packed-up-and-put-away-for-storage/2022/01/14/24bb31de-627e-11ec-a7e8-3a8455b71fad_story.html (accessed January 23, 2022).

76 Dominic-MadoriDavis, "TheActionGeneration," *BusinessInsider,*June10,2020, https://www.businessinsider.com/how-gen-z-feels-about-george-floyd-protests-2020-6 (accessed July 29, 2021).

77 Amy Harmon and Sabrina Tavernise, "One Big Difference about George Floyd Protests: Many White Faces," *New York Times,* June 12, 2020, https://www.nytimes.com/2020/06/12/us/george-floyd-white-protesters.html (accessed February 7, 2022).

78 Candis Watts Smith and Christopher DeSante, "The Racial Views of White Americans—Including Millennials—Depend on the Questions Asked," *Scholars Strategy Network,* January 12, 2018, https://scholars.org/contribution/racial-views-white-americans-including-millennials-depend-questions-asked (accessed August 17, 2020); and Christopher D. DeSante and Candis Watts Smith, *Racial Stasis: The Millennial Generation and the Stagnation of Racial Attitudes in American Politics* (Chicago, IL: University of Chicago press, 2020).

79 Harmon and Tavernise, "One Big Difference about George Floyd Protests."

80 Jennifer Chudy and Hakeem Jefferson, "Support for Black Lives Matter Surged Last Year. Did It Last?," *New York Times,* https://www.nytimes.com/2021/05/22/opinion/blm-movement-protests-support.html (accessed July 1, 2022).

81 Ibid.

82 Theodore Allen, *The Invention of the White Race: Racial Oppression and Social Control* (London: Verso, 1994), pp. 19–21.

83 W. E. B. du Bois, *Black Reconstruction in America 1860–1880* (New York: Harcourt, Brace and Co., 1935), p. 27.

84 James Horton, "Race: The Power of an Illusion," pt. 2, California Newsreel, 2003, https://newsreel.org/transcripts/race2.htm (accessed July 5, 2022).

85 "Public Opinion on Civil Rights: Reflections on the Civil Rights Act of 1964," *Roper Center Blog,* July 2, 2014, https://ropercenter.cornell.edu/blog/-public-opinion-civil-rights-reflections-civil-rights-act-1964-blog (accessed April 14, 2022).

86 See Du Bois, *Black Reconstruction in America 1860–1880.*

87 Manuel Pastor, *State of Resistance: What California's Dizzying Descent and Remarkable Resurgence Mean for America's Future* (New York: The New Press, 2018), pp. 20–21.

88 Ibid. My italics.

89 Ibid., pp. 57–58.

90 Ibid., pp.195–204.

91 "Michael R. Bloomberg sees California as Model on Climate Change, Guns," *AP News,* January 6, 2020, https://apnews.com/article/3e132696097bf5f9abc adf408d4d7cbb (accessed December 15, 2021).

92 Ibid.

93 David Lesher, "Here's Your Primer: What California State Government Has Been up to in 2021," Calmatters.Org, December 10, 2021, https://calmatters.org/politics/2021/12/california-state-government-primer-2021/ (accessed December 19, 2021).

94 John Halpin, Karl Agne, and Nisha Jain, "Americans Want the Federal Government To Help People in Need," Center for American Progress, March 10, 2021 (accessed August 18, 2021).

95 Ian Haney Lopez, Anat Shenker-Osorio, and Heather McGhee, "Race-Class: A Winning Electoral Narrative," *Race-Class Narrative Project*, https://ianhaneylopez.com/race-class-narrative (accessed February 8, 2022).

96 Ibid.

97 Ibid.

98 Ibid.

99 Ian Haney Lopez, "Can Democracy (and the Democratic Party) Survive Racism as a Strategy?" Medium.com, December 1, 2021, https://medium.com/@halo.politics/can-democracy-and-the-democratic-party-survive-racism-as-a-strategy-47257b3b450#_ftn4, (accessed February 15, 2022).

100 Ian Haney López, et alia, "Project Juntos: Latinx Race-Class," *Latino Research Partners, Way to Win and Equis Research*, https://static1.squarespace.com/static/5ef377b623eaf41dd9df1311/t/5fc55c8d4e98326c02c48eb6/1606769814244/Project+Juntos.summary+briefing.092620.pdf (accessed September 28, 2021).

101 Ibid.

102 Tory Gavito and Adam Jentleson, "The Powerful G.O.P. Strategy Democrats Must Counter if They Want to Win," *New York Times*, https://www.nytimes.com/2021/11/04/opinion/democrats-republicans-virginia-race.html?smid=tw-nytopinion&smtyp=current (accessed February 8, 2022).

103 See Micah English and Joshua Kalla, "Racial Equality Frames and Public Policy Support: Survey Experimental Evidence," Yale University, OSF Preprint, April 23, 2021, file:///C:/Users/Joe/OneDrive/Desktop/English_Kalla_Race_Class_Issue_Support-27.pdf. doi:10.31219/osf.io/tdkf3 (accessed July 5, 2022).

104 Heather McGhee, *The Sum of Us: What Racism Costs Everyone and How We Can Prosper Together* (New York: One World, 2021).

105 Ibid., p. 15.

106 See, for example, Sam Gindin, "Unmaking Global Capitalism," *Jacobin Magazine*, June 2014, https://jacobinmag.com/2014/06/unmaking-global-capitalism (accessed May 11, 2022). I am indebted here to discussions with social scientist Anthony Weems.

107 Steve Phillips, *Brown Is the New White* (New York: The New Press, 2016), p. 172.

108 Ibid., p. xix.

109 Ibid., p. 172.

110 Ibid., p. 253.

111 Stacey Abrams, *Our Time Is Now* (New York: Henry Holt and Co., 2020), pp. 136–137.

112 Ronald Brownstein, "The Price Republicans Paid in Georgia," *The Atlantic*, January 6, 2021, https://www.theatlantic.com/politics/archive/2021/01/georgia-senate-results-trump-hurt-republicans/617568/ (accessed February 22, 2021).

113 Karim Farishta and Jackson Miller, "Reclaiming the Southern Strategy: How Democrats Win Back the South in the 2020s," *Harvard Capstone*, April 2020, https://harvardgradcapstone.wixsite.com/reclaimingthesouth (accessed July 5, 2022).

114 Abrams, *Our Time Is Now*, pp. 136–137.

115 Emma Hurt and Thomas Wheatley, "The Stacey Abrams Blueprint," *Politics & Policy*, March 12, 2022, https://www.axios.com/the-stacey-abrams-blueprint-9de92a2a-3f4e-481c-9e0b-0b190d649721.html?deepdive=1 (accessed May 4, 2022).

116 Richard C. Fording and Sanford F. Schram, *Hard White: The Mainstreaming of Racism in American Politics* (New York: Oxford University Press, 2020), p. 222.

117 Ibid., p. 222.

118 George Yancy, as interviewed by Marshall Kupka-Moore, "The Emory Professor behind Dear White America Explains His Side," *The Tab*, 2015, https://thetab.com/us/emory/2016/02/06/emory-professor-behind-dear-white-america-explains-side-114 (accessed December 28, 2017). For more insight on dealing with white anti-humanism, see George Yancy, *Backlash: What Happens When We Talk Honestly about Racism in America* (Rowman & Littlefield, 2018).

119 Richard L. Hasen, "No One Is Coming to Save Us from the 'Dagger at the Throat of America,'" *New York Times*, January 1, 2022, https://www.nytimes.com/2022/01/07/opinion/trump-democracy-voting-jan-6.html (accessed January 7, 2022).

120 Molly Ball, "How Big Business Got Woke and Dumped Trump," *Time*, November 1, 2021, https://time.com/6111845/woke-big-business-dumps-trump/ (accessed December 21, 2021).

121 "Business Roundtable Statement on Anniversary of January 6 U.S. Capitol Riot," January 6, 2022, https://www.businessroundtable.org/business-roundtable-statement-on-anniversary-of-january-6-us-capitol-riot (accessed January 30, 2022).

122 "Interview with Noam Chomsky—Marx's Old Mole is Right Beneath the Surface," *Boston Review*, April 8, 2021, https://bostonreview.net/articles/marxs-old-mole-is-right-beneath-the-surface/ (accessed February 6, 2022).

123 "Fortune 500 Corporations and Industry Groups Gave Over $725K To 'Sedition Caucus' in October," December 20, 2021, https://www.accountable.us/news/report-fortune-500-corporations-and-industry-groups-gave-over-725k-to-sedition-caucus-in-october/ (accessed July 5, 2022).

124 Judd Legum, Rebecca Crosby, and Tesnim Zekeria, "Seven Major Corporations Pledge Not to Support GOP Objectors in 2022," *Popular Information*, January 4, 2022, https://popular.info/p/seven-major-corporations-pledge-not (accessed January 7, 2022).

125 Judd Legum, "The Truth about Corporate Contributions to Republican Objectors since January 6," *Popular Information*, January 3, 2022, https://popular.info/p/the-truth-about-corporate-contributions (accessed January 7, 2022).

126 Stephen L. Klineberg, *Prophetic City: Houston on the Cusp of a Changing America* (New York: Simon & Schuster, 2020), p. 286.

127 Hasen, "No One Is Coming to Save Us From the 'Dagger at the Throat of America.'"

128 Sam Kille, "Report for America Fights Crisis in Local News, Expands into 200-Plus Newsrooms with 300 Journalists," *Report for America*, April 27, 2021, https://www.reportforamerica.org/2021/04/27/report-for-america-fights-crisis-in-local-news-expands-into-200-plus-newsrooms-with-300-journalists/ (accessed February 28, 2022).

129 Karen Kornbluh, "Disinformation, Radicalization, and Algorithmic Amplification: What Steps Can Congress Take?" *JustSecurity.org*, https://www.justsecurity.org/79995/disinformation-radicalization-and-algorithmic-amplification-what-steps-can-congress-take/ (accessed February 7, 2022).

130 Stanley Augustin, "National Civil Rights Group Secures Critical Victory in Effort to Combat White Supremacy on Facebook Platform," *Lawyer's*

Committee for Civil Rights under Law, March 26, 2019, https://www.lawyers committee.org/national-civil-rights-group-secures-critical-victory-in-effort-to-combat-white-supremacy-on-facebook-platform/ (accessed March 7, 2022).

131 Ibid.

132 Kornbluh, "Disinformation, Radicalization, and Algorithmic Amplification."

133 See their websites in order here: https://nabjonline.org; https://nahj. orghttps; www.aaja.org; and https://najanewsroom.com. I am indebted here to suggestions by sociologist Kirk Johnson.

134 Leadership Conference, "Our Common Purpose," https://civilrights.org/ about/the-coalition/# (accessed March 1, 2022). I draw in this section on Joe R. Feagin, *White Party, White Government: Race, Class, and U.S. Politics* (New York: Routledge, 2012), passim.

135 "Biden-Harris Administration and Congress Must Continue to Advance Civil and Human Rights," *Leadership Conference*, https://civilrights.org/ 2022/02/28/biden-harris-administration-and-congress-must-continue-to-advance-civil-and-human-rights/# (accessed March 1, 2022).

136 I am indebted here to discussions with ASDIC founder Herb (Okogyeamon) Perkins.

137 ASDIC, "Our Story," https://www.asdicircle.org/our-story (accessed March 1, 2022).

138 I draw on notes from Herb (Okogyeamon) Perkins, Bundy Trinz, Margery Otto, and Tim Johnson.

139 Robert P. Jones, *White Too Long: The Legacy of White Supremacy in American Christianity* (New York: Simon & Schuster, 2020), p. 16.

140 Jennifer Richeson, "Americans Are Determined to Believe in Black Progress," *The Atlantic*, August 2020, https://www.theatlantic.com/magazine/ archive/2020/09/the-mythology-of-racial-progress/614173/ (accessed January 30, 2021).

141 Ronald Brownstein, "When and Where America's Culture War Was Won," CNN.com, March 30, 2021, https://www.cnn.com/2021/03/30/politics/ conservatives-culture-war-los-angeles-1970s/index.html (accessed March 30, 2021).

142 Phillip Martinez, "Read Amanda Gorman's Full Inauguration Poem 'The Hill We Climb,'" *Newsweek*, https://www.newsweek.com/amanda-gorman-inauguration-poem-hill-we-climb-words-video-1563148 (accessed February10, 2022).

143 Franklin Roosevelt, "State of the Union," http://www.presidency.ucsb.edu/ ws/index.php?pid=16518 (accessed February 28, 2005).

144 See Cushing Strout, *The Spirit of American Government* (Cambridge, MA: Harvard University Press, 1965), pp. liv–lv.

145 Frederick Douglass, "The Significance of Emancipation in the West Indies," in *The Frederick Douglass Papers*, ed. John W. Blassingame (New Haven, CT: Yale University Press, 1986), Volume 3, p. 204.

Index

Note: Page numbers followed by "n" denote endnotes.

Summers, Lawrence 127
superficial liberalism 150–152
systemic racism 115, 200, 202; systemic
  inequality 25, 222

Tanaka, Janice 32
Tea Party movement 86
Tech Transparency Project (TTP) 104
Telemundo 89
"terra nullius" 9
terrorism 34, 66, 72
Texas 181–185; Black voters in 147;
  community welfare problems 183;
  democratic voting institutions 184;
  politics 183–184; voters of color
  in 145
Texas Public Policy Foundation 181
Texas vs. California (Miller) 182
The Coming White Minority (Maharidge)
  179
Thornhill, Ted 31
Time Warner 89
Trinity Broadcasting networks 94
Trump, Donald 2, 3, 6, 34, 42, 146,
  150, 154, 156, 165, 166, 188,
  190, 191, 192; "Make America Great
  Again" slogan 63; Make America
  Great rhetoric 66; and white
  insurrectionists 71; white nationalistic
  demagoguery 56–58
Trump, Mary 6, 7n15
Twitter 90, 91, 101, 217

undemocratic political institutions
  158–160
undocumented immigration 59
unions 134, 166, 180, 198, 208, 214
United Farm Workers (UFW) 198
United Nations 118
United States (U.S.): Chamber
  of Commerce 114, 117, 215;
  concentration camps 32; immigration
  laws 55, 145; industrial revolution 10;
  political system 30, 72, 156, 158–159,
  177, 179; politics 104–106, 154–155
Unite the Right 2, 42
unjust enrichment 11, 33, 121, 125–126
unjust impoverishment 121, 129
upper-class 28, 86, 102, 137, 159, 183;
  see also elite white men
U.S. Commission on Civil Rights 144
U.S. Congress 45, 50, 52, 97, 101
U.S. Constitution 159, 222–223; Article
  V of 193; Article VI, Section III, of
  66; First Amendment 132–133, 221;

Fourteenth Amendment 59, 133, 198;
  Second Amendment 112
U.S. Constitutional Convention 193
U.S. Department of Education 136
U.S. racism 85, 89, 130–132, 151, 155,
  184, 202, 220; *see also* racism; systemic
  racism
U.S. society: Latin Americanization of
  175–177; South Africanization of
  177–179
U.S. Supreme Court 88, 101, 106, 133,
  159, 163, 166, 167, 186, 188, 189

VDARE website 55
ViacomCBS 89
violence: collective 66, 194; individual
  66; -oriented activism 34; political
  71, 104, 194, 214; racialized 102–104;
  right-wing 103; social 214
Virginia 2, 35, 42, 46, 54, 69, 120,
  145–146, 148, 156
virtuousness 9–10; of white civilization
  54; of white male workers 14
Volpe, John Della 150
voters: browning of 145–147; nonwhite
  154–157; younger and well-educated
  157–158
voters of color: Republican suppression
  of 163–166
voting: generational diversity and
  change 149–150; groups 64, 160;
  institutions 184; policies 87
Voting Rights Act 1965 106; renewal 4

"wage of whiteness" 84, 204
Waisbord, Silvio 102
Walker, Darren 117
Wallace, George 51
Wall Street 116, 129
Wall Street Journal 89, 93
Walter, Barbara F. 190
Washington, DyAnna 152
Washington, George 44, 66, 98, 120
Washington D.C. 3, 13, 70, 217
Washington Post 60, 91, 196
Watchmen on the Wall 95
wealth, intergenerational transmission
  of 125–127
The Wealth of Nations (Smith) 113–114
Weems, Anthony 194
welfare 61, 114, 119, 125, 179, 183
West, Cornel 198
Western capitalism 210
Western civilization 56, 67
Western imperialism 92